Revised and Expanded
Third Edition

THE
PERIGEE
VISUAL
DICTIONARY
OF
SIGNING

Revised and Expanded
Third Edition

THE PERIGEE VISUAL DICTIONARY OF SIGNING

Includes more than
1,350 signs of
American Sign Language

ROD R. BUTTERWORTH
and MICKEY FLODIN

A PERIGEE BOOK

*D*edicated to all who take the time
to learn this beautiful and expressive language.

———————————

A PERIGEE BOOK
Published by the Penguin Group
Penguin Group (USA) Inc.
375 Hudson Street, New York, New York 10014, USA
Penguin Group (Canada), 90 Eglinton Avenue East, Suite 700, Toronto, Ontario M4P 2Y3, Canada
(a division of Pearson Penguin Canada Inc.)
Penguin Books Ltd., 80 Strand, London WC2R 0RL, England
Penguin Group Ireland, 25 St. Stephen's Green, Dublin 2, Ireland (a division of Penguin Books Ltd.)
Penguin Group (Australia), 250 Camberwell Road, Camberwell, Victoria 3124, Australia
(a division of Pearson Australia Group Pty. Ltd.)
Penguin Books India Pvt. Ltd., 11 Community Centre, Panchsheel Park, New Delhi—110 017, India
Penguin Group (NZ), 67 Apollo Drive, Rosedale, North Shore 0632, New Zealand
(a division of Pearson New Zealand Ltd.)
Penguin Books (South Africa) (Pty.) Ltd., 24 Sturdee Avenue, Rosebank, Johannesburg 2196,
South Africa

Penguin Books Ltd., Registered Offices: 80 Strand, London WC2R 0RL, England

While the author has made every effort to provide accurate telephone numbers and Internet addresses
at the time of publication, neither the publisher nor the author assumes any responsibility for errors,
or for changes that occur after publication. Further, the publisher does not have any control over and
does not assume any responsibility for author or third-party websites or their content.

PRINTING HISTORY
Perigee trade paperback edition / August 1995

Library of Congress Cataloging-in-Publication Data

Butterworth, Rod R.
The Perigee visual dictionary of signing : includes more than 1,350 signs of American sign
language / Rod R. Butterworth : illustrated by Mickey Flodin.
    p.   cm.
Includes index.
ISBN 978-0-399-51952-9
    1. American sign language—Dictionaries.   I. Flodin, Mickey.   II. Title.
HV2475.B87   1995   95-1380 CIP
                                                                   419—dc20

PRINTED IN THE UNITED STATES OF AMERICA

29   28   27   26

Most Perigee Books are available at special quantity discounts for bulk purchases for sales promo-
tions, premiums, fund-raising, or educational use. Special books, or book excerpts, can also be created to fit specific needs. For details, write: Special Markets, Penguin Group (USA) Inc., 375 Hudson
Street, New York, New York 10014.

Acknowledgments

The *Perigee Visual Dictionary of Signing* has become a reality because of the willing cooperation of many people. If it were not for their assistance, this dictionary would have been supremely more difficult to complete. Special thanks are due to the following people it has been our privilege to work with:

Lynn Lutjen, instructor in deaf education for the Department of Speech and Theater, Southwest Missouri State University, Springfield, Missouri. Her willingness to act as a consultant from the early stages of the development of this dictionary has resulted in many profitable suggestions concerning the descriptions and illustrations.

Marybeth Herens, instructor of reading and language at Colorado State School for the Deaf and Blind, Colorado Springs, Colorado. Her expertise in sign language and language disciplines has provided valuable input throughout the preparation of this dictionary.

Many friends who are deaf and interpreters for deaf people, who have given encouragement and advice along the way.

Sam Mitnick, former publisher, Perigee Books, The Putnam Publishing Group. In appreciation of his vision and belief in this work as a valuable contribution to the field of sign language.

Christine Butterworth, for assistance in typing and correcting the manuscript.

Joanna Butterworth, for moral support as a devoted wife and sacrificial giving of her time to editing and correcting the manuscript.

Barbara J. Holland, for her valuable editorial suggestions regarding the improvement of the text, and many hours spent proofreading.

The rest of the Butterworth family, who all shared in the work at various stages: Winifred Butterworth, Michael, Donna, and Geoffrey.

Carol Flodin, for her enthusiasm and for her extensive labors in numerous ways during the production of this book.

Daniel Flodin, who helped when he could and who waited patiently for his dad to return to a more normal schedule.

—R.R.B.
—M.F.

Contents

Introduction

This latest revision and expanded third edition of *The Perigee Visual Dictionary of Signing* makes it an even more valuable tool for those learning sign language. Eighty-seven new signs have been added, making a total of over 1,350 of the same beautifully illustrated and clearly described signs. Also additional helps have been included which further aid the student of sign language to gain as thorough an understanding as possible of this fourth most used language in the United States.

Classes in sign language have become increasingly popular in universities, colleges, churches, and other organizations across the country, making it easier for people to learn this fascinating language. In fact, a wide variety of people in professional occupations, such as ambulance and rescue teams, police and security officers, and others participating in water sports such as scuba diving and skin diving, are also finding sign language an invaluable asset. As the skill of sign language is developed, these people are able to enjoy the benefits of communicating with deaf people. Practicing consistently will reap the reward of proficiency. Persons who are deaf look with favor upon those who seek to learn their language, and they have much patience and understanding with the beginning signer.

Both the classroom student and the person interested in learning sign language from this book independently will experience the satisfaction of being able to communicate with deaf people, and the joy of learning a language that is beautiful and expressive. There are approximately twenty million hard-of-hearing people living in the United States. Almost two million of this number are classified as being deaf. Those who are born deaf are referred to as *congenitally deaf,* while those who become deaf as a result of accident or illness are referred to as *adventitiously deaf.*

Just as the English language constantly evolves, so does the language of signing used by those who are deaf. Great care has been taken to review all the signs and descriptions in *The Perigee Visual Dictionary of Signing* and to revise those that required updating in order to correspond with current usage. New signs are often created among deaf people and sometimes spread across the country until they become generally accepted. The signs used in this book are commonly used and accepted in North America, but within various geographical communities one will often find slight differences and preferences concerning the way to make a particular sign.

The ultimate purpose of this book is to provide a basic and adequate vocabulary in sign language which the student can use to communicate effectively with those who are deaf. We believe that learning the information in this dictionary will enable the student to achieve this goal, while at the same time finding the experience both enjoyable and rewarding.

History of Sign Language

It was in the sixteenth century that Geronimo Cardano, a physician of Padua, in northern Italy, proclaimed that deaf people could be taught to understand written combinations of symbols by associating them with the thing they represented. The first book on teaching sign language to deaf people that contained the manual alphabet was published in 1620 by Juan Pablo de Bonet.

In 1755 Abbé Charles Michel de L'Epée of Paris founded the first free school for deaf people. He taught that deaf people could develop communication with themselves and the hearing world through a system of conventional gestures, hand signs, and fingerspelling. He created and demonstrated a language of signs whereby each would be a symbol that suggested the concept desired.

The abbé was apparently a very creative person, and the way he developed his sign language system was by first recognizing, then learning the signs that were *already being used* by a group of deaf people in Paris. To this knowledge he added his own creativeness which resulted in a signed version of spoken French. He paved the way for deaf people to have a more standardized language of their own—one which would effectively bridge the gap between the hearing and nonhearing worlds.

Another prominent deaf educator of the same period (1778) was Samuel Heinicke of Leipzig, Germany. Heinicke did not use the manual method of communication but taught speech and speechreading. He established the first public school for deaf people that achieved government recognition. These two methods (manual and oral) were the forerunners of today's concept of total communication. Total communication espouses the use of all means of available communication, such as sign language, gesturing, fingerspelling, speechreading, speech, hearing aids, reading, writing, and pictures.

In America the Great Plains Indians developed a fairly extensive system of signing, but this was more for intertribal communication than for deaf people, and only vestiges of it remain today. However, it is interesting to note some similarities existing between Indian sign language and the present system.

America owes a tremendous debt of gratitude to Thomas Hopkins

Gallaudet, an energetic Congregational minister who became interested in helping his neighbor's young deaf daughter, Alice Cogswell. He traveled to Europe in 1815, when he was twenty-seven, to study methods of communicating with deaf people. While in England he met Abbé Roche Ambroise Sicard, who invited him to study at his school for deaf people in Paris. After several months Gallaudet returned to the United States with Laurent Clerc, a deaf sign language instructor from the Paris school.

In 1817 Gallaudet founded the nation's first school for deaf people, in Hartford, Connecticut, and Clerc became the United States' first deaf sign language teacher. Soon schools for deaf people began to appear in several states. Among them was the New York School for the Deaf, which opened its doors in 1818. In 1820 a school was opened in Pennsylvania, and a total of twenty-two schools had been established throughout the United States by the year 1863.

An important milestone in the history of education for deaf people was the founding of Gallaudet College, in Washington, D.C. in 1864, which remains the only liberal arts college for deaf people in the United States and the world.

Thomas Hopkins Gallaudet passed on his dream of a college for deaf people to his son, Edward Miner Gallaudet, who with the help of Amos Kendall made the dream a reality. Edward Miner Gallaudet became the first president of the new college.

Today we are fortunate to have one of the most complete and expressive sign language systems of any country in the world. We owe much to the French sign system, from which many of our present-day signs, though modified, have been derived.

It might be noted here that many deaf people use a different grammatical structure when signing, usually among themselves, known technically as American Sign Language, or ASL. But signing in English word order continues to grow in popularity and is widely used by both deaf people and hearing people. It is easier for a hearing person to learn sign language in English syntax than to learn signing with the grammatical structure of ASL.

Interest continues to grow in sign language, and it is now the fourth most used language in the United States. Many sign language classes are offered in communities, churches, and colleges.

How to Use
This Dictionary

Direction and Orientation of Illustrations

The illustrations are drawn as you would see another person signing to you. This is not the same as looking into a mirror, for then the
right hand would appear to be the left hand. To make the signs clearer
and more easily understood, some illustrations are shown from an
angle or profile perspective.

Arrows

Great care has been taken to guide the student's comprehension
of a sign movement by the use of arrows. However, it is sometimes
possible to perceive a different movement from the actual one in
question if the reader is not extremely careful. Read the descriptions thoroughly when learning a new sign. They will guide and aid
the beginning sign language student in understanding the correct
movement.

Clockwise, Counterclockwise

Unless otherwise stated, these terms are to be understood from
the viewpoint of the signer, as if the signer is looking at the face of
a clock. This is true whether or not the imaginary clock be straight
ahead, flat, or at an angle. For example, the term clockwise corre-
sponds to the normal movement of the clock's hands, whereas
counterclockwise means to move your hands in a reverse direction.

Memory Aids

The addition of memory aids will help the beginning student
retain and recall the signs with their positions and movements. The
memory aids are not necessarily related to what may be considered
as the origin of a sign.

Main Entry and Synonym Index

The Main Entry and Synonym Index is a list of all the main entry words and all the synonyms following the main entries. This list is not to be considered exhaustive, but the sign language student will find it a rich resource and an invaluable aid to versatility of expression. It will also assist the student in locating a basic sign when he or she can think only of a synonym.

Suggestions and Tips for Easier Signing

The Signing Area

Most signs are made in an area extending from head to waist, and shoulder to shoulder. The majority of these signs are formed at or near the head, face, and neck area. This makes it easier for the person receiving the signs to observe and understand them more readily. When you are in between sentences or waiting for a response, hold your hand in a comfortable position at chest level or at your side.

Facial expression is extremely important when signing to deaf people. The deaf person relies heavily upon the combination of facial expressions, body language, and speaking or mouthing the words. Therefore, be sure to include these as you sign.

Punctuation

When asking a question either use the question mark sign at the end of a sentence, or make a questioning facial expression and hold the last sign a little longer. Punctuation can be used for exactness and emphasis when needed or desired but it is often omitted in favor of facial expressions and gestures.

Gender Signs

The male and female gender signs are identified more easily by their location. Many male-related signs are made adjacent to the forehead, while the cheek or chin is the location for many female-related signs.

The Person (Personalizing Word Ending)

This sign usually relates to a person's occupation or position in life and is made after another sign. Some examples of its use would be: sign *bake* plus the *person ending* for *baker*; sign *America* plus the *person ending* for *American*.

Signs with Similar Shapes, Movements, and Characteristics

There are several factors that help make sign language a little easier to learn and remember. Certain signs have similar shapes and movements, and in some cases signs simply reverse the movement while the hand shapes remain unchanged. For example: *come* and *go*; *open* and *close*; and *get in* and *get out*.

In addition, some signs resemble or remind one of the actual physical concept they represent. For example: the sign for *elephant* portrays the elephant's trunk, while the sign for *golf* portrays the use of a golf club.

Sometimes recognizing the origin of a sign helps to recall it more easily. For example: the sign for *milk* has its origin in the action of hand milking a cow.

There are also signs that are initialized by using the hand shape of the first letter of the English word. Some examples are: *parents, family*, and *nephew*. Initialization of signs appears to be a growing trend, and one that certainly aids signers and receivers of signs who desire to communicate in English syntax.

Present, Past, and Future

To understand the sign language concept of present, past, and future, the student should think of the area immediately in front of the body as representing *present* time. Therefore, signs dealing with present time are made in front of the body. Signs referring to the future (*tomorrow, next*) have a forward movement away from the body. Signs that deal with the past (*last week, yesterday*) move backward.

Basic Hand Shapes

This book refers to certain basic hand shapes which are used in the description to aid the student in forming the signs correctly. Familiarize yourself with the following illustrations.

THE *AND* HAND

Note that unless otherwise stated, the expression refers only to the ending position of the *and* hand as illustrated.

OPEN HAND

BENT HAND

FLAT HAND

The fingers are touching unless otherwise indicated by the use of a term such as "flat *open* hand."

CLOSED HAND

CURVED HAND

The fingers are touching unless otherwise indicated by the use of a term such as "curved *open* hand."

CLAWED HAND

The Manual Alphabet

It is highly recommended that the manual alphabet is memorized at the outset of learning sign language. The right hand is preferred to form the letters of the alphabet, although if you are left-handed the left hand may be used. The letter signs are illustrated as seen by the observer, or in some cases at a slightly different angle for the sake of clarity. Generally speaking, the hand should be held comfortably at shoulder level and in front of the body, with the palm facing forward.

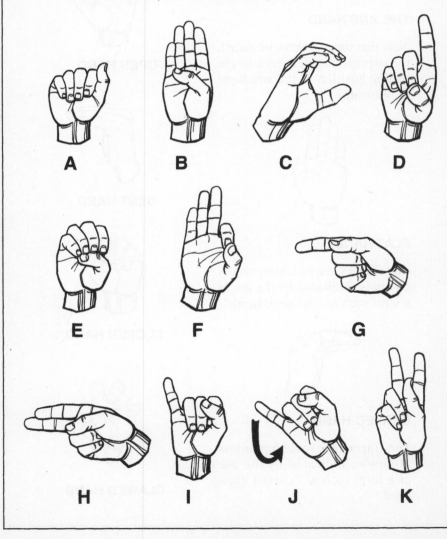

A   B   C   D

E   F   G

H   I   J   K

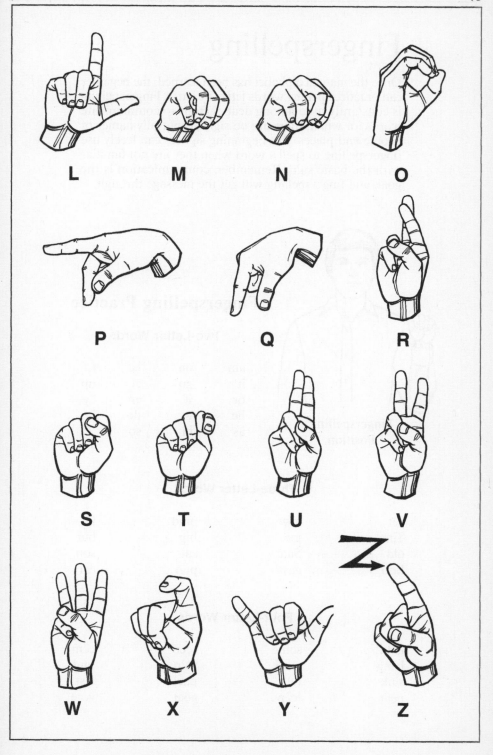

L M N O

P Q R

S T U V

W X Y Z

Fingerspelling

Once the manual alphabet has been learned, the beginner can practice spelling words letter by letter. Fingerspelling is constantly used among deaf persons to communicate words for which there are no signs, especially names of people and places. But beginning signers can freely use fingerspelling to spell a word when they are not familiar with the basic sign. Remember, communication is the goal, and fingerspelling will get the message through.

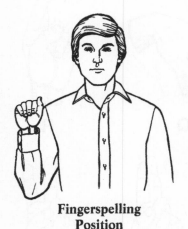

**Fingerspelling
Position**

Fingerspelling Practice

Two-Letter Words

am	on	be	to
it	go	at	up
or	if	an	by
he	we	do	in
as	hi	so	

Three-Letter Words

yet	new	mud	hit
Tim	Joe	big	but
old	Sam	cat	son
Bob	gas	pen	car

Four-Letter Words

land	some	seen	cent
bang	weak	vain	sank
sink	felt	pack	last
near	leap	goat	vote

Numbers

The palm generally faces forward unless otherwise indicated by illustration or description. Sign numbers, money, and years as they are spoken in English. For example: $38.75 is signed "38" "dollars" "75" "cents"; and 1997 is signed "19" "97."

1. Zero to a Million

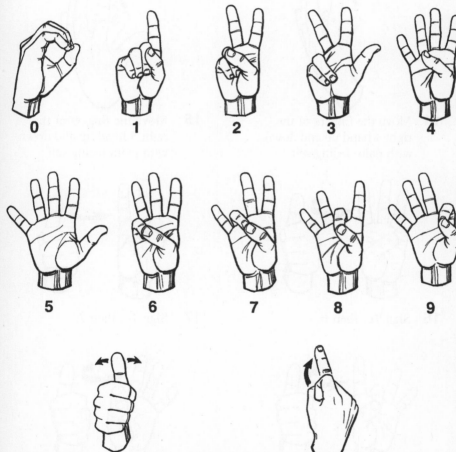

10 Shake the *A* hand.

11 Flick the right index finger up with palm facing self.

12 Flick the right index and middle finger up with palm facing self.

13 Move the fingers of the right hand up and down with palm facing self.

14 Move the fingers of the right *4* hand up and down with palm facing self.

15 Move the fingers of the right *5* hand up and down with palm facing self.

16 Sign *10*, then *6*.

17 Sign *10*, then *7*.

18 Sign *10*, then *8*.

19 Sign *10*, then *9*.

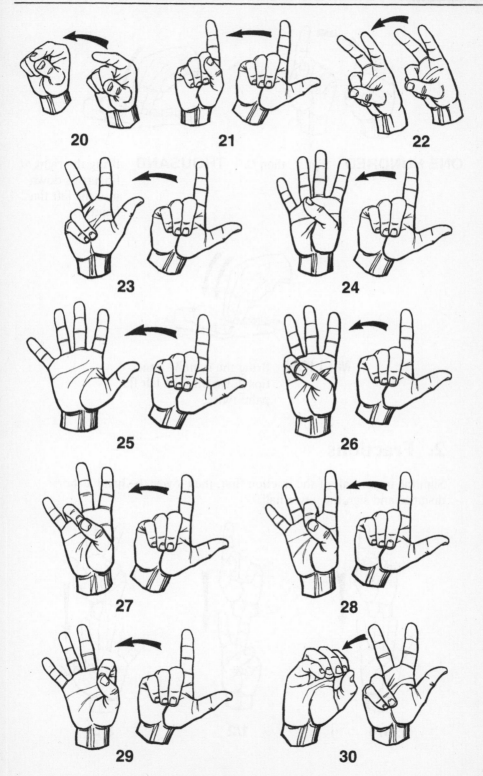

20

21

22

23

24

25

26

27

28

29

30

ONE HUNDRED Sign *1*, then *C*. **THOUSAND** Bring the right *M* fingertips down into the left flat hand.

MILLION Bring the right *M* fingertips down into the left flat palm twice.

2. Fractions

Sign the upper half of the fraction first, then lower the hand a short distance and sign the lower half.

1/4   **1/2**   **3/5**

3. Money

A. CENTS

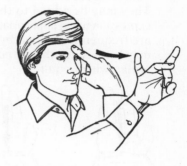

1¢ (penny)   **8¢**

B. DOLLARS

The palm faces forward, then dips and turns so that the palm faces self.

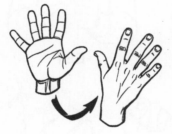

$1.00   **$5.00**   **$9.00**

4. Numbers for Practice

8	77	346	716	6,347
10	89	371	753	9,219
17	94	482	891	15,413
23	122	423	838	17,526
35	139	555	964	39,892
48	174	548	939	1,324,948
52	293	601	1,549	43,268,512
61	227	686	4,858	579,643,810

Inflections

Following are some of the word endings commonly used. They may be added to the basic signs for more exact expression when appropriate. *Note:* Possessives and plurals are frequently omitted by most signers. However, they may be used for the purpose of conveying exact English syntax when required.

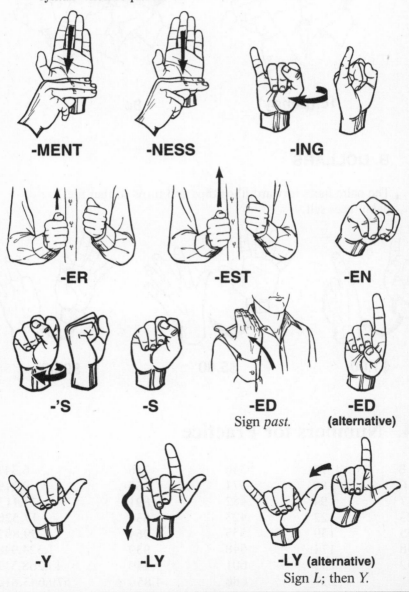

-MENT

-NESS

-ING

-ER

-EST

-EN

-'S

-S

-ED
Sign *past.*

-ED (alternative)

-Y

-LY

-LY (alternative)
Sign *L*; then *Y.*

Definite and Indefinite Articles

Most of the time signers omit the definite and indefinite articles (*a, an, the*), if the meaning of the sentence is not altered. Deaf adults do not use articles when signing. Obviously this would speed up the interchange of conversation. However, when young deaf children are being taught English language structure in the classroom setting, all words are signed.

A (indefinite article)

Hold the right *A* hand to the front with palm facing forward, and make a small arc to the right.

Memory aid: The initial is self-explanatory.

Example: Jenny's English grade was *a* good one.

AN (indefinite article)

Fingerspell *A-N.*

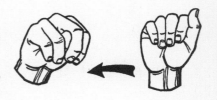

Memory aid: The initials are self-explanatory.

Example: It is correct English to write "I have '*an*' appointment, not '*a*' appointment."

THE (definite article)

Hold the right *T* hand up with palm facing left and rotate it to the right.

Memory aid: The initialized hand, context, and lipreading will convey the meaning.

Example: In English, "*the*" is the definite article.

*Revised and Expanded
Third Edition*

THE
PERIGEE
VISUAL
DICTIONARY
OF
SIGNING

A

ABANDON, DISCARD, FORSAKE, LEAVE, NEGLECT

With the palms facing each other, point both flat hands to the left (or to the right); then pivot both hands downward from the wrists.

Memory aid: Suggests putting something to the side.

Examples: Rose decided to *abandon* her plans. Don't just *leave* me here.

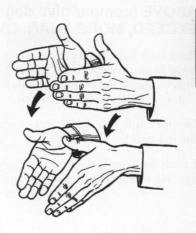

ABOUT, CONCERNING

Move the right index finger in a forward circular direction around the fingers of the left *and* hand.

Memory aid: The circular movement suggests the meaning.

Example: The students are learning *about* scientific principles.

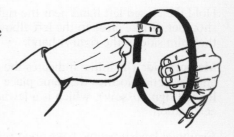

ABOVE, OVER

Make a counterclockwise circle with the right flat hand over the left flat hand.

Memory aid: Suggests one level that is higher than another.

Examples: He is honest and *above* deception. She has authority *over* thirty assistants.

ABOVE (comparative degree), EXCEED, MORE THAN, OVER

Hold both bent hands to the front of the body with the right fingers on top of the left fingers. Raise the bent right hand a short distance. *Note:* Compare *below.*

Memory aid: The right hand moves *above* the left hand.

Examples: Carolyn's grades are *above* average. He took *more than* his brother.

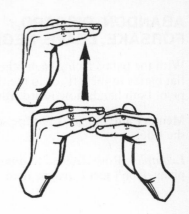

ABRAHAM

Hold the closed left hand near the right shoulder. Strike close to the left elbow with the palm side of the right *A* hand.

Memory aid: The initial indicates the word, and the action locates the same place used for the sign *Passover,* which is a Jewish celebration.

Example: Jewish people have great respect for *Abraham.*

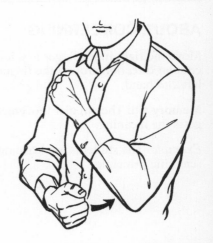

ACCEPT

Hold both open hands to the front of the body. Move them toward the chest while simultaneously forming *and* hands, which then come to rest on the chest.

Memory aid: Suggests bringing something toward oneself.

Example: I want you to *accept* this gift.

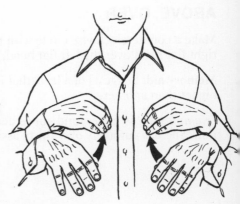

ACCIDENT, COLLISION, CRASH, WRECK

Strike the knuckles of both clenched hands together.

Memory aid: Symbolizes a *collision*.

Example: Be careful not to *collide* with anyone.

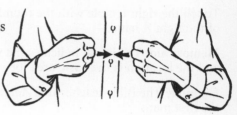

ACROSS, CROSS, OVER

With the left flat hand facing down, move the little-finger edge of the right flat hand over the knuckles of the left hand.

Memory aid: One hand crosses *over* the other.

Examples: Tomorrow we will go *across* the mountain. The horse jumped *over* the fence.

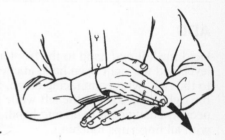

ACTOR, ACTRESS

Rotate both *A* hands inward toward the body with the palms facing each other; then add the sign for *person (personalizing word ending)*.

Memory aid: The initialized hands indicate the words, and the movement suggests the action that accompanies drama.

Example: This play requires nine *actors*.

1.

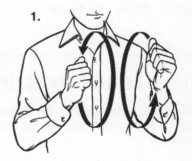

2.

ADAM

Touch the right temple with the thumb tip of the right *A* hand.

Memory aid: The initial indicates the word, and the location is the basic area for *male.*

Example: The Bible teaches that *Adam* was the first man.

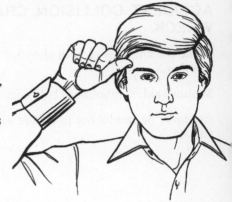

ADD

Hold the left *and* hand to the front at chest level, and the right open hand at chest level to the right with palm facing down. Move the right hand toward the left while simultaneously changing it to an *and* hand. End with all fingertips touching.

Memory aid: Suggests that the right hand grasps something and *adds* it to the left hand.

Example: Please *add* 43 and 96.

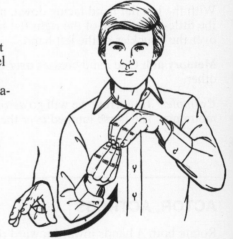

ADOPT, ASSUME, TAKE UP

With palms facing down, simultaneously lift the open hands up while closing them into *S* hands.

Memory aid: Simulates the act of grasping something.

Example: The committee voted to *adopt* the plan suggested by Nathan.

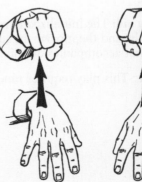

ADULT

Place the right *A*-hand thumb first at the right temple, then at the right side of the chin. *Note:* Compare *parents.*

Memory aid: The initial indicates the word, and the two locations refer to the basic positions for *male* and *female.*

Example: Every *adult* should take advantage of the right to vote.

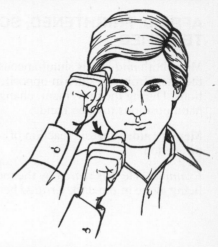

ADVERTISE, COMMERCIAL, PUBLICIZE

Place the left *S* hand in front of the mouth area with the palm facing right and the right *S* hand in front of the left. Move the right *S* hand forward and backward a few times.

Memory aid: Suggests the expression Blowing one's horn, which is used to boast of personal accomplishment.

Example: Ralph decided to *advertise* his car in the newspaper.

ADVICE, ADVISE, COUNSEL

Touch the back of the left flat hand with the fingertips of the right *and* hand. Form an open right hand while moving it forward across the left hand.

Memory aid: Suggests giving out information in many directions.

Example: How would you *advise* me?

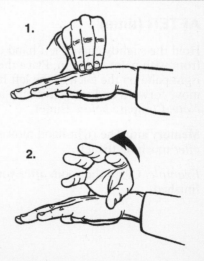

1.

2.

AFRAID, FRIGHTENED, SCARED, TERRIFIED

Move both *and* hands simultaneously across the chest from the sides in opposite directions. During the movement, change the hand positions to open hands.

Memory aid: Suggests reaction of self-protection.

Examples: He was *scared* by the movie. Being alone in the dark *terrified* her.

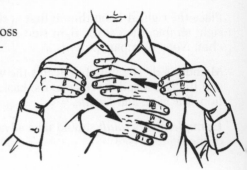

AFRICA, AFRICAN

Make a counterclockwise circle in front of the face with the right *A* hand. The palm faces left. Add the sign for *person (personalizing word ending)* when signing *African* with reference to a person.

Memory aid: The initial indicates the word, which requires context and simultaneous lipreading for full comprehension.

Example: Many different languages are spoken in *Africa*.

AFTER (time)

Hold the slightly curved left hand out to the front with palm facing in. Place the curved right palm on the back of the left hand and move forward and away from the left hand. *Note:* Compare *before* (time).

Memory aid: The right hand moves forward *after* touching the left.

Example: Clean the room *after* you have finished.

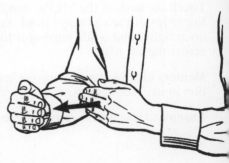

AFTERNOON

Hold the left arm in a horizontal position pointing to the right. The left hand is flat with palm facing down. Place the right forearm on the back of the left hand at a 45-degree angle.

Memory aid: Symbolizes the sun making its descent.

Example: Please come this *afternoon* at 4:00 P.M.

AGAIN, ENCORE, REPEAT

Hold the left flat hand pointing forward with palm up and the bent right hand palm up and parallel to the left hand. Move the bent right hand upward and turn it over until the fingertips are placed in the left palm. Sometimes the left hand is pointed up with palm facing right.

Memory aid: Similar to a clapping action, indicating the desire for *repetition*.

Example: I will visit London *again*.

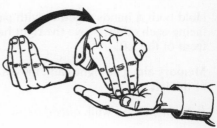

AGAINST, OPPOSE

Thrust the fingertips of the right flat hand into the palm of the left flat hand.

Memory aid: Suggests one hand attacking the other.

Example: I am *opposed* to his decision.

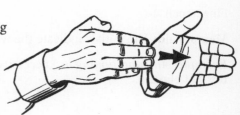

AGREE, ACCORD, COINCIDE, CONSENT, CORRESPOND

Touch the forehead with the right index finger; then move both *D* hands to chest level with palms down and sides of index fingers touching. The latter is the sign for *same*.

Memory aid: A meeting of minds in unison.

Examples: So you *agree*? Let's be in *accord* about this. Does Richard *consent* to the new plan? The information doesn't *correspond*.

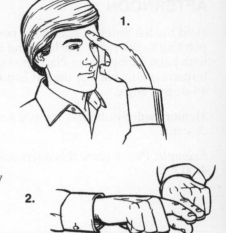
1.

2.

AHEAD

Hold both *A* hands together with palms facing each other. Move the right hand in front of the left.

Memory aid: The right hand moves *ahead* of the left.

Example: Don't walk *ahead* of me.

AIR CONDITIONING

Fingerspell *A-C*.

Memory aid: The initials indicate the words.

Example: Air conditioning is a necessity in this hot climate.

AIRPLANE, FLY, JET

Use the *Y* hand with index finger extended and palm facing down. Make a forward-upward sweeping motion.

Memory aid: Suggests the wings and fuse-lage of an *airplane* taking off.

Example: Do you enjoy *flying*?

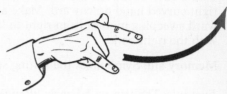

ALIGN, LINE UP

Place both open hands in front of chest with the left palm facing right and the right palm facing left. Put one hand in front of the other and touch the little finger and thumb. Both hands may pivot back and forth slightly in opposite directions.

Memory aid: The fingers can suggest people *lined up*.

Example: The fence posts were *aligned* perfectly.

ALL, ENTIRE, WHOLE

Hold the left flat hand to the front with palm facing the body. Move the right flat hand, with palm facing out, over-down-in-up, ending with the back of the right hand in the palm of the left hand.

Memory aid: The circular action suggests an encompassing and a completeness.

Example: The board members *all* agreed.

ALL NIGHT, OVERNIGHT

Hold the left arm in a horizontal position with the fingers of the left downturned flat hand pointing right. Place the right forearm on the back of the left hand and point the right curved hand downward. Make a downward sweeping motion from right to left with the right hand.

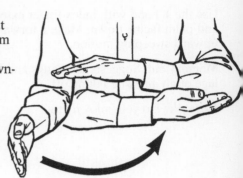

Memory aid: Symbolizes the setting sun.

Example: The trip took nearly *all night.*

ALLOW, GRANT, LET, PERMIT

Hold both flat hands forward with palms facing. Swing them upward simultaneously so that the fingertips point slightly outward. The *L* hands may be used for *let* and the *P* hands for *permit.*

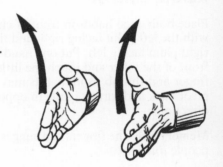

Memory aid: The slight widening of the hands suggests flexibility.

Example: Please *allow* me to assist you.

ALL RIGHT, OK

Hold the left flat hand with palm facing up. Move the little-finger edge of the right flat hand across the face of the left hand from the heel to the fingertips. *OK* is often fingerspelled.

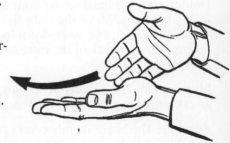

Memory aid: The movement suggests a straight line with agreement to move ahead.

Examples: Your plan seems *all right* to us. It's *OK* with me.

ALMOST, NEARLY

Brush the little-finger edge of the right hand upward over the fingertips of the curved left hand. Both palms face up.

Memory aid: The left hand *almost* stops the upward movement of the right hand.

Example: It's *almost* time to go.

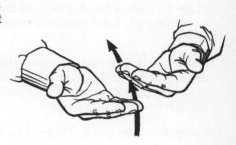

ALTAR

Touch the *A* thumbs in front with the palms facing down. Move them apart sideways a short distance, then down a short distance with the palms now facing.

Memory aid: The initials indicate the word, and the movement outlines the tablelike shape of an *altar*.

Example: The bride and groom knelt at the *altar*.

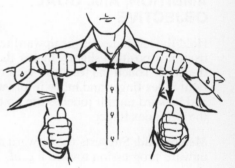

ALWAYS, CONSTANTLY, EVER

Point the right index finger forward-upward with palm up, then move it in a clockwise circle.

Memory aid: The circle suggests continuance.

Example: That boy is *always* getting into trouble.

AM, ARE

Place the right A-hand thumb on the lips and move the right hand straight forward. Use R for *are*.

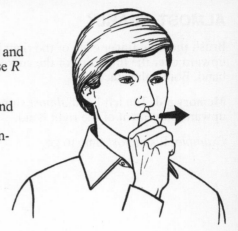

Memory aid: The initial suggests the sound of the word, and the action indicates a breathing person and thus a symbolic connection with the verb *to be*.

Examples: I *am* going. They *are* clever.

AMBITION, AIM, GOAL, OBJECTIVE

Hold the left index finger upward to the front in a position slightly higher than the head. Touch the forehead with the right index finger and move it forward and upward until it touches the tip of the left index finger.

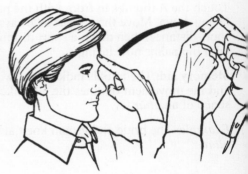

Memory aid: Suggests the forward and upward progression toward a *goal*.

Examples: She has a lot of *ambition*. I *aim* to win.

AMERICA, AMERICAN

Interlock the fingers of both slightly curved open hands and move them from right to left in an outward circle. For *American* add the sign for *person (personalizing word ending)* in reference to a person.

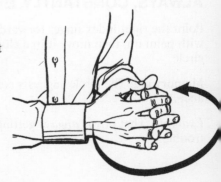

Memory aid: The interlocked fingers suggest the log fences made by *America's* early settlers.

Example: America is blessed with abundant resources.

AMESLAN (American Sign Language)

Rotate both *A* hands alternately toward the body with palms facing forward. Then point both *L* hands toward each other and move them to the sides with a twisting motion from the wrists.

Memory aid: The first part of the movement is the sign for *signs,* and the second part is the sign for *language.*

Example: How good are you at signing *Ameslan?*

AMONG

Interweave the right index finger in and out of the fingers of the left open hand.

Memory aid: Suggests the mingling of one person *among* others.

Example: Phil is looked upon as *among* the best of tennis players.

ANALYZE

Place both crooked *V* hands in front of the body with palms facing down. Pull the hands apart sideways a few times. *Note:* Compare *separate.*

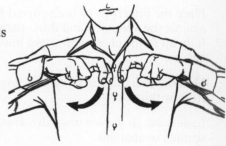

Memory aid: Suggests pulling something apart to examine the inner workings.

Example: We must *analyze* the reasons for his success.

AND

Place the right open hand in front with palm facing in and fingers pointing to the left. Move the hand to the right while bringing the fingertips and thumb together.

Memory aid: Symbolizes a stretching action. The conjunction *and* stretches sentences.

Example: Please make biscuits *and* gravy.

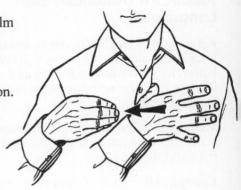

ANGEL, WINGS

Touch the shoulders with the fingertips of both hands (sometimes only one hand is used). Point the fingers of both downturned hands outward to the sides; then flap the hands up and down a few times.

Memory aid: Suggests the general location and action of *wings*.

Example: An albatross has very large *wings*.

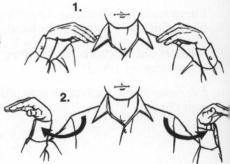

ANGER, FUME, RAGE, WRATH

Place the fingertips of both curved hands against the abdomen and draw them forcefully up to the chest with slight inward curves.

Memory aid: Suggests *angry* feelings rising from within.

Examples: He *fumed* inwardly. Dan's *rage* seemed unabatable.

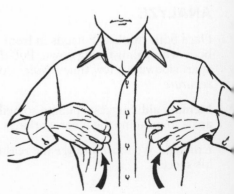

ANIMAL

Place the fingertips of both bent hands on the chest. Maintain the position of the fingertips while rocking both hands in and out sideways.

Memory aid: Suggests the often pronounced breathing movements of an animal that has exerted itself physically.

Example: Donna is a real *animal* lover.

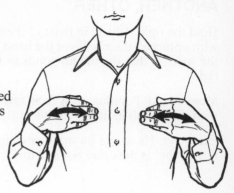

ANNOUNCE, DECLARE, PROCLAIM

Touch the lips with both index fingers and swing them forward and to the sides.

Memory aid: Something is *proclaimed* from the mouth that expands to a wide group of hearers.

Example: Malcolm decided to *announce* an early retirement.

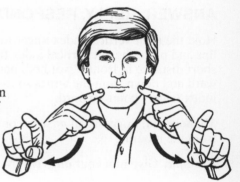

ANOINT

Place the right *C* hand slightly above head level with palm facing forward. Tilt the *C* hand toward the head.

Memory aid: Symbolizes pouring onto the head.

Example: David was *anointed* by Samuel before he became king.

ANOTHER, OTHER

Hold the right *A* hand in front of the chest with upturned thumb. Pivot the hand from the wrist so that the thumb points to the right.

Memory aid: Pointing away from oneself with the thumb indicates *another*.

Examples: He works for *another* company now. What is the *other* boy's name?

ANSWER, REPLY, RESPOND

Hold the right vertical index finger to the lips and place the left vertical index finger a short distance in front. Pivot both hands forward and down from the wrists so that the index fingers point forward.

Memory aid: Suggests an *answer* coming from the mouth.

Example: Give him your *answer* now.

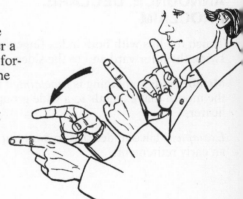

ANY

Place the right *A* hand in front of the body with the palm facing in. Move the *A* hand forward to the right until the palm faces forward.

Memory aid: The thumb seems to be searching for something or someone.

Example: We will consider *any* apartment available.

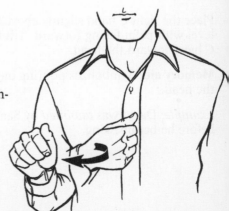

ANYHOW, ALTHOUGH, ANYWAY, DOESN'T MATTER, NO MATTER, REGARDLESS

Hold both slightly curved hands to the front with palms facing up and fingertips pointing toward each other. Brush the fingertips back and forth over each other a few times.

Memory aid: A vague type of action that suggests many possibilities.

Examples: No matter what you say, I am going. He kept going, *regardless* of the pain. It *doesn't matter* to me.

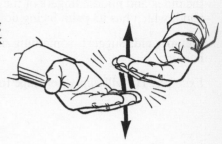

ANYONE, ANYBODY

Place the right *A* hand in front of the body with the palm facing in. Move the *A* hand forward to the right until the palm faces forward. Follow with the numerical sign for *one*, which is done by pointing up with the right index finger.

Memory aid: The hand seems to be engaged in a wide-angled search for something or someone.

Example: Does he know *anyone* here?

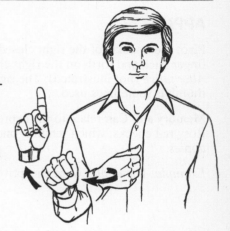

ANYTHING

Sign *any* followed by *thing. Any* is signed by placing the right *A* hand in front of the body with the palm facing in. Move the *A* hand forward to the right until the palm faces forward. *Thing* is signed by dropping the right hand slightly a few times as it is moved to the right. Compare *thing* and *substance*.

Memory aid: The hand movements suggest the idea of presenting several alternatives.

Example: Do you have *anything* we can use?

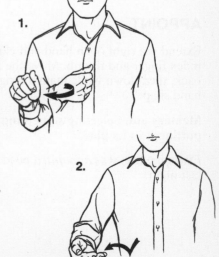

APPEAR, POP UP, RISE, SHOW UP

Move the right index finger upward between the index and middle fingers of the left flat hand, which has its palm facing down.

Memory aid: Suggests something *rising* from below.

Example: He will *appear* onstage tonight.

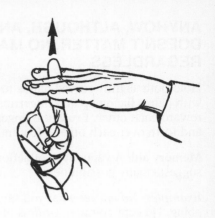

APPLE

Pivot the knuckle of the right closed index finger back and forth on the right cheek. *Alternative* (not illustrated): The right *A* thumb is sometimes used.

Memory aid: Can relate to the expression Rosy red cheeks, which reminds one of *apples*.

Example: The *apples* were cheap.

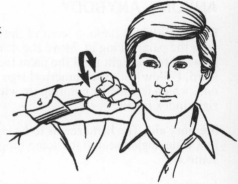

APPOINT

Extend the right open hand and close the index finger and thumb. Move the right hand back, then down while maintaining the same hand shape.

Memory aid: Selecting something and putting it in its place.

Example: Bob was *appointed* head coach last night.

APPOINTMENT, ENGAGEMENT, RESERVATION

Circle the palm-down right *A* hand above the palm-in left *S* hand in a counterclockwise direction. Bring the right wrist down onto the left and move both hands down together a short distance.

Memory aid: Indicates a binding together of the hands in commitment.

Examples: I must not miss my *appointment.* My luncheon *engagement* has been postponed. There are two seats *reserved* for you.

APPRECIATE

Make a counterclockwise circle with the right middle finger over the heart. The sign for *please* may also be used.

Memory aid: Suggests feelings of the heart.

Example: I *appreciate* good music.

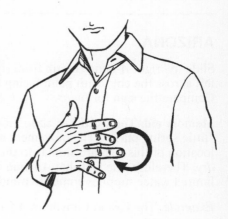

ARCHERY

Stretch the left *S* hand out sideways; then bring the right curved *V* fingers backward from behind the left hand to a closed-hand position just under the chin.

Memory aid: Symbolizes an arrow being pulled back in a bow.

Example: Do you belong to an *archery* club?

ARGUE, DISPUTE, DEBATE, CONTROVERSY

First strike the left palm with the right index finger and then the right palm with the left index finger. Repeat several times.

Memory aid: The movement suggests two sides or opposing opinions.

Example: Jim is one of those people who seems to enjoy an *argument*.

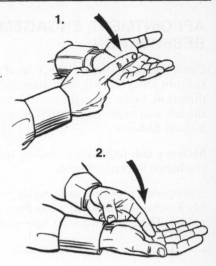

ARIZONA

Slide the right *A*-hand thumb from right to left across the chin with palm facing left. Compare the sign for *twins*.

Memory aid: The word *"Arizona"* means "little spring place." The movement and location of this sign are similar to those for *dry*. Therefore, the fact that *Arizona* has limited water supplies comes to mind.

Example: The Grand Canyon in *Arizona* is awesome.

ARM

Move the fingertips of the upturned curved right hand down the left arm.

Memory aid: The length of the *arm* is pointed out.

Example: His *arms* are strong.

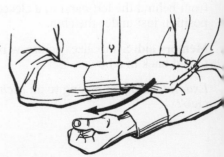

ARMY, MILITARY

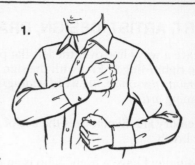

Place palm side of right *A* hand just below left shoulder and palm side of left *A* hand several inches below right hand. Then hold both *C* hands upright before the chest with palms facing. Move hands outward in a circle until little fingers touch.

Memory aid: A combination of the signs for *soldier* and *group*.

Example: John decided to join the *army* just as his father and grandfather had before him.

AROUND, SURROUND

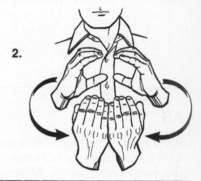

Make a counterclockwise circle with the right index finger around the left upturned *and* hand.

Memory aid: Suggests circling *around* something.

Example: The shark swam *around* the boat.

ARRIVE, GET TO, REACH

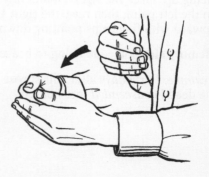

Move the back of the right curved hand forward into the palm of the left curved hand.

Memory aid: Destination is *reached.*

Examples: Please *arrive* on time. How do you *get to* Main Street?

ART, ARTIST, DESIGN, DRAW

Trace a wavy line over the left flat palm with the right *I* finger. End with the sign for *person (personalizing word ending)* when signing *artist*.

Memory aid: Symbolizes the use of a pencil or brush.

Example: I have a friend who is an *artist*.

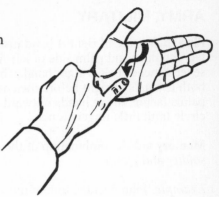

AS

Point both index fingers forward together with a short distance between them and the palms facing down. Maintain this position as both hands are moved to the left. *Note:* Compare *same* and *too*.

Memory aid: The repeated action indicates something extra or added.

Example: The air felt as hot *as* a furnace.

ASCENSION

Hold the left flat hand to the front with palm facing up. Place the right *V*-hand fingertips on the left palm; then raise the right *V* hand upward with fingertips pointing down.

Memory aid: Someone rising to heaven.

Example: Forty days after Christ rose from the dead He *ascended* into heaven.

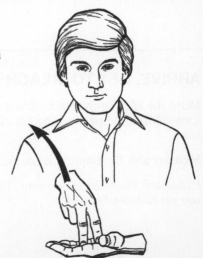

ASK, REQUEST

Bring both flat hands together with palms touching and move them in a backward arc toward the body.

Memory aid: Suggests the traditional hand position of a person engaged in prayer.

Example: I'll *ask* my boss for a raise.

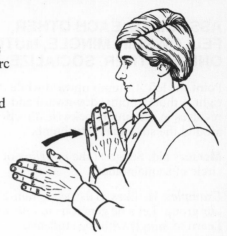

ASSEMBLIES OF GOD

Put thumb of right *A* hand on forehead; then point right *G* finger forward and upward at head level. (Some use the flat hand with palm facing left.) Move right hand in a downward arc toward self, ending with a *B* hand in front of the chest. The second part is the sign for *God.*

Memory aid: The *A* hand indicates the name; the pointing finger suggests God is above all.

Example: Do you attend the *Assemblies of God* church?

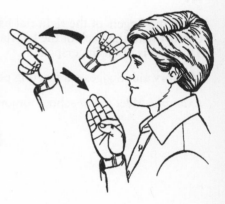

ASSISTANT

Bring the right *L* hand up under the closed left hand and touch the little-finger edge of the left hand with the right thumb. Sometimes the left hand remains open.

Memory aid: Suggests support from underneath.

Example: Pat is one of my *assistants.*

ASSOCIATE, EACH OTHER, FELLOWSHIP, MINGLE, MUTUAL, ONE ANOTHER, SOCIALIZE

Point the left *A* thumb upward while the right *A* thumb points downward and revolves in a counterclockwise direction around the stationary left thumb.

Memory aid: Suggests the *mingling* of a circle of acquaintances.

Examples: He likes to *associate* himself with our group. Let's be generous to *one another.* Learn to *mingle* with the students.

AT

Bring the fingers of the right flat hand in contact with the back of the left flat hand. This sign is often fingerspelled.

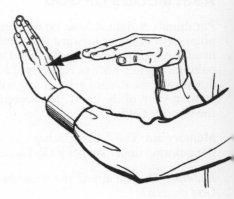

Memory aid: Suggests a meeting point.

Example: Meet me *at* school tomorrow.

ATTEMPT, EFFORT, TRY

Hold both *S* hands to the front with palms facing; then move them forward with a pushing motion. *Effort* and *try* may be initialized.

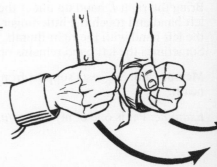

Memory aid: Pushing takes *effort.*

Example: Will you *attempt* to race again?

ATTENTION, CONCENTRATION, FOCUS, PAY ATTENTION

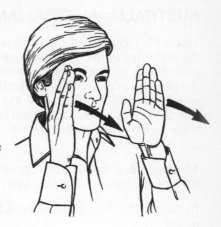

Hold both flat hands at the sides of the face with palms facing; then move them both forward simultaneously.

Memory aid: Suggests *concentration* in one direction without deviating, and also reminds one of the blinders attached to some horse bridles that allow the horse to see only straight ahead.

Examples: Give me your *attention*. We must *focus* our thoughts on the problem.

AUDIOLOGY

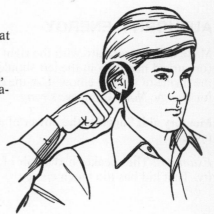

Circle the right *A* hand in a forward circle at the right ear.

Memory aid: The initial indicates the word, and the action suggests a continuing emphasis on the ear.

Example: Audiology concerns itself with the study of the science of hearing.

AUNT

Place the right *A* hand close to the right cheek and shake back and forth from the wrist.

Memory aid: The initial *A* is placed near the *female* sign position.

Example: His *aunt* likes to baby-sit.

AUSTRALIA, AUSTRALIAN

Touch the right side of the forehead with the fingertips of the right flat hand with the palm facing in; then twist the hand so that the palm faces out with the fingertips again touching the forehead. Add the sign for *person (personalizing word ending)* when signing *Australian* with reference to a person.

Memory aid: Suggests the wide upturned brim of the traditional *Australian* bush hat.

Example: The *Australian* outback is enormous.

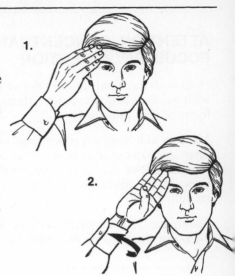

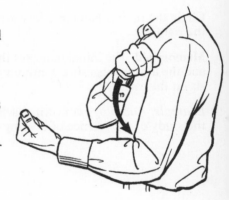

AUTHORITY, ENERGY

Make a downward arc with the right *A* hand (or curved hand) from the left shoulder to the inside of the left elbow. Use the *E* hand for *energy*. *Note:* Compare *strong*.

Memory aid: Suggests the power of a biceps muscle.

Examples: The speaker had an air of *authority*. That kid has too much *energy*.

AVOID, EVADE, SHUN

Place both *A* hands to the front with palms facing and the right hand slightly behind the left. Move the right hand backward away from the left with a wavy motion. *Alternative* (not illustrated): Push to left with the palms of both flat hands while making an appropriate facial expression.

Memory aid: The first sign suggests that the right hand is attempting to *avoid* the left and the second suggests the gesture of pushing something aside.

Example: Tax *evasion* is a serious crime.

AWAKE, AROUSE, WAKE UP

Place the closed thumbs and index fingers of both *Q* hands at the corners of the eyes; then open eyes and fingers simultaneously.

Memory aid: Symbolizes the eyes opening.

Example: It's time to *wake up*.

AWAY

Move the curved right hand away from the body and to the right, ending with the palm facing forward and downward. Sometimes the *A* hand is used at the beginning of the sign.

Memory aid: A natural gesture that suggests separation.

Example: Mickey moved *away* from the store window.

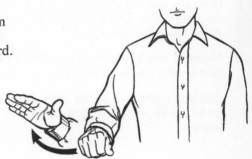

AWFUL, CATASTROPHIC, DREADFUL, FEARFUL, HORRIBLE, TERRIBLE, TRAGIC

Place both *O* hands near the temples and flick the fingers out while forming open hands with palms facing.

Memory aid: Suggests that a person's attention is riveted to something unpleasant.

Examples: The accident was *awful* to behold. There was a *fearful* explosion.

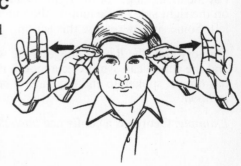

AWKWARD, BUNGLING, CLUMSY

Point both 3 hands forward with the palms facing down. Move them back and forth or up and down with an *awkward* jerking motion.

Memory aid: Suggests a person trying to walk with some toes missing.

Example: I've noticed how *awkward* she's becoming.

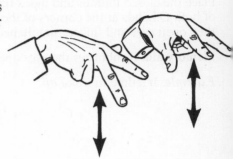

B BABY, INFANT

Hold the arms in the natural position for cradling a baby and rock the arms sideways. *Note:* Compare *fool.*

Memory aid: The natural movement of comforting a *baby* in the arms.

Examples: She was a cute *baby. Infants* up to age two are provided for in the nursery.

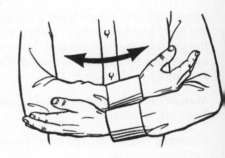

BACHELOR

Put the index finger of the right *B* hand first on the right side of the mouth, then on the left. Some signers reverse this action.

Memory aid: The *B* hand suggests the word, and the action can symbolize a mouth that has not yet spoken to end the state of *bachelorhood.*

Example: George is a confirmed *bachelor.*

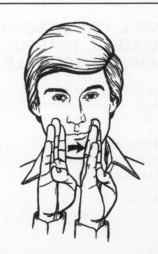

BACK AND FORTH

Move the right *A* hand *back and forth* a few times.

Memory aid: The movement indicates the meaning.

Example: She drove *back and forth* every day.

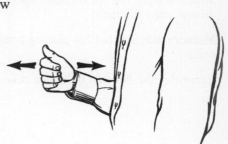

BACON

Touch the fingertips of both *U* hands in front of the chest. Move both hands out sideways in opposite directions while waving the *U* fingers up and down.

Memory aid: Suggests the wavy shape of *bacon* as it is being cooked.

Example: I like *bacon* and eggs for breakfast.

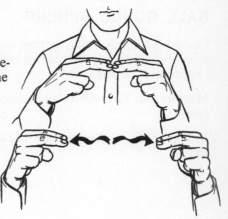

BAD

Place the fingertips of the right flat hand at the lips; then move the right hand down and turn it so that the palm faces down.

Memory aid: Suggests something that has been tasted and disapproved of.

Example: This fruit has gone *bad*.

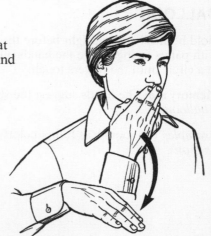

BAKE, OVEN

Slide the right flat (or *B*) hand under the left downturned flat hand.

Memory aid: Symbolizes placing bread in an *oven.*

Example: She *baked* a delicious cake.

BALL, ROUND, SPHERE

Curve both hands with fingertips touching as if holding a ball. Let the thumbs and index fingers face the observer.

Memory aid: The round shape identifies a *ball.*

Examples: So you have a *ball?* The earth is a *sphere.*

BALLOON

Hold both *C* hands upright before the mouth with palms facing. Move the hands outward in a circle until the fingers touch.

Memory aid: The hands suggest the shape of a *balloon.*

Example: The room was full of colorful *balloons.*

BANANA

Hold the left index finger up with the palm facing in; then make a few grasping downward movements around it with the fingers and thumb of the right hand.

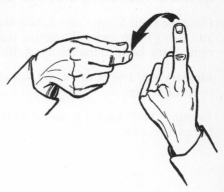

Memory aid: Suggests peeling a *banana*.

Example: Bananas contain valuable vitamins.

BAPTIST, BAPTISM, IMMERSION

Hold both *A* hands to the front with palms facing. Move both hands to the right and down slightly, while at the same time turning the hands so that the thumbs point to the right.

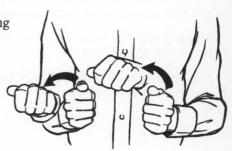

Memory aid: Symbolizes water *baptism* by *immersion*.

Example: I have a cousin who is *Baptist*.

BAPTIZE, CHRISTEN (sprinkling)

Place the closed *S* (or *and*) hand above the head and thrust downward toward the head simultaneously opening the hand.

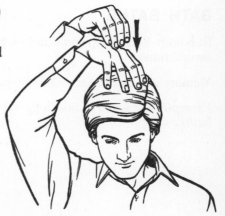

Memory aid: Symbolizes water falling on the head.

Example: Last summer we *baptized* new converts in a river in Albania.

BASEBALL, BAT, SOFTBALL

Place the right *S* hand above the left *S* hand and swing them forward together from the right of the body to the center of the body.

Memory aid: The position and action of a *baseball* batter.

Example: Professional *baseball* players have to practice a lot.

BASKETBALL

Hold both curved open hands at head level and move them forward and upward.

Memory aid: The natural position and action for throwing a *basketball*.

Example: I found *basketball* to be an extremely strenuous game.

BATH, BATHE

Rub both *A* hands up and down on the chest several times.

Memory aid: Symbolizes washing the body.

Example: She loved to take long, relaxing *baths*.

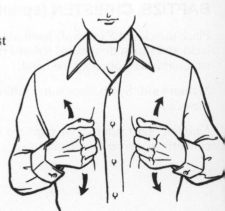

BATTLE, WAR

Hold both open bent hands at chest level with fingertips pointing toward each other. Move both hands simultaneously to the left and then to the right a few times.

Memory aid: Suggests the advance and retreat of military forces.

Example: We will win the *war*.

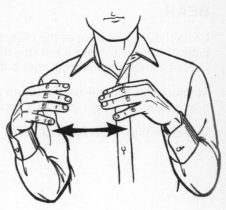

BAWL OUT

Place the little-finger edge of the right *S* hand over the thumb edge of the left *S* hand. Move both hands forward while quickly forming open hands that are crossed at the wrists.

Memory aid: The fingers are thrust vigorously toward another person, representing a barrage of words.

Example: He got *bawled out* by the boss today.

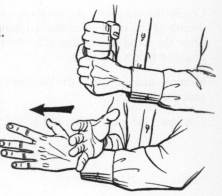

BE

Move the right *B* hand forward from the mouth.

Memory aid: The initial suggests the word, and the action indicates a breathing person and thus a symbolic connection with the verb *to be*.

Example: Please *be* careful.

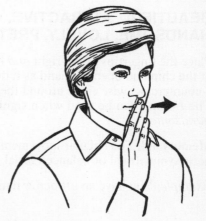

BEAR

Cross the arms in front of the chest with palms facing self. Make a few downward and inward clawing movements with both hands.

Memory aid: Symbolizes the action of a *bear's* claws while grasping at something.

Example: Watch out for wild *bears*.

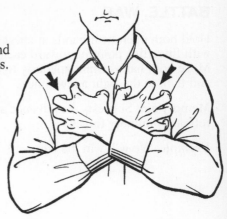

BEARD

Cradle the chin with the fingertips and thumb of the right open curved hand; then draw the hand down until it forms the *and* position below the chin.

Memory aid: Suggests the position and shape of a *beard*.

Example: Ed grew a fine red *beard*.

BEAUTIFUL, ATTRACTIVE, HANDSOME, LOVELY, PRETTY

Place the fingertips of the right *and* hand at the chin and open the hand as it describes a counterclockwise circle around the face. The *H* hand can be used when signing *handsome*.

Memory aid: The circular movement suggests symmetrical or balanced facial features.

Example: You have an *attractive* daughter.

BECAUSE

Place the right index finger on the forehead. Move slightly to the right and upward while forming the *A* hand.

Memory aid: Touching the forehead can indicate the thought that there is a reason for everything.

Example: I appreciate you *because* you are honest.

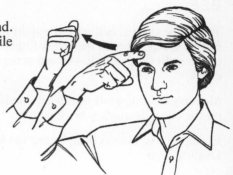

BECOME, GET

Place the curved hands in front with the right palm facing forward and the left palm facing self; then reverse positions.

Memory aid: Suggests a change around.

Example: John *became* a licensed pilot recently.

BED

Hold both hands palm to palm and place the back of the left hand on the right cheek. *Alternative* (not illustrated): Place the slightly curved right hand on the right cheek and tilt the head to the right.

Memory aid: Both signs symbolize resting the head on a pillow.

Example: It's time to go to *bed*.

BEE

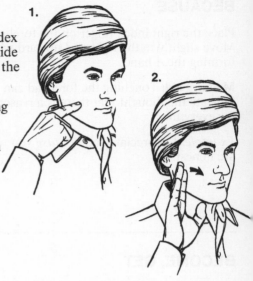

Touch the right cheek with the right index finger. Quickly brush the index-finger side of the right flat hand downward across the cheek.

Memory aid: Suggests that a *bee* landing on the cheek is quickly brushed off.

Example: I've always been interested in keeping *bees*.

BEER

Draw the index-finger side of the right *B* hand down at the right side of the mouth.

Memory aid: The initial *B* suggests the word, and the downward action suggests drinking.

Example: Jack's drinking problem started with just a few *beers*.

BEFORE (location), FACE TO FACE, PRESENCE

Hold the left flat hand at eye level with palm facing in. Move the right flat hand upward with a sweeping motion until palms are facing.

Memory aid: Suggests one person moving in front of another.

Example: The bride and groom stood *before* the altar.

BEFORE (time)

Hold the slightly curved left hand out to the front with palm facing in. Hold the right curved hand near the palm of the left and then draw the right hand in toward the body. *Note:* Compare *after.*

Memory aid: The right hand is *before* the palm of the left.

Example: Let me read that book *before* you return it.

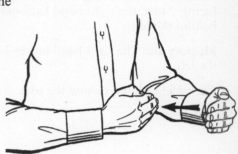

BEG, ENTREAT, PLEAD

Pull the right upturned curved hand backward across the back of the left downturned closed hand. *Alternative* (not illustrated): Clasp both hands together and shake them slightly as in the traditional gesture of begging for mercy.

Memory aid: The upturned hand suggests a desire to grasp something.

Example: She may end up *begging* for help.

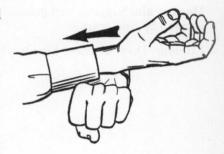

BEHAVIOR

Hold both *B* hands, side by side with palms forward, in front of the body and swing them simultaneously back and forth.

Memory aid: Displaying one's actions for all to see.

Example: Jason's *behavior* was not expected.

BEHIND

Hold both *A* hands together with palms facing. Move the right hand backward *behind* the left.

Memory aid: The right hand moves *behind* the left.

Example: Josh hid *behind* the tree.

BELIEVE

1.

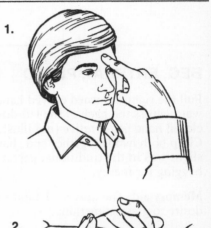

Touch the forehead with the right index finger; then bring the right hand down until it clasps left hand in front of chest.

Memory aid: Suggests that *belief* is something to be held onto.

Example: Do you *believe* her story?

2.

BELOW, BENEATH, UNDER

Make a counterclockwise circle with the right flat hand below the left flat hand. *Note: Under* is also signed by moving the right *A* hand under the left flat hand, and sometimes by circling the *A* hand counterclockwise in that position.

Memory aid: Suggests one level lower than another.

Example: The water remained *below* his knees.

BELOW (comparative degree), LESS THAN, UNDER

Hold both bent hands to the front with the left fingers on top of the right fingers. Lower the right hand a short distance. *Note:* Compare *above.*

Memory aid: The right hand moves *below* the left hand.

Examples: Earl's estimate was *below* his competitor's. The temperature is *less than* 30 degrees.

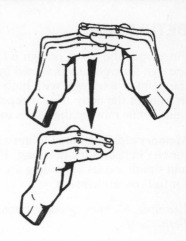

BERRY

Make a twisting motion with the right fingers and thumb while they hold the left little finger.

Memory aid: Suggests the action of picking a *berry.*

Example: That bush is full of *berries.*

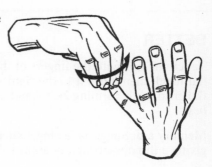

BEST

Touch the lips with the fingers of the right flat hand; then, while closing it into an *A*-hand shape, move it to the right side of the head above head level. *Note:* See *better.*

Memory aid: Suggests tasting something and giving a thumbs-up sign of approval.

Example: It's the *best* store for novelties that I know of.

BETHLEHEM

Fingerspell the word, or sign *B* followed by the sign for *city*. *City* is signed by making the point of a triangle with both flat hands in front of the body. This is repeated a few times while moving the hands to the right.

Memory aid: The initial followed by the sign for *city* indicates the meaning. The context and simultaneous lipreading are required for full comprehension.

Example: Many religious groups visit *Bethlehem*.

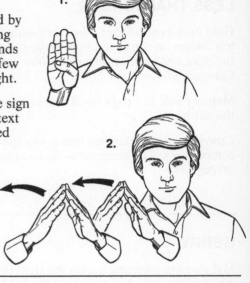
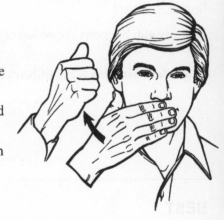

BETTER

Touch the lips with the fingers of the right flat hand; then move it to the right side of the head while forming an *A* hand. *Note:* See *best*.

Memory aid: Suggests tasting something and giving a thumbs-up sign of approval.

Example: This year's concert was *better* than previous ones.

BETWEEN

Put the little-finger edge of the right flat hand between the thumb and index finger of the left flat hand. Pivot the right hand back and forth while keeping the right little-finger edge anchored.

Memory aid: The right hand is *between* two sides.

Example: Put the table *between* the two windows.

BEYOND

Hold both flat hands to the front with palms facing in. Move the right hand over the stationary left hand and continue with the forward movement. *Note:* Compare *next.*

Memory aid: Can symbolize the other side of a wall and *beyond.*

Example: The store is *beyond* the second set of lights.

BIBLE, GOD'S BOOK

Hold both open hands to the front with palms facing. Touch left palm with right middle finger; then touch right palm with left middle finger. This is the sign for *Jesus.* An alternative (not illustrated) is to point both flat hands up with palms touching in a "praying hands" position. Last, point both hands forward with palms touching; then open them.

Memory aid: The alternatives indicate *Jesus' Book* or *God's Book* respectively. The last part is the sign for *book.*

Example: Do you own a *Bible?*

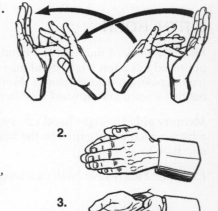

1.

2.

3.

BICYCLE, CYCLE, TRICYCLE

Move both downturned *S* hands forward in alternate circles.

Memory aid: Symbolizes the action of pedaling a *bicycle.*

Example: Riding a *bicycle* is good for the health.

BIRD

Place the right *Q* hand at the right side of the mouth with the fingers pointing forward. Close and open the *Q* fingers a few times.

Memory aid: Suggests the movement of a *bird's* beak.

Example: It's fun to feed the *birds* in our yard.

BIRTH, BORN

Place the back of the right flat hand into the upturned left palm (right hand may start from a position near stomach). Move both hands forward and upward together.

Memory aid: The right hand can symbolize a baby which is presented to the left hand, and then to all.

Example: Helen gave *birth* two weeks early.

BIRTHDAY

Place back of right flat hand into upturned left palm. Move hands forward and upward together. Point left index finger to right, palm down. Rest right elbow on left index finger with right index finger pointing upward. Move right index finger and arm in partial arc across body from right to left.

Memory aid: The signs for *birth* and *day*.

Example: Mom's *birthday* is next month.

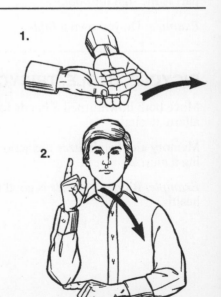

1.

2.

BISCUIT

Place the right *C* thumb and fingertips into the left flat palm and raise right hand a few times.

Memory aid: Suggests a *biscuit* rising.

Example: A favorite American breakfast includes *biscuits* and gravy.

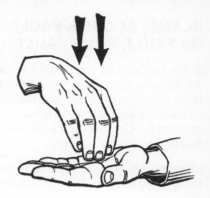

BLACK

Move the right index finger sideways across the right eyebrow.

Memory aid: Suggests the cosmetic makeup of the eyebrow.

Example: I need some *black* shoes.

BLACKBERRY

Move the right index finger sideways across the right eyebrow. Make a twisting motion with the right fingers and thumb while they hold the left little finger.

Memory aid: The signs for *black* and *berry*.

Example: We used to go *blackberry* picking when we were younger.

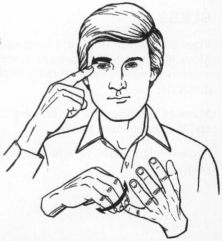

BLAME, ACCUSE, FAULT, MY FAULT, YOUR FAULT

Strike the back of the closed left hand with the little-finger edge of the right *A* hand. Point the right knuckles and thumb to self or another depending on who is being referred to. Combine the movements together smoothly as one.

Memory aid: Suggests that someone needs to have the back of the hand slapped.

Example: The accident is *your fault.*

BLANKET

Hold both open hands to the front with palms facing down and fingers pointing down. Lift both hands to shoulder level while closing the thumbs on the index fingers.

Memory aid: Symbolizes pulling up a *blanket* to cover oneself.

Example: You will need three *blankets.*

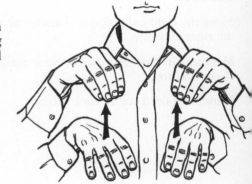

BLESS

Place the thumbs of both *A* hands at the lips. Move both hands in a forward-downward movement while changing them to palm-down flat hands.

Memory aid: Suggests the *blessing* of a kiss and the laying on of hands.

Example: Do I have your *blessing* on this project?

BLIND

Place the fingertips of the right curved *V* fingers in front of the eyes and lower slightly. Sometimes the eyes are closed momentarily.

Memory aid: Suggests that the eyes are closed.

Example: Do you know any *blind* people?

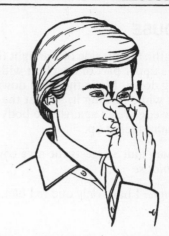

BLOOD, BLEED, HEMORRHAGE

Wiggle the fingers of the right open hand as they move down the back of the left open hand. Sometimes the lips are touched first with the right index finger, which is the sign for *red*.

Memory aid: Symbolizes a *bleeding* left hand with *blood* trickling down.

Example: Some people faint at the sight of *blood*.

1.

2.

BLOSSOM, BLOOM

Point both curved hands upward with palms facing and fingertips touching. Move the hands outward and upward while forming open curved hands.

Memory aid: Suggests the process of budding and *blooming*.

Example: Your roses are *blooming*.

BLOUSE

Place the thumb side of the right flat hand on the upper part of the chest with the palm facing down. Move the hand down to the waist while turning it, so that the little-finger edge rests against the body with the palm facing up.

Memory aid: Suggests the area covered by a *blouse.*

Example: I have only one red *blouse.*

BLUE

Move the right *B* hand to the right while shaking it from the wrist.

Memory aid: The initial indicates the meaning.

Example: My new shirt is *blue.*

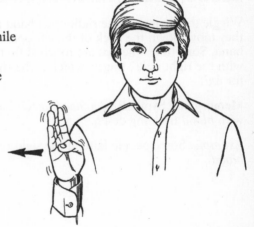

BLUEBERRY

Move the right *B* hand to the right while shaking it from the wrist. Make a twisting motion with the right fingers and thumb while they hold the left little finger.

Memory aid: The signs for *blue* and *berry.*

Example: Carol makes the most delicious *blueberry* pie.

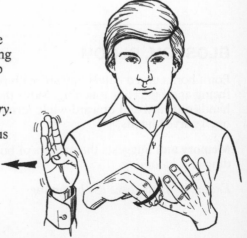

BLUSH

Stroke the right index finger down across the lips. Raise both open hands in front of the face with palms facing in.

Memory aid: Suggests red coming over the face in embarrassment.

Example: The surprise birthday party made Mom *blush.*

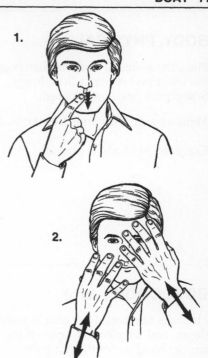

BOAST, BRAG, SHOW OFF

Move one or both *A*-hand thumbs in and out at the sides just above the waist.

Memory aid: Pointing continually to self suggests a self-centered person.

Example: He *brags* about his ability constantly.

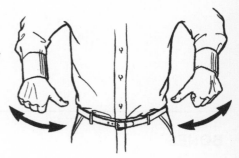

BOAT

Form a cupped shape with both curved hands and move forward with a bouncing motion.

Memory aid: Suggests the hull of a *boat* going over waves.

Example: Do you have a fishing *boat*?

BODY, PHYSICAL

Place the palms of both flat hands against the chest and repeat a little lower. Sometimes one hand is used.

Memory aid: The hands feel the *body*.

Example: My *body* is bruised.

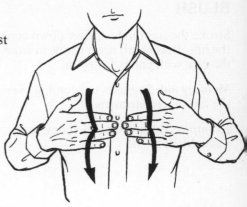

BOIL, COOK (verb)

Hold the horizontal left arm in front, palm down, and wiggle the fingers of the right curved hand under the left palm.

Memory aid: Suggests fire under a pan.

Example: *Boil* the water for the spaghetti.

BONES

Close the downturned left hand and tap the knuckles with the right *X* finger.

Memory aid: An obviously bony part of the hand is indicated.

Example: Many people get broken *bones* while skiing.

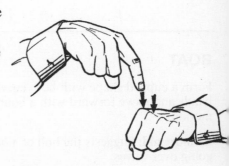

BOOK, TEXTBOOK, VOLUME

Place the hands palm to palm, with fingers pointing forward. Open both hands to the palm-up position while maintaining contact with the little fingers.

1.

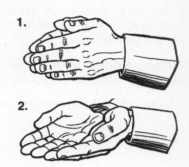

Memory aid: Pictures the opening of a *book.*

Examples: Don't forget your *book.* Study your *textbook.* Please give me *volume* two.

2.

BOOTS

Strike the thumb sides of both closed hands together a few times; then place the right flat hand at the left elbow.

1.

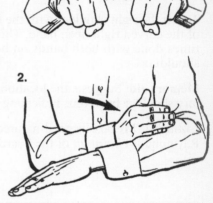

Memory aid: Suggests heels clicking together in military fashion followed by the length of the left forearm shown to indicate the length of the *boots.*

Example: My *boots* are muddy.

2.

BORING, DULL, MONOTONOUS, TEDIOUS

Touch the side of the nose with the right index finger and twist forward slightly. Assume an appropriate facial expression.

Memory aid: Shutting off the airflow of the nose suggests there is nothing interesting to smell.

Example: They found the trip *dull.*

BORROW

Cross the *V* hands at the wrists (the sign for *keep*) and move them toward the body. *Note:* Compare *lend.*

Memory aid: The inward action suggests the keeping of something to oneself for a while.

Example: May I *borrow* some cash?

BOSS, CAPTAIN, CHAIRMAN, GENERAL, OFFICER

Touch the right shoulder with the fingertips of the curved right open hand. This is sometimes done with both hands on both shoulders.

Memory aid: Suggests the location of military shoulder bars, thus indicating authority.

Examples: My *boss* is good-natured.
Raymond is *chairman* of the board.

BOSTON

Place the *B* hand near the right shoulder with the palm facing forward, and then make a few short downward movements.

Memory aid: The initial indicates the word, which requires context and simultaneous lipreading for full comprehension.

Example: I went to *Boston* last summer.

BOX 81

BOTH, PAIR

Hold the left *C* hand to the front with palm facing in. With the right palm facing in, draw the right open *V* fingers down through the left *C* hand and close the *V* fingers.

Memory aid: Suggests two becoming one.

Example: Both paintings are beautiful.

BOWLING

Swing the right curved hand forward from behind the body to the front.

Memory aid: The action for *bowling*.

Example: The *bowling* alley opens at 10:00 A.M.

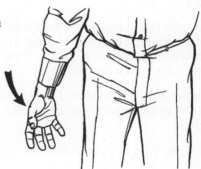

BOX

Point the fingertips of both flat hands up with the palms facing each other in front of the chest. Bend both hands with the right hand positioned over the left. Can also be done with hands in the horizontal position. *Note:* Compare *room*.

Memory aid: The hands outline the shape of a *box*.

Example: Do you have a small cardboard *box*?

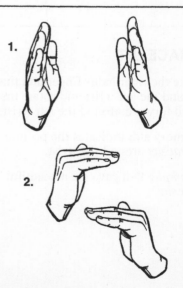

BOXING, FIGHTING

Place the right *S* hand close to the body and the left *S* hand a short distance from the body. Reverse positions a few times.

Memory aid: The position and action for *boxing*.

Example: Boxing matches draw large crowds.

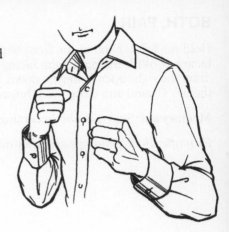

BOY

Move the right hand to the forehead as though gripping the peak of a cap or hat between the fingers and thumb; then move it forward a few inches.

Memory aid: Old-fashioned tipping of caps by men, especially when greeting women.

Example: That *boy* can swim well.

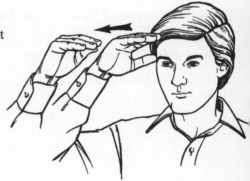

BRACELET

Place the right index finger and thumb around the left wrist and rotate the right hand forward around the left wrist.

Memory aid: Indicates the position of a *bracelet* around the wrist.

Example: Jodi gave me a beautiful *bracelet*.

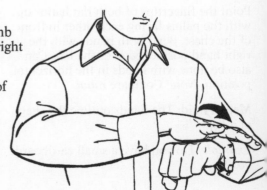

BRAVE, COURAGEOUS, FEARLESS

Touch the chest below the shoulders with the fingertips of both open hands; then move them forward forcefully into *S* positions.

Memory aid: Suggests strong shoulders prepared for a battle.

Example: His *bravery* was exceptional.

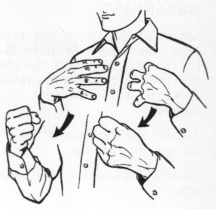

BREAD

Draw the little-finger edge of the right hand downward a few times over the back of the flat left hand, which has its palm facing the body.

Memory aid: Symbolizes cutting slices of *bread*.

Example: I'd like my *bread* toasted.

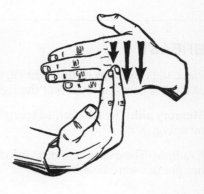

BREAK, FRACTURE, SNAP

Hold the thumb and index-finger sides of both *S* hands together; then twist them both sharply outward and apart.

Memory aid: Can symbolize *breaking* a stick.

Examples: The glass was *broken*. The window cord *snapped*.

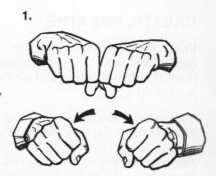

BREAKFAST

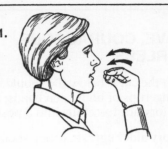

Move the fingers of the right closed *and* hand to the mouth a few times. Place the left flat hand into the bend of the right elbow; then raise the right forearm upward. *Note:* This sign is a combination of *eat* and *morning.*

Memory aid: The nighttime fast is broken by eating in the morning.

Example: I did not feel hungry at *breakfast* time.

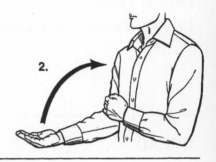

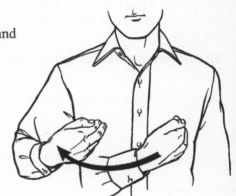

BREAST

Place the fingertips of the right curved hand at the left breast and then at the right.

Memory aid: The location suggests the meaning.

Example: The examination revealed that her *breasts* were healthy.

BREATH, BREATHE

Place both open hands, palms in and left hand above right, on the chest and move them simultaneously on and off the chest several times.

Memory aid: Indicates the expansion and contraction of the chest when *breathing.*

Example: Shelby took a deep *breath* and jumped into the swimming pool.

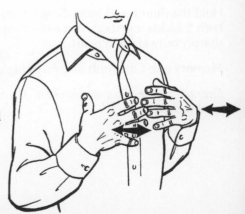

BRIDGE

Hold the left closed hand to the front with the forearm almost horizontal. Touch the underside of the forearm with the tips of the right *V* fingers, first under the wrist and then under the forearm.

Memory aid: Suggests the pillars supporting a *bridge*.

Example: The *bridge* was swept away in the flood.

BRING, FETCH

Hold both open hands to the front with palms facing up and one hand slightly in front of the other. Move both hands toward self, another, or to the right or left, depending on who is indicated.

Memory aid: Symbolizes something being *brought* closer.

Example: Please *bring* my umbrella.

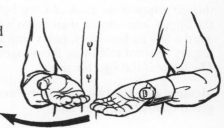

BROAD-MINDED, OPEN-MINDED

Position both flat hands forward with palms facing each other just in front of the forehead. Move the hands forward and outward with a widening *V* shape.

Memory aid: Suggests an expanding mind.

Example: The new president has an *open mind.*

BROKE, BANKRUPT

Strike the neck with the little-finger edge of
the right bent hand.

Memory aid: Symbolizes the head being
cut off.

Example: He gambled until he was *broke*.

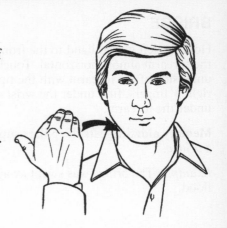

BROTHER

Move the right hand to the forehead as
though gripping the peak of a hat between
the fingers and thumb; then move it forward a few inches. Next, point both index
fingers forward and bring them together.
The latter is the sign for *same*.

Memory aid: The two signs combined suggest a male of the same family.

Example: His *brother* is a good worker.

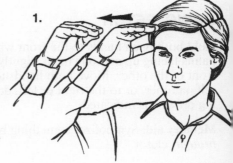

BROWN

Move the index finger of the right *B* hand
down the right cheek.

Memory aid: Suggests the skin color.

Example: He wore a *brown* jacket.

BUG, INSECT

Touch the nose with the thumb tip of the right 3 hand. Bend and unbend the index and middle fingers a few times.

Memory aid: Suggests the moving antennae or feelers of many *insects*.

Example: There's a *bug* on your blouse.

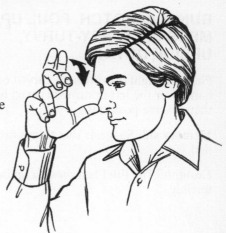

BUILD, CONSTRUCT, ERECT

Place both bent hands to the front with palms down. Position the fingers of the hands one above the other alternately a few times.

Memory aid: Suggests building blocks going up.

Example: How is the *construction* project doing?

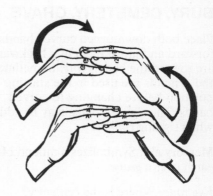

BUILDING

Place both bent hands in front with palms down. Position the fingers one above the other and rotate positions alternately a few times. Form the point of a triangle at head level with both flat hands; then move them apart and straight down simultaneously with the fingers pointing up. This is a combination of the signs for *build* and *house*.

Memory aid: Suggests the action of *building* and the shape of a house.

Example: This is a beautiful *building*.

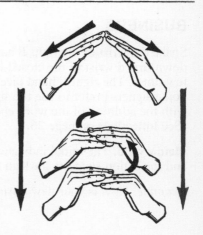

BUNGLE, BOTCH, FOUL UP, MESS UP, TOPSY-TURVY, UPSIDE DOWN

Place the right downturned curved open hand over the left upturned curved hand; then reverse positions.

Memory aid: Suggests that things are unsettled.

Example: The thief had *messed up* her room terribly.

BURY, CEMETERY, GRAVE

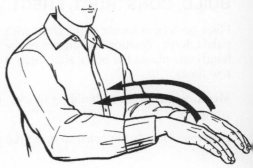

Place both downturned curved hands forward and move them in a backward arc toward the body. *Note:* Sometimes the *A* hands are used in the starting position before changing to curved hands. The sign for *place* may be added when signing *cemetery*.

Memory aid: Symbolizes a mound of earth over a *grave*.

Example: Where is the *cemetery*?

BUSINESS

Strike the wrist of the right *B* hand on the downturned wrist of the closed left hand a few times. The right *B* hand faces forward. Some signers prefer to use the sign for *busy* with the addition of the word ending *ness*. (See Inflections on page 26.)

Memory aid: The initial indicates the word, and the action suggests the sign for *work.*

Example: How is your new *business* doing?

BUSY

Tap the wrist of the left closed palm-down hand with the wrist of the right *B* hand, which has palm facing forward. The right hand moves from right to left as it taps the left wrist.

Memory aid: The initial indicates the word, and the action suggests the sign for *work*.

Example: I'm too *busy* to come now.

BUT, ALTHOUGH, HOWEVER

Cross both index fingers with palms facing out; then draw them apart a short distance. *Note:* See *different*.

Memory aid: Indicates that an opposite or alternative suggestion may be forthcoming.

Examples: Boxing is an exciting *but* dangerous sport. Judy is efficient; *however,* Elaine is even more so.

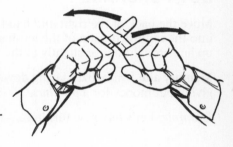

BUTTER

Quickly brush the fingertips of the right *H* hand across the left palm a few times.

Memory aid: Suggests spreading *butter* on bread.

Example: Put plenty of *butter* on my muffin.

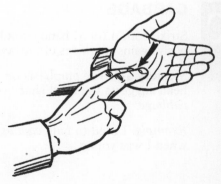

BUTTERFLY

Interlock the thumbs of both open hands in the crossed position in front of the chest with the palms facing self. Wiggle the fingers and flap the hands.

Memory aid: Symbolizes the shape and flying motion of a *butterfly*.

Example: It was the biggest *butterfly* I had ever seen.

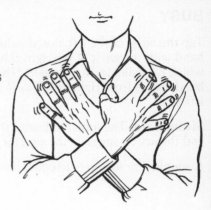

BUY, PURCHASE

Move the back of the right *and* hand down into the upturned palm of the left hand, then up and straight out or slightly to the right.

Memory aid: Symbolizes laying down and giving out money for a *purchase*.

Example: Let's *buy* new furniture.

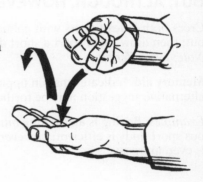

CABBAGE

Strike both *A* (or *S*) hands simultaneously against the sides of the head.

Memory aid: The emphasis on the head suggests the head shape of the *cabbage*.

Example: I used to hate *cabbage* when I was young.

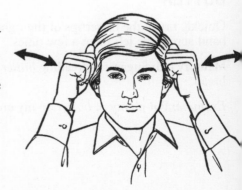

CAKE

Move the fingertips and thumb of the right
C hand forward across the left flat hand
from wrist to fingertips.

Memory aid: Suggests sliding a piece of *cake*
from a serving dish onto someone's plate.

Example: Thank you for my birthday *cake*.

CALIFORNIA

Touch the right ear with the right index finger, or grasp the right earlobe between the
right index finger and thumb. Shake the
right *Y* hand as it moves down and forward.

Memory aid: Suggests the idea of earrings
and the color of gold reminiscent of
California gold rush days.

Example: California has frequent earth-
quakes.

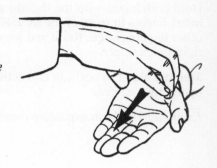

CALL, SUMMON

Place fingers of right slightly curved hand on
the back of the left flat hand. Pull right hand
up toward the body while forming an *A*
hand. *Alternative* (not illustrated): Place the
right curved hand around the mouth with
palm facing left.

Memory aid: The first sign indicates that
deaf persons may need to be touched to get
their attention. The alternative sign is the
natural gesture of cupping the mouth to
project the voice.

Example: Joan was *called* to the front.

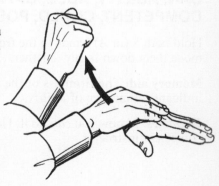

CAMERA

Hold both hands with the thumbs and bent index fingers in front of the face. Keep the other fingers closed. Raise and lower the right index finger.

Memory aid: The position and action for operating a *camera*.

Example: That's an expensive *camera*.

CAMP

Form the point of a triangle with the fingers of both *V* hands, then separate them by moving them down and to the sides a short distance. Repeat the sign a few times while moving the hands to the right.

Memory aid: Symbolizes the shape of a tent used for *camping*.

Example: We *camped* near a small stream.

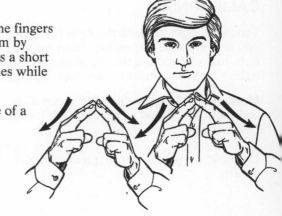

CAN, ABILITY, ABLE, CAPABLE, COMPETENT, COULD, POSSIBLE

Hold both *S* (or *A*) hands to the front and move them down firmly together.

Memory aid: The firmness of the action indicates assurance of *ability*.

Examples: I know you *can* do it. He is a *competent* instructor.

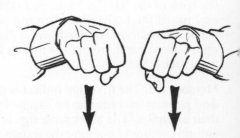

CANADA, CANADIAN

Grasp the right jacket or coat lapel (or an imaginary one) and shake it. Add *person (personalizing word ending)* when signing *Canadian* with reference to a person.

Memory aid: Suggests shaking snow from one's coat.

Example: Many areas of *Canada* have long winters.

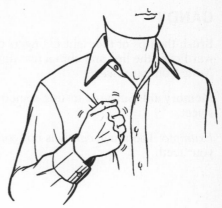

CANCEL, ANNUL, CORRECT, CRITICIZE

Trace an *X* on the left palm with the right index finger.

Memory aid: Suggests the idea of crossing something out.

Examples: I decided to *cancel* my subscription. Professor Smith is *correcting* his students' papers.

CANDLE

Hold the left open hand up with palm facing forward and the right index finger at the base of the left hand. Wiggle the fingers of the left hand.

Memory aid: Suggests the flickering flame of a *candle*.

Example: We need some *candles* for emergencies.

CANDY

Brush the tips of the right *U* fingers downward over the lips and chin a few times. *Note:* Compare *sweet*.

Memory aid: Suggests tasting something sweet.

Example: Too much *candy* is not good for your teeth.

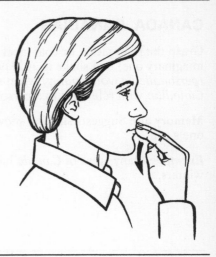

CANNOT, IMPOSSIBLE, INCAPABLE, UNABLE

Strike the left index finger with the right index finger as it makes a downward movement. The left index maintains its position.

Memory aid: The left index *cannot* be moved.

Example: I *cannot* speak French.

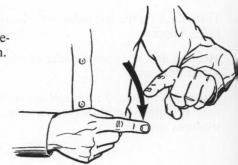

CANOEING

Hold the right *S* hand over the left *S* hand to the right or left of the body. Move them simultaneously down and backward.

Memory aid: The natural action for paddling a *canoe*.

Example: Canoeing can be fun if you're careful.

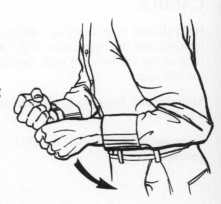

CAR, AUTOMOBILE, DRIVE

Use both closed hands to manipulate an imaginary steering wheel.

Memory aid: Holding a steering wheel.

Examples: Please wash the *car.* I'm learning to *drive.*

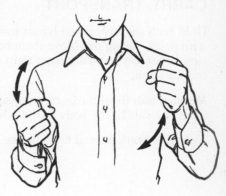

CAREFUL

Cross the wrist of the right *V* hand over the wrist of the left *V* hand. Strike the right wrist on the left wrist a few times.

Memory aid: The fingers can symbolize four watchful eyes.

Example: The waiter was *careful* not to spill the overloaded tray.

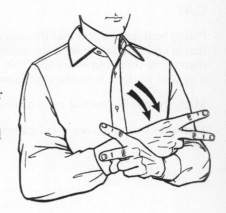

CARELESS, RECKLESS, THOUGHTLESS

Place the right *V* hand in front of the forehead with palm facing left. Move back and forth across the forehead a few times.

Memory aid: The *V* hand can suggest a mind void of common sense.

Example: He was fired for *careless* driving.

CARRY, TRANSPORT

Hold both slightly curved hands to the front with palms facing up. Move them both simultaneously in an arc from right to left, or vice versa.

Memory aid: Symbolizes *carrying* something from one side of the body to the other.

Example: Mark *carried* her suitcase.

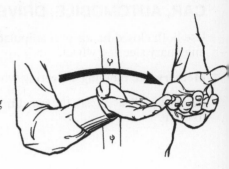

CAT

Place the index fingers and thumbs of the *F* hands under the nose with the palms facing, then move them out sideways. This sign may also be done with the right hand only.

Memory aid: Suggests a *cat's* whiskers.

Example: I used to own a *cat* named Tiger.

CATCH, CAPTURE, GRAB, GRASP, SEIZE

The curved open hand moves quickly into an *S* hand as it rests on the back of the closed left hand.

Memory aid: The act of *catching* an object.

Example: Jerry tried his best to *catch* the ball.

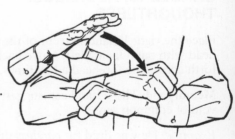

CATHOLIC

Outline a cross in front of the forehead with the right *U* fingers. Move down first, then from left to right.

Memory aid: Symbolizes the cross of Christ, which is central to *Catholic* belief.

Example: My religious background is *Catholic.*

CELEBRATE, CELEBRATION, CHEER, TRIUMPH, VICTORY

Hold up one or both closed hands with the thumb tips and index fingertips touching. Make small circular movements. The *V* hands can be used for *victory.*

Memory aid: Symbolizes the waving of small flags.

Example: The crowd *cheered* loudly.

CENT, CENTS, PENNY

Touch the forehead with the right index finger and then sign the appropriate number.

Memory aid: Suggests the heads on coins.

Example: I need 75¢ (*cents*).

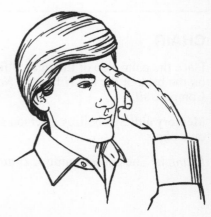

CENTER, CENTRAL, MIDDLE

Make a clockwise circle with the right curved hand above the left flat hand; then lower the fingertips of the right hand into the left palm.

Memory aid: Suggests something standing up in the *middle* of a circle.

Example: Where is the *central* office?

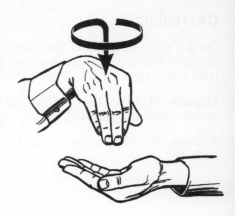

CHAIN

Interlock both index fingers and thumbs a few times. Alternate the position of each thumb so that one thumb is first above, then beneath.

Memory aid: Pictures the links of a *chain*.

Example: The door was *chained*.

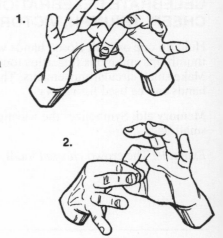

1.

2.

CHAIR

Place the palm side of the right *H* fingers on the back of the left *H* fingers. *Note:* Compare *sit*.

Memory aid: Symbolizes a person sitting on a *chair*.

Example: She collects antique *chairs*.

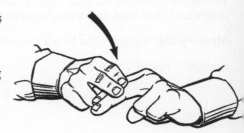

CHANGE, ADAPT, ADJUST, ALTER

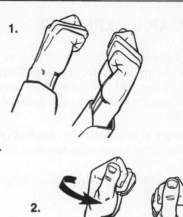

Place the thumb tips of both closed hands into the crook of the bent index fingers. Hold the palms facing with the left palm facing the chest and the right palm facing out; then reverse positions so that the right palm faces in. The *A* hands can also be used.

Memory aid: Suggests a *change* around.

Example: When did you *change* jobs?

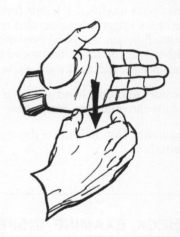

CHAPTER

Move the thumb and fingertips of the right *C* hand downward across the left flat palm.

Memory aid: The initial position of this sign is similar to that for *paragraph,* but the action suggests something of greater length than a paragraph.

Example: Which *chapter* are you reading now?

CHARACTER (individual)

Put the thumb side of the right *C* hand against the left flat hand and make a circular movement as illustrated.

Memory aid: The initial indicates the word, and the action suggests a circle of personal activities.

Example: His *character* imitations were hilarious.

CHEAP, INEXPENSIVE

Hold the left flat hand with fingers pointing forward and palm facing right. Brush the index-finger side of the slightly curved right hand downward across the palm of the left hand.

Memory aid: Something brushed off easily cannot be of great consequence.

Example: I bought this lamp *cheap* at a sale.

CHEAT, BETRAY, DECEIVE, FRAUD

Point both modified *Y* hands forward with the index fingers also extended and palms down. Position one hand over the other (either is acceptable), and move the top one forward and backward a few times.

Memory aid: One hand seems to be trying to hide the other one from view.

Examples: Don't *cheat* on the test. He is a *fraud.*

CHECK, EXAMINE, INSPECT, INVESTIGATE

Point the right index finger to the right eye, then move it forward and down, and then forward across the upturned left palm until it goes beyond the fingers.

Memory aid: The right index finger is *checking* the left hand.

Example: I had my car *inspected* yesterday.

CHECK (bank)

Draw the fingertips of the right *C* hand, palm down, across the flat open palm and fingers of the left upturned hand.

Memory aid: The initial indicates the word, and the movement indicates the size of the *check*.

Example: The *check* was late in arriving.

CHEESE

Place the heels of both hands together and rotate them back and forth in opposite directions.

Memory aid: Suggests the action of shaping *cheese*.

Example: I like a variety of *cheeses*.

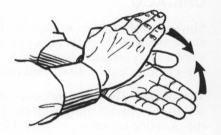

CHEF, COOK (noun)

Place first the palm side and then the back of the right flat hand on the upturned palm of the left flat hand. Add the sign for *person* (*personalizing word ending*).

Memory aid: Suggests a *chef* turning over food in a frying pan.

Example: This restaurant has a *chef* who was trained in Paris.

1.

2.

3.

CHEWING GUM

Place the right *V* fingertips on the right cheek and move the right hand up and down. The fingertips of the right *V* remain in place on the right cheek during this movement.

Memory aid: Suggests constant chewing.

Example: Don't forget to buy *chewing gum*.

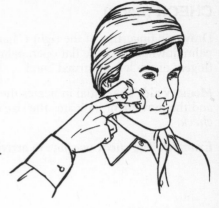

CHICAGO

Move the right *C* hand to the right from just above shoulder level; then move it downward a short distance. Some use a slight wavy motion for the downward movement.

Memory aid: The initial indicates the word, and the downward movement can symbolize the changing directions of wind. *Chicago* is known as the "windy city."

Example: Chicago is on the southern shore of Lake Michigan.

CHICKEN, HEN

Open and close the right index finger and thumb in front of the mouth. Sometimes these fingers are also brought down into the upturned left palm with a pecking motion.

Memory aid: Indicates a *chicken's* beak.

Example: I love roast *chicken*.

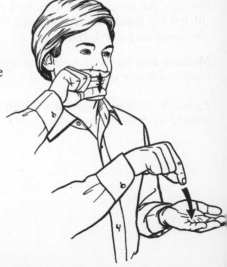

CHILD, CHILDREN

Place the right flat downturned hand before the body and motion as if patting the head of a child. When referring to more than one child, move the hand to another position and repeat the sign.

Memory aid: *Children* are shorter than adults.

Examples: Geoffrey is an exceptional *child*. The *children* like their new teacher.

CHINA, CHINESE

Touch the left side of the chest then the right side of the chest with the extended right index finger, palm facing body, then move the index finger straight down. Add the sign for *person (personalizing word ending)* when signing *Chinese* with reference to a person.

Memory aid: Suggests the shape of *Chinese* military uniforms.

Examples: China is a fascinating country. I like *Chinese* food.

CHOCOLATE

Make a few small circles with the thumb of the right *C* hand over the back of the left flat hand.

Memory aid: The *C* hand indicates the word, and the action suggests mixing *chocolate* icing.

Example: Chocolate cake is my favorite dessert.

CHOOSE, PICK, SELECT

Use the right thumb and index finger to
make a picking motion from the front as the
hand is drawn back toward self. The remaining right fingers are extended. Sometimes
the fingers of the left hand are held up in
front of the right, and the right appears to
be deciding which finger to choose. *Note:*
Compare *find*.

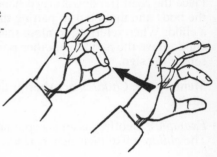

Memory aid: An item is *selected* with great
care.

Example: Bill *chose* the blue suit.

CHRISTIAN

1.

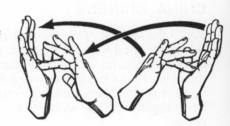

Hold both open slightly curved hands to the
front, palms facing each other. Touch the
left palm with the right middle finger; then
touch the right palm with the left middle
finger. Add the *person (personalizing word
ending)* sign.

Memory aid: This is a combination of the
signs for *Jesus* and *person (personalizing
word ending)*.

2.

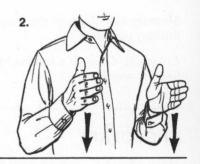

Example: A *Christian* is a follower of Jesus
Christ.

CHRISTMAS

Move the right *C* hand in a sideways arc
to the right with the palm facing forward.

Memory aid: The initialized movement
requires context and simultaneous
lipreading for full comprehension.

Example: What does Susan want for
Christmas?

CHURCH, CHAPEL, DENOMINATION

Tap the thumb of the right *C* hand on the back of the closed left hand.

Memory aid: The initial indicates the word (except for *denomination*), and the position suggests that the *church* is built on a solid foundation.

Example: Our *church* has a seminar next week.

CIGARETTE

Point the left index finger in a forward direction. Extend the right index and little finger with other fingers closed. Place the right index finger on the left index knuckle and the right little finger on the left index tip.

Memory aid: Suggests the length of a *cigarette*.

Example: Cigarette smoke hurts my throat.

CITY, COMMUNITY, TOWN, VILLAGE

Make the point of a triangle with both flat hands in front of the chest. Repeat a few times while moving the hands to the right.

Memory aid: Symbolizes the roofs of many houses.

Example: Our *city* has clean streets.

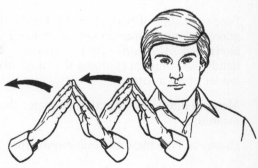

CLAP, APPLAUD, OVATION, PRAISE

Clap the hands as many times as desired.

Memory aid: The action represents the word.

Example: They gave him a standing *ovation*.

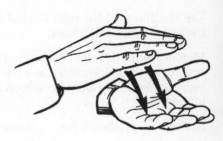

CLEAN, NICE, PURE

Move the palm of the right flat hand across the palm of the left flat hand from wrist to fingertips.

Memory aid: Symbolizes the washing of the hands.

Example: Do you have a *clean* shirt?

CLIMB, ASCEND

Face the palms of both curved *V* hands, then make a *climbing* motion with each hand alternately. *Alternative* (not illustrated): The hands can simulate *climbing* the rungs of a ladder or up a rope.

Memory aid: Upward action indicates the meaning.

Example: Pete likes to *climb* mountains.

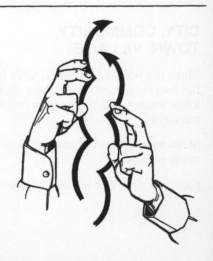

CLOSE, SHUT

Bring both flat hands together from the sides with palms facing forward.

Memory aid: Suggests the *closing* of window drapes.

Example: The restaurant is *closed*.

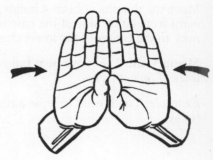

CLOTHES, DRESS, GARMENT, GOWN, SUIT, WEAR

Brush the fingertips of both flat open hands down the chest a few times.

Memory aid: Suggests the smoothing of *clothes* over the body.

Examples: This *dress* is very colorful. I'd like a gray *suit* this time.

CLOUD, GALE, STORM

Hold both open curved hands to the front at head level with palms facing. Move both hands from one side to the other while making circular and up-and-down movements from the wrists. Make the movement more pronounced and vigorous when signing *gale* and *storm*.

Memory aid: Symbolizes the movement and formation of *clouds*.

Example: A sudden *gale* descended upon us.

COAT, JACKET, OVERCOAT

Move the thumbs of both *A* hands downward from either side of the base of the neck to the center of the lower chest.

Memory aid: The movement follows the lines of *jacket* lapels.

Example: You'll need to wear a *coat* today.

COFFEE

Make a counterclockwise circular movement with the right *S* hand over the left *S* hand.

Memory aid: Symbolizes grinding *coffee* beans by hand.

Example: I drink too much *coffee*.

COINS

Make a small circle on the left flat palm with the right index finger.

Memory aid: Suggests the size and shape of a *coin*.

Example: Some people collect *coins*.

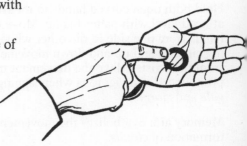

COLD, CHILLY, FRIGID, WINTER

Hold up both *S* hands in front of the chest and shake them.

Memory aid: Suggests a person shivering in the *cold*.

Example: It's too *cold* to go out.

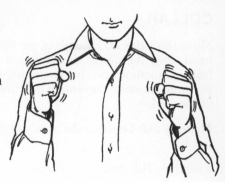

COLD (sickness)

Place the thumb and bent index finger on either side of the nose and draw down a few times.

Memory aid: Symbolizes wiping the nose.

Example: I had a terrible *cold* last week.

COLLAPSE, BREAKDOWN

Place the fingertips of both flat hands together in an upside-down *V* shape. Quickly bend the fingers of both hands down so that a regular *V* shape is formed.

Memory aid: Suggests a roof *collapsing*.

Examples: She *collapsed* with exhaustion. The trade talks *broke down*.

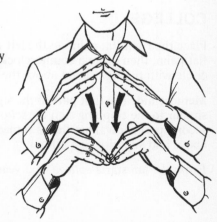

COLLAR

Move the index and thumb of the right Q hand along the side of the neck from back to front. Sometimes two hands are used to perform the same movement on either side of the neck.

Memory aid: Outlines the area and shape of a *collar*.

Example: This *collar* is too tight.

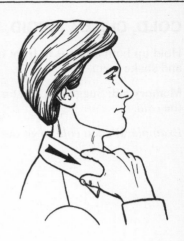

COLLECT, ACCUMULATE, EARN, SALARY, WAGES

Move the little-finger edge of the right curved hand across the upturned left flat hand from fingertips to wrist. End with the right hand closed.

Memory aid: The action of gathering to oneself.

Example: How much did you *earn* on that job?

COLLEGE

Place the right flat palm on the left upturned flat palm, then make a counterclockwise circle with the right hand above the left.

Memory aid: The first part of the sign is similar to the clapping sign for *school*. The second part shows that this is something above and superior to a school.

Example: Jan starts *college* next year.

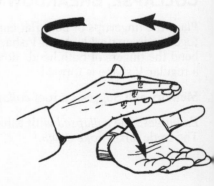

COLOR

Point the fingertips of the open right hand toward the mouth and wiggle them as the hand moves slightly out. Some signers begin this sign by touching the lips with the fingertips.

Memory aid: The fingers can suggest the different *colors* of a rainbow.

Example: What is your favorite *color*?

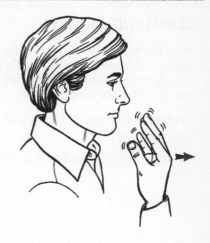

COME

Point both index fingers toward each other and rotate them around each other while simultaneously moving them toward the body. *Note:* See *go*. *Alternative* (not illustrated): The common action of beckoning with the hand or index finger.

Memory aid: Both signs symbolize the idea of *coming* closer to self.

Example: When will you *come* to see me?

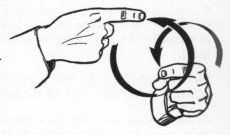

COMFORT

Rub the right curved hand over the back of the left, and vice versa.

Memory aid: The movement suggests smooth hands that lack roughness.

Example: This chair is *comfortable*.

1.

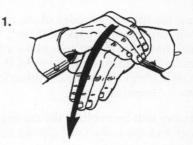

2.

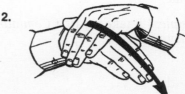

COMMAND, ORDER

Point the right index finger to the mouth and then move it forward and slightly down with considerable emphasis. The index finger ends pointing forward.

Memory aid: Suggests strong words coming from the mouth.

Example: The *command* came to set up camp.

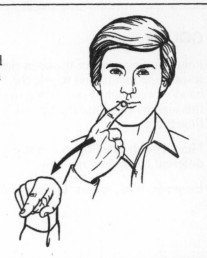

COMMANDMENTS

Place the index and thumb side of the right *C* hand on the front of the palm-forward left hand near the top; then move it downward in an arc until it rests at the base of the left hand.

Memory aid: The right hand seems to be pointing out written rules on the left hand.

Example: God wrote the ten *commandments* on stone tablets and gave them to Moses.

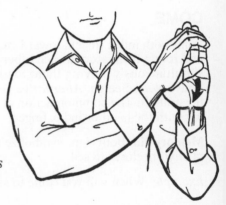

COMMUNION, EUCHARIST

Draw the little-finger edge of the right hand downward over the back of the left flat hand, which has palm facing self. Make a forward circular movement with the right *W* hand on the right cheek. This is a combination of the signs for *bread* and *wine*.

Memory aid: Symbolizes the cutting of bread slices and the redness of cheeks caused by wine.

Example: I'll take my first *Communion* this Sunday.

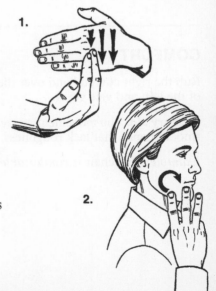

1.

2.

COMPARE, CONTRAST

With palms facing each other, hold both curved hands up near the head; then rotate the hands with an inward twist from the wrists so that both palms face the head.

Memory aid: Suggests a side-by-side *comparison.*

Examples: You'd better *compare* both jobs before deciding. The colors created a vivid *contrast.*

COMPLAIN, GRIPE, GRUMBLE, OBJECT, PROTEST

Strike the fingertips of the curved right hand sharply against the chest. Repeat a few times.

Memory aid: Suggests the expression Something on his chest.

Examples: Joe *complained* bitterly. Stop *grumbling.*

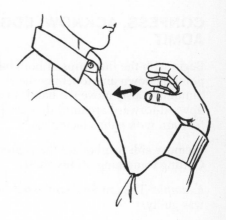

COMPLETE, CONCLUDE, DONE, END, FINISH

Hold the left flat hand with fingers pointing forward and palm facing right. Move the fingers of the right flat hand outward along the index-finger edge of the left until it drops off the end.

Memory aid: Suggests coming to the *end.*

Examples: He *completed* his work. Let's *conclude* our research.

COMPUTER

Move the right *C* hand across the forehead in two arcs from left to right.

Memory aid: The initial indicates the word, and the location of the movement in front of the brain suggests that *computers* are smart.

Example: What brand of *computer* do you use?

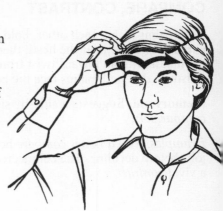

CONFESS, ACKNOWLEDGE, ADMIT

Begin with the fingertips of both hands pointing down and touching the chest. Simultaneously move the hands in an upward-forward arc until they are pointing forward with palms facing up.

Memory aid: Symbolizes the expression Getting something off his chest.

Example: The criminal *confessed* that he was guilty.

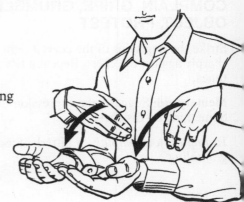

CONFIDENCE, TRUST

Begin with slightly curved open hands. Move the right *S* hand slightly under the left *S* hand in front of the left shoulder. *Note:* Compare *faith*.

Memory aid: Suggests preparing to plant a flagpole into the ground.

Example: I have complete *confidence* in you.

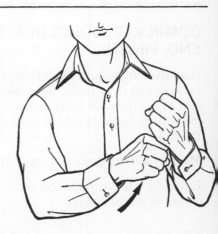

CONFLICT

Point the left index finger to the right and the right index finger to the left at right angles. Move them forward so that they cross.

Memory aid: The action suggests two people going in different directions.

Example: My class schedule *conflicts* with my work schedule.

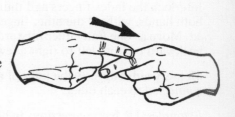

CONFUSE, MIX, SCRAMBLE

Place the left curved open hand in front with palm facing up. Circle the right curved open hand in a counterclockwise direction above the left.

Memory aid: The circular action suggests the meaning.

Example: Don't *confuse* the issue.

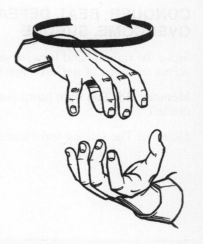

CONGRATULATE

Touch the lips with the fingers of the right flat hand and then clap the hands as much as desired.

Memory aid: A combination of *good* and *praise*.

Example: Ed is to be *congratulated* for his success.

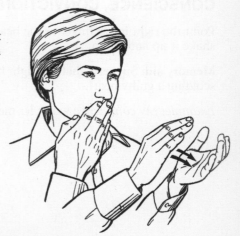

CONNECTION, BELONG, RELATIONSHIP

Interlock the index fingers and thumbs of both hands, with all the other fingers extended. Move as one unit either forward and backward or from left to right a few times.

Memory aid: Suggests the links of a chain *connected* to each other.

Examples: He has *connections* in high places. Our *relationship* is friendly.

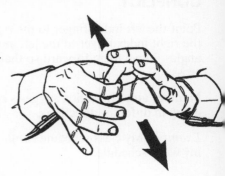

CONQUER, BEAT, DEFEAT, OVERCOME, SUBDUE

Move the right *S* hand forward and down across the wrist of the left *S* hand.

Memory aid: The right hand dominates the left.

Example: The visiting team was *defeated*.

CONSCIENCE, CONVICTION

Point the right index finger at the heart and shake it up and down.

Memory aid: Suggests that the right hand is scolding a guilty heart.

Example: My *conscience* won't let me lie.

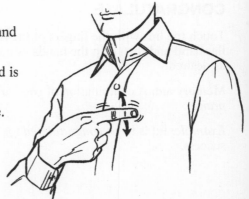

CONSTITUTION, PARLIAMENTARY, PRINCIPLES

Place the index and thumb side of the right *C* hand on the front of the palm-forward left hand near the top; then move it downward in an arc until it rests at the base of the left hand. *Note:* Use initialized right hand positions according to word used.

Memory aid: The right hand seems to be pointing out written *rules* on the left hand, which can represent the printed page.

Example: Do you have a *constitution* yet?

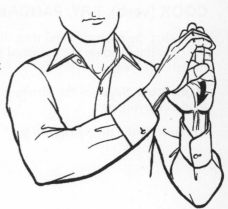

CONTINUE, ENDURE, LASTING, PERMANENT, PERSEVERE

Place the tip of the right *A* thumb behind the left *A* thumb and move both hands forward together. The palms face down.

Memory aid: Suggests a determination to *continue* forward.

Examples: He received a *lasting* impression. *Persevering* practice will produce results.

CONTROL, DIRECT, GOVERN, MANAGE, OPERATE, REGULATE, REIGN, RULE

Close both hands with the thumb tips in the crook of the index fingers. Hold both hands parallel; then move them back and forth with a slight pivoting action from the wrists.

Memory aid: Suggests holding the reins of a horse.

Examples: Who is in *control*? Will Michael be able to *manage* the business?

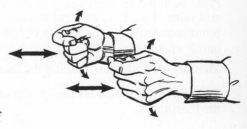

COOK (verb), FRY, PANCAKE

Place first the palm side and then the back of the right flat hand on the upturned palm of the left flat hand.

Memory aid: Suggests the turning over of food in a *frying* pan.

Example: Is the turkey *cooked* yet?

1.

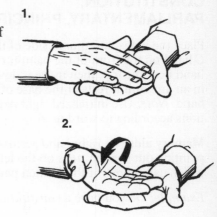

2.

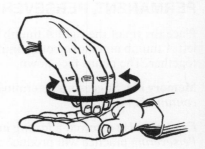

COOKIE

Place the right *C* thumb and fingertips into the left flat palm and twist. Repeat a few times.

Memory aid: Suggests using a *cookie* cutter.

Example: Cream-filled *cookies* are a real temptation to me.

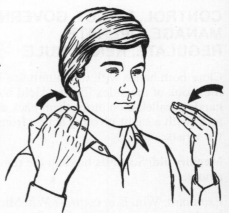

COOL, REFRESH

Place both flat or open hands to the front and sides of the face with palms facing in. Simultaneously flap the fingers of both hands up and down.

Memory aid: Suggests fanning the face.

Example: A nice *cool* breeze sprang up in the morning.

COOPERATE

Interlock the index fingers and thumbs of both hands, with the other fingers extended. Move as one unit in a counterclockwise circle.

Memory aid: The links of a chain are moving in harmony.

Example: Please *cooperate* with me.

COPY, DUPLICATE, IMITATE

Move the right open hand into the left flat palm while simultaneously closing into the *and* hand shape.

Memory aid: The right hand seems to be impressing its message onto the left hand.

Example: Please make five *copies* of this page.

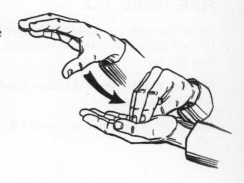

CORN

Rotate the right index finger back and forth in front of the mouth. The movement is from the wrist.

Memory aid: Suggests the action of eating an ear of *corn*.

Example: Corn plants usually grow quite high.

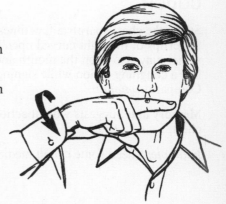

CORNER

Point either the flat-hand fingers or the index fingers at right angles to each other.

Memory aid: A *corner* is pictured.

Example: Meet me at the *corner* delicatessen.

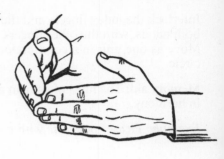

COST, CHARGE, EXPENSE, FEE, FINE, PRICE, TAX

Strike the right crooked index finger against the left flat palm with a downward movement.

Memory aid: Suggests the idea of making a dent in one's finances.

Examples: What will it *cost* me? I'll have to pay the *fine*.

COUGH

Strike the chest sharply a few times with the fingertips of the right curved open hand. The signer may also open the mouth and simulate a coughing action while signing. *Note:* Compare *complain*.

Memory aid: Suggests violent action in the chest.

Example: I need some *cough* medicine.

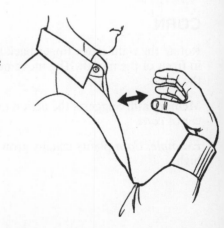

COUNT

Hold up the left flat hand with the palm facing right. Move the thumb and index finger of the right *F* hand upward over the left hand from wrist to fingertips.

Memory aid: Can symbolize the moving of beads on an abacus or old-fashioned *counting* board.

Example: Shirley is learning to *count*.

COUNTRY (national territory)

Rub the palm side of the right *Y* hand in a counterclockwise direction on the underside of the left forearm near the elbow.

Memory aid: Can suggest a patriotic willingness to wear out one's elbow for one's *country*. The *Y* hand indicates the last letter of the word and is necessary to distinguish it from the sign for *farm*.

Example: The tour covers six *countries*.

COURSE

Place the little-finger edge of the right *C* hand against the fingers of the left flat hand. The left palm can face up or toward self. Move the *C* hand down to the base of the left hand. *Note:* Compare *lesson*.

Memory aid: The initial indicates the word, and the action is similar to the sign for *lesson*.

Example: I am satisfied with the *courses* I have chosen.

COUSIN

Place the right *C* hand either close to the right temple for a male or close to the right cheek for a female; then shake back and forth from the wrist. Place between the *male* and *female* positions for neuter reference.

Memory aid: The initial *C* is placed wherever appropriate.

Example: I have two male *cousins* and three female *cousins*.

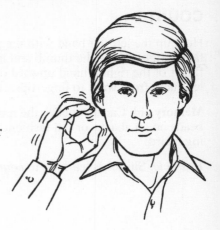

COVER

Slide the curved right hand over the back of the curved left hand from fingertips to wrist.

Memory aid: Shows one hand *covering* the other.

Example: His desk was *covered* with dust.

COW

Place the thumb tips of both *Y* hands against the temples and twist upward so that the little fingers point up (sometimes the action is reversed). This sign is often done with the right hand only.

Memory aid: Suggests a *cow's* horns.

Example: There's a lot of cream in fresh *cow's* milk.

CRACKER

Strike the right *S* hand near the left elbow.
Note: Compare *Passover*.

Memory aid: Suggests an old European method of crumbling *crackers* into soup.

Example: Crackers make a nice snack.

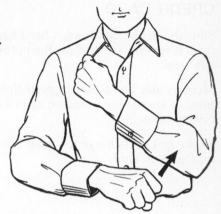

CRAZY, NUTS (adjective)

Point the right curved open hand to the temple and rotate back and forth from the wrist. *Alternative:* Point the right index finger to the temple and make a small circular movement.

Memory aid: Both signs symbolize a scrambled brain.

Example: He has to be *crazy* to attempt that.

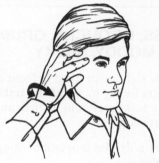

or:

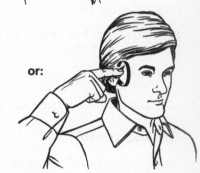

CREAM

Move the little-finger edge of the curved right hand across the left flat palm from fingertips to wrist.

Memory aid: Suggests skimming the *cream* off the top of milk.

Example: Do you like *cream* with your coffee?

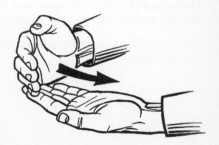

CREDIT CARD

Slide the right palm-down *A* hand back and forth across the palm of the flat upturned left hand.

Memory aid: The action suggests the movement of impressing a *credit card* in a credit card machine.

Example: Don't charge too many purchases on the *credit card*.

CROSS, GROUCHY, GRUMPY, MAD, MOODY, SULKY

Hold the right open hand in front of the face with palm facing in. Bend and unbend the fingers a few times, and assume an appropriate expression.

Memory aid: The movement suggests tension of the face.

Examples: Don't be *cross* with me. He is feeling *moody* today.

CROSS (noun)

Trace the outline of a cross with the fingers and thumb of the right *C* hand. First move down, then across from left to right.

Memory aid: The initial indicates the word, and the action portrays the shape of a *cross*.

Example: The Romans crucified many people on *crosses*.

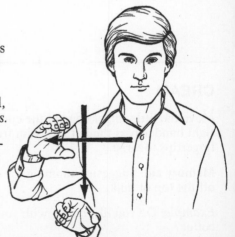

CRUCIFY, CRUCIFIXION

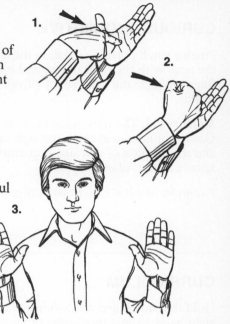

Thrust the right index finger into the palm of the left open hand; then strike the left palm with the little-finger edge of the closed right hand. Hold both flat open hands up to the front with palms facing forward.

Memory aid: Symbolizes the nails being hammered through the hands and the final position on a cross.

Example: Crucifixion is an extremely painful method of execution.

CRY, BAWL, SOB, TEARDROP, TEARS, WEEP

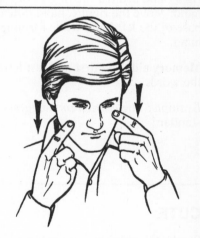

Move one or both index fingers down the cheeks from underneath the eyes a few times.

Memory aid: Suggests falling *tears*.

Examples: She was *bawling*. His eyes were red from *weeping*.

CUP

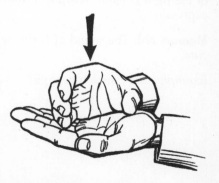

Put the little-finger edge of the right *C* hand on the left flat palm.

Memory aid: Indicates the size and shape of a *cup*.

Example: Give me a *cup* of coffee.

CURIOUS, INQUISITIVE

Pinch a small portion of skin in the front of the neck with the right thumb and index finger. Wiggle the hand slightly from side to side.

Memory aid: The traditional apple in the Garden of Eden was eaten through *curiosity,* and the location of this sign is commonly known as the Adam's Apple.

Example: She has the *curiosity* of a cat.

CURRICULUM

Hold the thumb and index-finger side of the right hand against the fingers of the left flat hand. Move the right *C* hand down to the base of the left hand while forming an *M* hand.

Memory aid: The first and last letters of the word.

Example: The *curriculum* suggests a high standard.

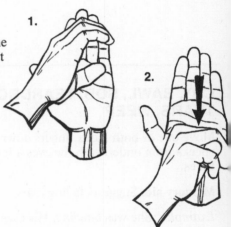

CUTE

Stroke the chin several times with the fingers of the right *U* hand. Assume a smiling expression.

Memory aid: The sound of *U* rhymes with *cute.*

Example: She's such a *cute* girl.

DAILY, EVERYDAY

Place the right *A* hand on the right cheek with the palm facing the cheek. Rub it forward several times.

Memory aid: Indicates a constant continuation by the repeated rubbing action.

Examples: You should exercise *daily*. It's an *everyday* occurrence.

DANCE, BALL

Point the left flat upturned hand to the right; then swing the downturned fingers of the right *V* hand from side to side over the left palm.

Memory aid: The fingers of the *V* hand represent the *dancing* legs of a person.

Examples: Little Robin *danced* for joy. They're having a celebration *ball* tonight.

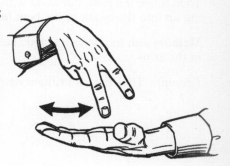

DANGER, PERIL

Hold the left closed hand to the front with the palm facing the body and the arm pointing right. Move the back of the right *A* thumb up across the back of the left hand a few times.

Memory aid: The left arm seems to be protecting the body from an attack by the right hand.

Example: There is *dangerous* quicksand just ahead.

DARK, DIM

Cross the palms of both flat hands down in front of the face.

Memory aid: *Darkness* is created by the eyes being covered.

Example: The room was plunged into *darkness.*

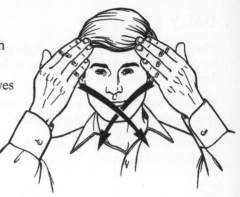

DAUGHTER

Trace the right jawbone from ear to chin with the palm side of the right *A* thumb. Then move the right flat hand with palm facing up into the crook of the bent left elbow.

Memory aid: Indicates a female baby cradled in the arms.

Example: They have a brilliant *daughter.*

1.

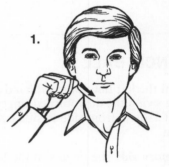

2.

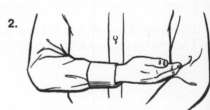

DAY, ALL DAY

Point the left index finger to the right with palm down. Rest the right elbow on the left index finger with the right index finger pointing upward. Move right index finger and arm in a partial arc across the body from right to left. To sign *all day,* hold right index finger as far to the right as possible before beginning to make arc across the body.

Memory aid: The left arm suggests the horizon; right arm the sun's movement.

Examples: On what *day* shall we go? Mark is on duty *all day.*

DEAF

Touch or point to the right ear with the right index finger. Place both downturned flat hands to the front and draw them together until the index fingers and thumbs touch. This last movement is the sign for *closed*.

Memory aid: Suggests that the ears are closed.

Example: I have many *deaf* friends.

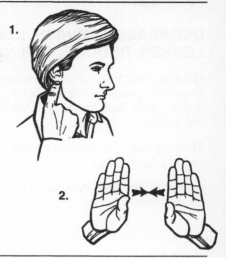

DEATH, DEAD, DIE, EXPIRE, PERISH

Hold both flat hands to the front with the right palm facing up and the left palm facing down. Move both hands in an arc to the left while changing the hand positions so that the palms reverse direction.

Memory aid: Symbolizes a body rolling over at the moment of *death*.

Example: The old dog quietly *expired*.

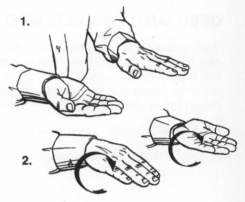

DECIDE, DECISION, DETERMINE, MAKE UP ONE'S MIND

Touch the forehead with the right index finger, then bring both *F* hands down with palms facing.

Memory aid: Suggests a mind that is free to act.

Examples: That is a wise *decision*. Please *make up your mind* now.

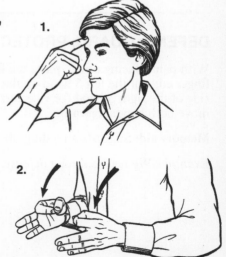

DECREASE, DIMINISH, LESS, LESSEN, REDUCE, SHRINK

Hold both slightly curved open hands to the front with palms facing and hands several inches apart. Reduce the distance between the hands.

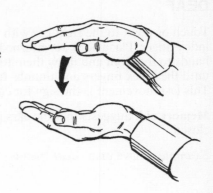

Memory aid: The distance between the two hands becomes *less*.

Example: The train passed, and the noise *diminished*.

DEER, ANTLERS, ELK, MOOSE

With palms facing forward, touch the temples with the thumbs of both open hands a few times. *Note: Moose* can be signed with the same movement but with the fingers closed rather than open.

Memory aid: Symbolizes the *antlers*.

Example: When is *deer* season?

DEFEND, GUARD, PROTECT

With palms facing down, place the little-finger edge of the left *S* hand on the thumb side of the right *S* hand (or vice versa) and move both hands forward.

Memory aid: Suggests a fending-off action.

Example: We need a strong *defense*.

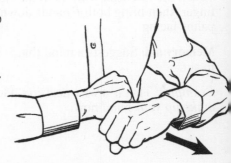

DEFLATE, FLAT TIRE

Put the thumb of the right *C* hand either on the palm or back of the left hand. Bring the right fingers down upon the right thumb.

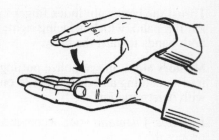

Memory aid: Symbolizes the air going out of a tire.

Examples: I'm glad his ego was *deflated.* Your car has a *flat tire.*

DELAY, POSTPONE, PROCRASTINATE, PUT OFF

Place both *F* hands to the front with palms facing and fingers pointing forward. Make a few short forward arcs.

Memory aid: Suggests moving an appointment further into the future.

Example: I'm afraid I must *postpone* the party again.

DELICIOUS

Touch the lips with the right middle finger. Sometimes the middle finger and thumb are rubbed together a few times as the hand moves forward. This is in addition to the first part of the sign.

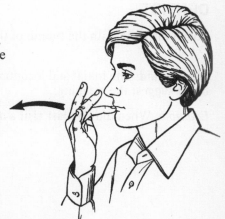

Memory aid: Suggests that something is tasted and approved of.

Example: Her apple pies are *delicious.*

DEMAND, INSIST, REQUIRE

Thrust the bent right index finger into the left flat palm, which is facing right; then pull both hands toward the body.

Memory aid: Can symbolize putting a hook into something and drawing it to oneself with determination.

Example: I *demand* your acceptance of this proposal.

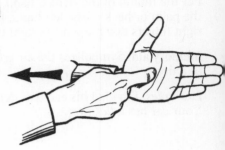

DEMOCRAT

Hold up the right *D* hand and shake it.

Memory aid: The initial suggests the word, which requires context and simultaneous lipreading for full comprehension.

Example: My grandfather always votes *Democratic.*

DENTIST

Touch the teeth with the thumb of the right *D* hand.

Memory aid: The initial and location combined suggest the meaning.

Example: When did you last visit a *dentist*?

DENY

Move the thumb tips of both *A* hands forward alternately from under the chin. *Note:* Compare *not*.

Memory aid: A stronger form of *not*.

Example: She *denied* it.

DENY (self)

Point the thumbs of both *A* hands downward in front of the chest, then move them down a short distance.

Memory aid: Suggests keeping one's own desires under control.

Example: The mother *denied* herself food for her children's sake.

DEPEND, RELY

Cross the right index finger over the top of the left index finger with palms facing down, then move both hands down a short distance. Sometimes this sign is made by using both the index and middle fingers and sometimes with the right *D* hand on the back of the left hand.

Memory aid: Suggests that the right finger can *rely* upon the support of the left.

Example: Can we *depend* on you?

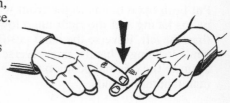

DEPRESSED, DISCOURAGED

Stroke the chest downward with both middle fingers simultaneously. Extend the remaining fingers.

Memory aid: Suggests sinking feelings.

Example: Why are you *depressed*?

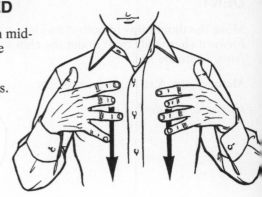

DESSERT

Bring the thumbs of both upright *D* hands together a few times.

Memory aid: The *D* hands suggest the word, and the repetition can suggest the desire for something in addition to the main course.

Example: What's for *dessert*?

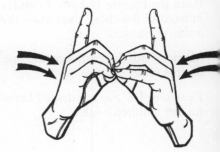

DESTROY, ABOLISH, DAMAGE, DEMOLISH

Put both open hands to the front with palms facing and the right hand lower than the left. Reverse the hand positions while forming *A* hands; then reverse them again to the original position while still maintaining *A* hands.

Memory aid: Suggests pulling something up and down with *destructive* force.

Example: The volcanic eruption *destroyed* the countryside.

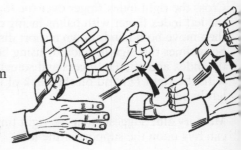

DETERIORATE, DECLINE, WORSEN

Move the little-finger edge of the right flat hand in small arcs down the back of the left forearm.

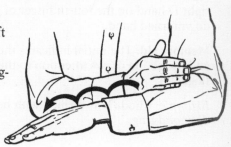

Memory aid: The downward movement suggests degrees of *deterioration.*

Example: Her health is rapidly *declining.*

DEVELOP

Place the *D* hand against the left flat palm, which faces right. Slide the *D* hand up to the left fingertips.

Memory aid: The initialized sign indicates the word.

Example: We *developed* the film yesterday.

DEVIL, DEMON, DEVILMENT, MISCHIEF, SATAN

Touch the temple with the thumb of the right palm-forward 3 hand. Bend and unbend the index and middle fingers a few times.

Memory aid: Suggests the medieval conception of a horned *devil.*

Examples: He's got the *devil* in him today. What wicked *mischief* are you up to now?

DIAMOND

Place the thumb and middle finger of the right *D* hand on the fourth finger of the left downturned hand.

Memory aid: The initial indicates the word, and the action draws attention to the ring finger.

Example: Rhoda was thrilled with her new *diamond* ring.

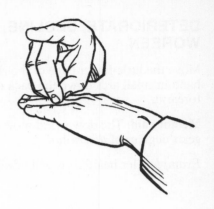

DICTIONARY

Hold the right *D* hand up and shake it.

Memory aid: The initial indicates the word, which requires context and simultaneous lipreading for full comprehension.

Example: You need a good *dictionary*.

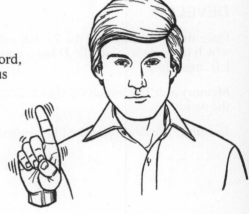

DIFFERENT, DIFFER, DIVERSE, UNLIKE, VARIED

Cross both index fingers with palms facing out; then draw them apart beyond the width of the body. *Note:* Compare *but*.

Memory aid: The movement in opposite directions indicates the meaning.

Example: The two sisters dressed very *differently*.

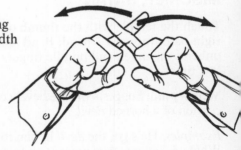

DIFFICULT, HARD

Strike the knuckles of both bent *V* hands as they are moved up and down.

Memory aid: The striking action makes it more *difficult* for the up-and-down movement.

Example: It is *difficult* to avoid problems with some people.

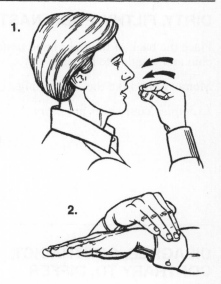

DINNER, SUPPER

Move the fingers of the right closed *and* hand to the mouth a few times and place the curved right hand over the back of the left flat hand. *Note:* This sign is a combination of *eat* and *night*.

Memory aid: Suggests the meal eaten when the sun has set.

Example: Joyce invited Sally to *dinner*.

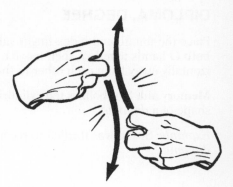

DINOSAUR

Point the left flat hand to the right with palm facing down. Rest the right elbow on the back of the left hand with the right arm in a vertical position and move the right bent *and* hand back and forth a few times.

Memory aid: The arm and the *and* hand suggest the neck and head of a *dinosaur*.

Example: Six-year-old Billy loves *dinosaurs*.

DIPLOMA, DEGREE

Place the thumb and index-finger sides of both *O* hands together, then move them horizontally away from each other to the sides.

Memory aid: Symbolizes the cylindrical shape of a *diploma*.

Example: Susan was thrilled to receive her *diploma*.

DIRTY, FILTHY, FOUL, NASTY

Place the back of the right hand under the chin and wiggle the fingers.

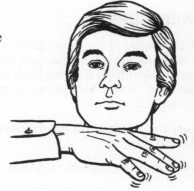

Memory aid: Like the sign for *pig*.

Example: Your shoes are *filthy*.

DISAGREE, CONTRADICT, CONTRARY TO, DIFFER

Touch the forehead with the right index finger; then bring both *D* hands to chest level with palms facing in and index fingertips touching. Move the hands outward sharply in opposite directions. *Note:* When someone is signing rapidly during conversation, the fingertips may not actually touch.

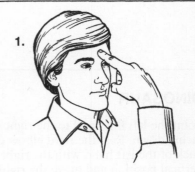

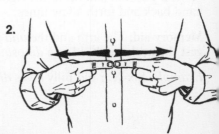

Memory aid: A separating of minds is suggested.

Examples: I have a right to *disagree*. Don't *contradict* me. Their intentions are *contrary to* ours.

DISAPPEAR

Move the right index finger downward between the index and middle fingers of the left palm-down flat hand.

Memory aid: Suggests something *disappearing* from view.

Example: Don't you *disappear,* young man.

DISAPPOINT, MISS

Place the tip of the right index finger on the chin, and assume the appropriate facial expression.

Memory aid: Suggests the expression Take it on the chin, which can indicate suffering as a result of *disappointment*.

Example: The results *disappoint* me.

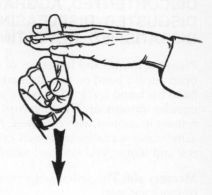

DISCONNECT, DETACH, RELEASE

Interlock the index fingers and thumbs of both hands with all other fingers extended. Pull them apart.

Memory aid: Suggests the links of a chain breaking.

Example: Be sure to *disconnect* the electricity.

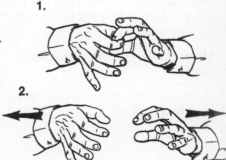

DISCONTENTED, AGGRAVATED, DISGUSTED, DISPLEASING, DISSATISFIED, REVOLTING

Place the thumb and fingertips of the right open curved hand on the chest and move the hand back and forth sideways or in a slight circular movement. The fingertips usually remain in contact with the chest. *Note:* The same concept can be expressed by signing *not* and *happy,* and *not* and *satisfied.*

Memory aid: The action suggests a churning of inner feelings.

Example: He always says something to *aggravate* me.

DISCUSS

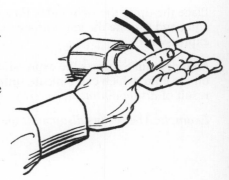

Strike the left palm with the right index finger several times.

Memory aid: The movement is a common gesture used when one wishes to emphasize a point.

Example: I had a long *discussion* with Al.

DISMISS, LAY OFF

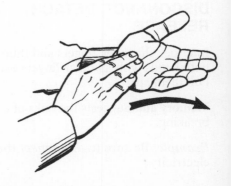

Slide the fingers of the right flat hand quickly over and off the lower edge of the left flat hand.

Memory aid: The right hand leaves the left hand.

Example: Ten percent of their employees have been *laid off.*

DISOBEY, DISOBEDIENCE

Hold one or both *A* hands close to the fore-head with palms facing in. Twist both hands so that the palms face forward.

Memory aid: Suggests a mind that will not cooperate.

Example: Don't *disobey* me.

DISTURB, BOTHER, INTERFERE, MEDDLE

Strike the little-finger edge of the right flat hand into the opening between the left thumb and index finger a few times.

Memory aid: The right hand jars the left.

Example: That noise *bothers* me.

DIVIDE

Cross the little-finger edge of the right flat hand over the index-finger edge of the left flat hand. Move both hands down and to the sides with the palms facing down.

Memory aid: Suggests separating into two sides.

Example: Please *divide* these apples equally.

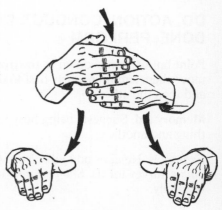

DIVORCE

Hold both *D* hands with palms facing and knuckles touching. Twist both hands outward and sideways until the palms face forward. *Alternative* (not illustrated): First sign *marriage,* then move the hands apart with palms facing each other to the *A* position.

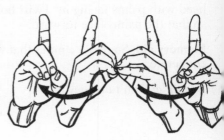

Memory aid: Two people once close to each other now separate.

Example: Larry is *divorced.*

DIZZY

Hold the palm side of the right curved open hand in front of the face and move it in a few slow counterclockwise circles.

Memory aid: Suggests that things seem to be going around in circles.

Example: Do you feel *dizzy?*

DO, ACTION, CONDUCT, DEED, DONE, PERFORM

Point both *C* hands down to the front and move them simultaneously first to one side and then the other.

Memory aid: Suggests being busy with one thing and another.

Examples: He *does* odd jobs. You will *conduct* a survey for us. She *performs* her duties faithfully.

DOCTOR, PHYSICIAN, SURGEON

Place the right *D* hand or *M* fingers on the upturned left wrist.

Memory aid: Suggests taking a person's pulse rate.

Example: What is your *doctor's* name?

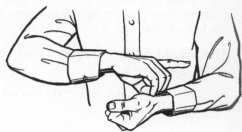

DOG

Slap the right flat hand against the right leg and snap the right middle finger.

Memory aid: A common gesture for attracting a *dog's* attention.

Example: Our two *dogs* are brother and sister.

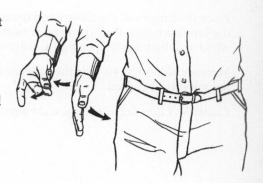

DOLL

Place the bent index finger across the bridge of the nose and move both head and hand downward simultaneously.

Memory aid: A *doll's* nose can be pulled, but a real person cannot be fooled the same way.

Example: Jessica wants a *doll* for Christmas.

DOLLARS, BILLS

Point the fingers of the left flat hand to the right. Grasp the left fingers between the right palm and fingers (or thumb and fingers), then pull the right hand away from the left a few times.

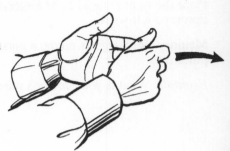

Memory aid: Suggests counting out individual paper *bills*.

Example: How many *dollars* do you need?

DON'T CARE

Place the fingers of the closed *and* hand on the forehead; then flick the hand forward while simultaneously opening the fingers.

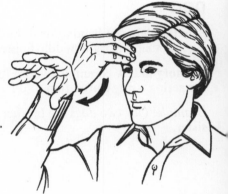

Memory aid: Suggests that the concern of the mind is discarded.

Example: I *don't care* what you do anymore.

DON'T KNOW, DIDN'T RECOGNIZE

Place the fingers of the right flat hand on the forehead (the sign for *know*); then move the right hand away from the forehead with the palm facing forward.

Memory aid: The turning-away action indicates the negative.

Examples: We *don't know* the way home. Jim *didn't recognize* me.

DON'T WANT

Move both open curved hands from a palm-up to a palm-down position.

Memory aid: Suggests throwing something down or away.

Example: He *doesn't want* to go.

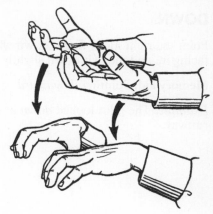

DOOR

Hold both *B* hands to the front with palms facing out and index fingers touching. Twist the right hand back and forth from the wrist.

Memory aid: Symbolizes the opening and closing of a *door*.

Example: Open the *door*.

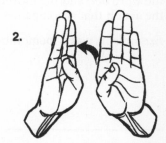

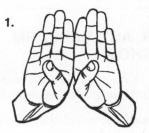

DOUGHNUT

Beginning at the lips, make a forward circle with both *R* hands.

Memory aid: Suggests the ring shape of a *doughnut*.

Example: I usually have a *doughnut* at break time.

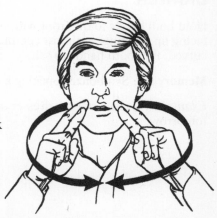

DOWN

Point the right index finger down with palm facing in, and move it down slightly.

Memory aid: Pointing *downward.*

Example: The pilot looked *down* at the runway.

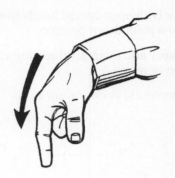

DRAMA, ACT, PERFORM, PLAY, SHOW

Rotate both *A* hands inward toward the body with the palms facing each other.

Memory aid: The initialed hands suggest the word *act,* and the movement suggests the action that accompanies *drama.*

Example: It was a memorable *performance.*

DRAWER

Hold both hands to the front with palms facing up and fingers almost completely curved. Pull both hands to self.

Memory aid: Symbolizes opening a *drawer.*

Example: I'll clean out my dresser *drawers* tomorrow.

DREAM, DAYDREAM

Touch the forehead with the right index finger and move it upward and forward while bending and unbending the index finger.

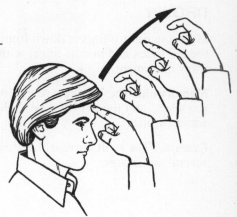

Memory aid: Suggests that the imagination goes on ventures of its own.

Example: Scientists claim that everyone *dreams.*

DRINK

Move the right *C* hand in a short arc toward the mouth.

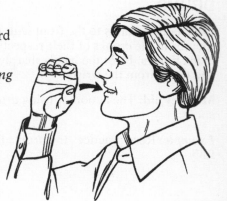

Memory aid: Suggests the action of *drinking* from a glass.

Example: I love to *drink* orange juice.

DROP

Hold both *S* hands to the front with palms down. Drop them sharply while simultaneously changing to open hands.

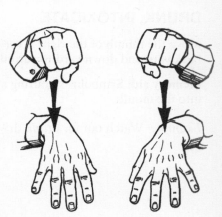

Memory aid: Suggests something slipping out of the hands.

Examples: Marion decided to *drop* the course. The catcher *dropped* the ball.

DROWN

Move the right *V* fingers down from between the left index and middle finger with a slight wavy movement.

Memory aid: The *V* fingers represent a person's legs, and the left hand symbolizes the water surface.

Example: The swift currents have caused several *drownings.*

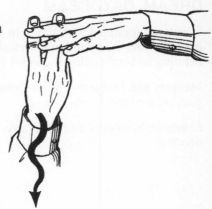

DRUMS

Place both *A* hands to the front with the thumbs in the crooks of their respective index fingers. Pivot the hands sharply up and down from the wrists.

Memory aid: The action of using *drumsticks.*

Example: Ross practices the *drums* faithfully.

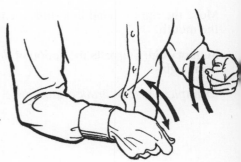

DRUNK, INTOXICATE

Move the thumb of the right *A* (or *Y*) hand backward and downward toward the mouth.

Memory aid: Symbolizes pouring alcohol into the mouth.

Example: Watch out for *drunk* drivers.

DRY, DROUGHT, PARCHED

Move the right curved index finger across the lips from left to right.

Memory aid: Suggests wiping *dry* lips.

Examples: The clothes would not *dry.* The ground was *parched.*

DRYER (clothes)

Move the right curved index finger across the mouth from left to right (the sign for *dry*). Next, hold both flat open hands to the front with palms facing each other and move them simultaneously downward a short distance.

Memory aid: Suggests that drying is purposely activated by a person.

Example: Our old clothes *dryer* needs replacing.

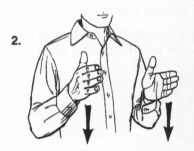

DUCK

Point the right *N* fingers and thumb forward in front of the mouth. Open and close the *N* fingers and thumb a few times.

Memory aid: Suggests the shape and movement of a *duck's* bill.

Example: The loud quacking of the *ducks* awoke me.

DURING, IN THE MEANTIME, WHILE

Point both index-finger hands forward with palms down and a small distance between them. Move them forward simultaneously in a slight down-forward-up curve.

Memory aid: The simultaneous movement suggests parallel activities or time.

Example: Rose always calls *during* mealtime.

DUST

The *A* hand, facing left with palm down, sweeps across the front of the body in a wavy motion.

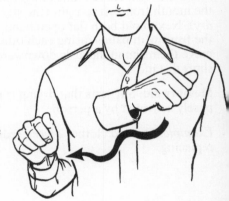

Memory aid: Suggests the movement of *dusting* with a cloth.

Example: Jill tried to *dust* the house before her mother-in-law's visit.

DUTY

Strike the wrist of the downturned left *S* hand with the right *D* hand a few times.

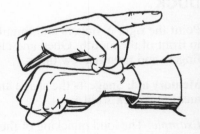

Memory aid: The position can suggest binding the hands and thus the idea of being bound by *duty*.

Example: It's my *duty* to be present.

E

EACH, EVERY

Hold the left *A* hand to the front with palm facing right. The knuckles and thumb of the right *A* hand rub downward on the left thumb a few times.

Memory aid: The right thumb seems to be giving recognition to the left thumb.

Example: Pete jogs thirty miles *each* week.

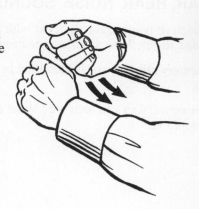

EAGER, AMBITIOUS, ANXIOUS, EARNEST, ENTHUSIASTIC, ZEAL

Rub the flat hands together enthusiastically.

Memory aid: Rubbing things together produces heat.

Examples: Frank *eagerly* anticipated his vacation. Please show some *enthusiasm*.

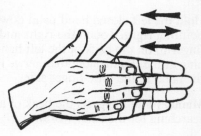

EAGLE

Place the right *X* hand in front of the nose with palm facing forward.

Memory aid: Symbolizes the hooked beak of an *eagle*.

Example: Eagles can fly to great heights.

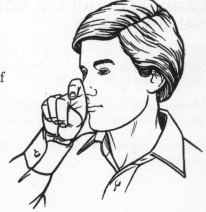

EAR, HEAR, NOISE, SOUND

Touch or point to the right ear with the right index finger. *Note:* Compare *hearing.*

Memory aid: The *ear* is identified by pointing.

Examples: Can you *hear* me? What does that *sound* like?

EARLY

Hold the left closed hand palm down and pointing right. Touch the right middle fingertip on the back of the left hand beginning at the thumb side; then move it across the hand to the little-finger side.

Memory aid: Suggests the beak of a bird searching for the *early* worm.

Example: Let's get up *early* tomorrow.

EARN, ACCUMULATE, COLLECT, SALARY, WAGES

Slide the little-finger edge of the right curved hand inward across the left flat hand. Some end with the right hand closed.

Memory aid: Suggests gathering coins into the hand from the edge of the table.

Example: My *salary* will increase next month.

EARTH, GEOGRAPHY, GLOBE, TERRESTRIAL

Grasp the back of the left closed hand between the right index and thumb and pivot the right hand from left to right (toward the left fingers and elbow).

Memory aid: The left hand symbolizes the *earth,* and the right thumb and finger identify the poles. The movement suggests the *earth's* rotation.

Example: I always found *geography* interesting.

EARTHQUAKE

1.

Grasp the back of the left closed hand between the right index finger and thumb; then pivot the right hand back and forth (toward the left fingers and elbow). Move both fists forward and backward in front of the body with forceful movements. *Note:* These movements combine the signs for *earth* and *thunder.*

Memory aid: Symbolizes the earth rotating on its poles and the vibrating effect of thunder, which has similarities to the tremors of an *earthquake.*

Example: Over three thousand homes were destroyed in the *earthquake.*

2.

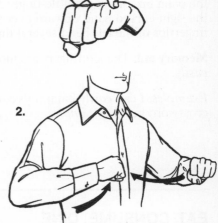

EAST

Move the right *E* hand to the right with palm facing forward.

Memory aid: The initial and direction of the movement indicate the meaning.

Example: The *eastern* sky was brilliant.

EASTER

Move the right *E* hand in a sideways arc to the right with the palm facing forward. *Alternative* (not illustrated): Hold up the right *E* hand with palm facing forward and shake it slightly by pivoting the wrist.

Memory aid: The initial suggests the word, and the arc can be symbolic of the resurrection.

Example: The resurrection of Christ is celebrated at *Easter*.

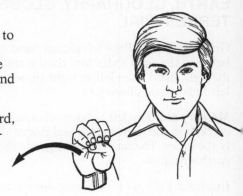

EASY, SIMPLE

Hold the left curved hand to the front with the palm up. Brush the little-finger edge of the right curved hand upward over the fingertips of the left hand several times.

Memory aid: The left fingers are moved *easily*.

Examples: I can *easily* paint my room. This crossword puzzle is *simple*.

EAT, CONSUME, DINE, FOOD, MEAL

The right *and* hand moves toward the mouth a few times.

Memory aid: Putting *food* into the mouth.

Examples: Don't *eat* too much. We have plenty of *food*.

EDUCATION

With palms facing each other, move both *E* hands forward from the forehead a few times. *Note:* The sign for *learn* can also be used.

Memory aid: Suggests the mind's involvement in giving and receiving information.

Example: My grandfather didn't have much *education*.

EGG

Bring the middle finger of the right *H* hand down upon the index finger of the left *H* and move both hands down and out. Most of the latter movement can be done from the wrists.

Memory aid: Suggests the action of removing an *egg* from its shell by breaking the shell.

Example: Some people prefer brown *eggs*.

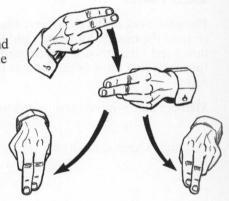

EGYPT, EGYPTIAN

With the right palm forward, form a *C* shape with the index finger and thumb and place it on the forehead. Add the sign for *person (personalizing word ending)* when signing *Egyptian* with reference to a person.

Memory aid: The *C* hand resembles the crescent on a Moslem flag.

Example: The famous Nile is the longest river in *Egypt*.

ELECTRICITY, PHYSICS

Strike the bent index and middle fingers of each hand (or just the index fingers) together a few times. The other fingers are closed.

Memory aid: Suggests *electrical* lines being brought together.

Example: Never play with *electricity*.

ELEPHANT

Place the back of the right curved hand in front of the mouth. Move the right hand down and then forward and upward. Let the fingertips lead the way throughout the movement.

Memory aid: Symbolizes an *elephant's* trunk.

Example: Our zoo has a new *elephant*.

ELEVATOR

Raise and lower the right *E* hand. *Alternative* (not illustrated): Place the fingertips of the right *V* fingers on the upturned left palm and raise both hands together.

Memory aid: The initial and movement of the first sign suggest the meaning. The second sign illustrates a person standing on a rising *elevator*.

Example: Where is the *elevator*?

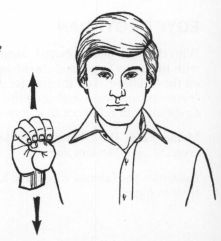

EMBARRASS, BASHFUL, SHY

Raise and lower both open hands alternately in front of the face with palms facing in. Sometimes the hands are rotated slightly forward at the same time.

Memory aid: Suggests the desire to hide the face because of *embarrassment*.

Example: I was so *embarrassed*.

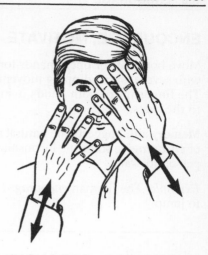

EMOTION

Stroke the chest a few times with the palm side of both *E* hands. Move them alternately in a forward-circular motion.

Memory aid: Suggests the beating of the heart with *emotion*.

Example: It was an *emotional* appeal.

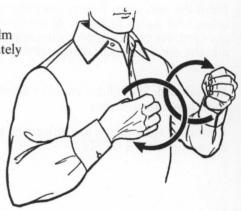

EMPTY, BARE, NAKED, VACANT

Place the right middle finger on the back of the downturned left hand and move it from the wrist to beyond the knuckles.

Memory aid: Symbolizes the idea that the back of a hand is *empty* and *bare*.

Example: The room was *empty*.

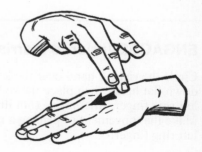

ENCOURAGE, MOTIVATE

Move both flat (or open) hands forward with several short dipping movements. The fingertips of both hands point out to the sides.

Memory aid: Suggests the natural action of *encouraging* someone by pushing the person forward.

Example: The fireman *encouraged* Tony to jump.

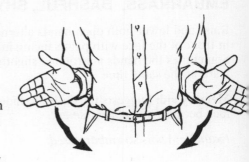

ENEMY, FOE, OPPONENT, RIVAL

1.

Point the two index fingers toward each other with palms facing in. Move them outward sharply in opposite directions; then add the sign for *person (personalizing word ending)*.

Memory aid: Symbolizes *enemies* drawing further and further apart.

Examples: He is acting like an *enemy*. John's chess *opponent* is skillful.

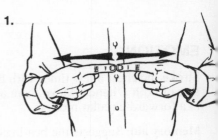

2.

ENGAGED (prior to marriage)

Circle the right *E* hand over the left palm-down flat hand; then place the right *E* on the left ring finger. *Alternative* (not illustrated): Make the movement of placing a ring on the left ring finger.

Memory aid: The *engagement* ring finger is given prominence.

Example: Jim and Sue were *engaged* six months ago.

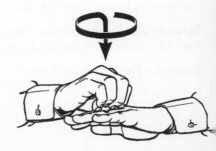

ENGLAND, ENGLISH

Grasp the outer edge of the left closed hand at the wrist with the curved right hand, and move both hands back and forth. Add the sign for *person (personalizing word ending)* when signing *English* with reference to a person.

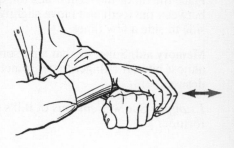

Memory aid: Symbolizes that *England* once ruled much of the world with a firm hand.

Example: Many old streets in *England* are very narrow.

ENOUGH, ADEQUATE, AMPLE, PLENTY, SUBSTANTIAL, SUFFICIENT

Hold the left *S* hand forward with palm facing right. Move the right flat open hand across the top of the left hand from left to right a few times.

Memory aid: Suggests that a container is filled to the brim.

Examples: Do you have *enough* apples?
I have *plenty* of potatoes.

ENVIRONMENT, CIRCUMSTANCE, SITUATION

Circle the right *E* hand in a counterclockwise direction around the front of the left vertical index finger. Initialize with a *C* for *circumstance* and an *S* for *situation*.

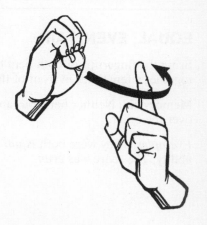

Memory aid: Suggests the surrounding area.

Example: Barbara's *circumstances* are ideal.

ENVY

Place the tip of the right index finger between the teeth and move slightly from side to side a few times.

Memory aid: Suggests that a person might almost bite off a finger to get something desired.

Example: Sue was *envious* of Bill's good fortune.

EPISCOPAL

Hold the left arm in front of the chest with the palm down and the hand closed. Touch the underside of the left forearm with the right index finger at the wrist; then dip the right index hand before touching the left elbow.

Memory aid: Suggests the enlarged sleeve of a priest's robe.

Example: Steve and Elaine attend an *Episcopal* church.

EQUAL, EVEN, FAIR

Bring the fingertips of both bent hands together a few times in front of the chest.

Memory aid: Neither hand has an advantage over the other.

Examples: They were both *equal* in their ability. The score was *even*.

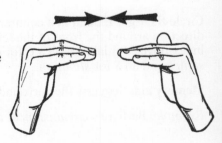

ESCAPE, FLEE, RUN OFF

Point the right index finger forward and place it under the left flat palm. Move the right index finger quickly forward and to the right.

Memory aid: Symbolizes someone breaking away from cover.

Example: The prison *escape* was thwarted.

ESTABLISH, BASED, FOUNDED

Hold the left closed hand in front with palm facing down. Make a counterclockwise circle with the right *A* hand above the left hand; then bring the little-finger edge of the right *A* hand down onto the back of the left hand.

Memory aid: The right hand finds a solid resting place on the back of the left hand.

Example: Our plan is *established* on principles gained from experience.

EUROPE, EUROPEAN

The right *E* hand moves in a small clockwise circle, with palm out, at the right side of the head. Add the sign for *person (personalizing word ending)* when signing *European* with reference to a person.

Memory aid: The initial indicates the word, and the movement suggests many countries.

Example: Geoffrey's college choir is going on a *European* tour this summer.

EVALUATE, CONSIDER

Move both *E* hands up and down alternately with palms facing forward.

Memory aid: The movement suggests scales and the idea of weighing first one side, then the other.

Example: Give me time to *evaluate* these facts.

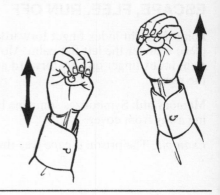

EVE

Swing the right *E* hand up to the right side of the chin.

Memory aid: The initial indicates the word, and the location conveys the meaning of female.

Example: The Bible teaches that *Eve* was the first woman.

EVERYONE, EVERYBODY

Hold the left *A* hand to the front with palm facing right. The knuckles and thumb of the right *A* hand rub downward on the left thumb a few times. Add the numerical sign for *one*.

Memory aid: The right thumb seems to be giving recognition to the left thumb.

Example: Everyone enjoyed the party.

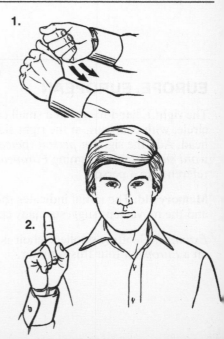

EVIL, CRIME, SIN, WICKED

Point both index fingers toward each other with palms facing self. Move them simultaneously in up-out-down-in circles. Sometimes this sign is preceded or replaced by the sign for *bad.*

Memory aid: The direction of the circles oppose each other, and likewise, that which is considered *evil* generates opposition.

Example: That was a *wicked* thing to do.

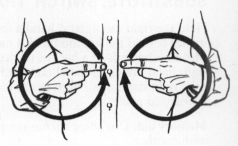

EXACT, ACCURATE, PRECISE, SPECIFIC

Place the thumb tips and index fingertips of each hand together. Position the right hand with palm facing forward and the left hand with palm facing the right hand. Move the hands together until the thumb and index fingers touch. *Note:* Compare *perfect.*

Memory aid: Suggests meeting at an *exact* point.

Example: Make sure your figures are *precise.*

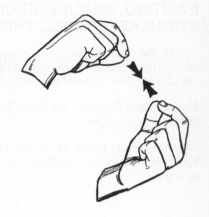

EXAGGERATE

Hold the left *S* hand in front of the chest with palm facing right. Place the right *S* hand in front of the left *S* hand and move it forward while pivoting it several times from the wrist.

Memory aid: The right hand seems to be stretching something held by the left hand.

Example: Uncle Phil always *exaggerates* his experiences.

EXCHANGE, REPLACE, SUBSTITUTE, SWITCH, TRADE

Hold the right modified *A* hand a few inches behind the left modified *A* hand. Move both hands in a backward circle, right hand under left hand and left hand over right hand, until both hands have exchanged places.

Memory aid: One thing *exchanges* place with another.

Example: Please *exchange* this shirt for a larger size.

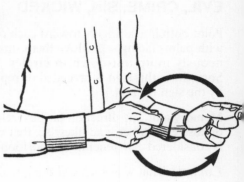

EXCITING, AROUSE, EXCITE, STIMULATE, THRILL, THRILLING

Stroke the chest a few times, using both middle fingers alternately with a forward circular motion. Extend the other fingers.

Memory aid: Suggests the heart beating faster in *excitement.*

Examples: I'm *excited* about this new business. Johnny was *thrilled* with his new toy.

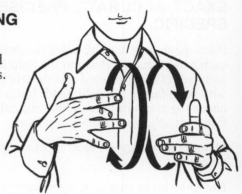

EXCUSE, EXEMPT, FORGIVE, PARDON

Stroke the lower part of the left flat hand with the right fingertips several times.

Memory aid: Suggests a wiping movement and the expression A clean slate.

Examples: Please *excuse* my ignorance. The prisoner was *pardoned.*

EXERCISE

Hold both *S* hands up to the front with palms facing forward. Move both hands up and down (or forward and backward) simultaneously.

Memory aid: Suggests using dumbbells for *exercise.*

Example: People need *exercise* to benefit their health.

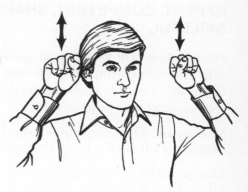

EXPENSIVE, COSTLY

Slap the back of the right *and* hand in the upturned palm of the left hand (the sign for *money*); then lift the right hand and open it while simultaneously pivoting it to the right.

Memory aid: Symbolizes throwing money away.

Example: The rent is too *expensive.*

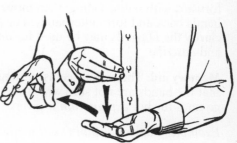

EXPERIENCE

Move the right curved open hand slightly outward from the right temple while simultaneously closing the hand to the *and* position.

Memory aid: Suggests an area of the head (sideburns) where an old and *experienced* man is still likely to have hair.

Example: Do you have enough *experience* to do the job?

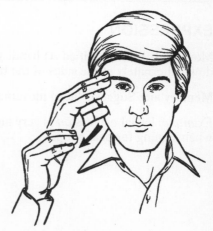

EXPERT, COMPETENT, SHARP, SKILLFUL

Point the fingers of the left hand upward with palm facing right. Grasp the little-finger side of the left hand with the right, and move the right hand forward.

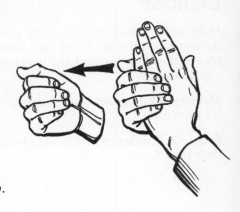

Memory aid: The action suggests that the edge of the left hand is being *sharpened*.

Examples: She is an *expert* at horseback riding. The whole class is unusually *sharp*.

EXPLAIN, DEFINE, DESCRIBE

Point the extended fingers of both *F* hands forward with palms facing; then move the hands back and forth alternately. For added clarity the *D* hands may be used for *define* and *describe*.

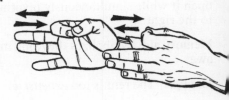

Memory aid: The action seems to suggest that the hands are not sure which way to go until further *explanation* is given.

Example: Can you *explain* your method to us?

EXPRESSION

Move both *X* (or modified *A*) hands up and down alternately at the sides of the face.

Memory aid: Suggests facial movements.

Example: Facial *expression* is very important when signing for deaf people.

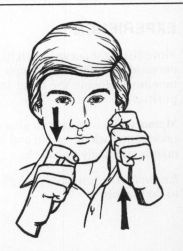

EYE

Point to the eye with the right index finger.

Memory aid: The *eye* is identified by pointing.

Example: I have gray *eyes*.

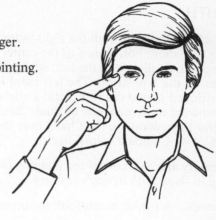

FACE

Move the right index finger in a counter-clockwise direction around the face.

Memory aid: The action points to the *face*.

Example: Your *face* is red.

F

FAIL

Slide the back of the right *V* hand across the upturned left hand and go beyond and below the left fingertips.

Memory aid: The downward movement can suggest *failure*. Or, victory has fallen.

Example: We *failed* to raise enough money.

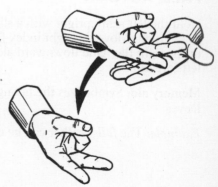

FAITH

Touch the forehead with the right index finger; then move both hands to the center of the chest, or slightly to the left, while closing them to the S position. The left hand is positioned above the right, and a slight downward movement can be made. Some prefer to position the right hand over the left. *Note:* Compare *confidence.*

Memory aid: Symbolizes the planting of a flag to show *faith* in one's country.

Example: A person needs *faith* to succeed.

FAITHFUL

Point both *F* hands forward with the right hand over the left. Move both hands forward while simultaneously striking the lower side of the right hand on the upper side of the left a few times. *Note:* Compare *regular.*

Memory aid: The repeated striking action indicates *faithfulness.*

Example: He is *faithful* to the cause.

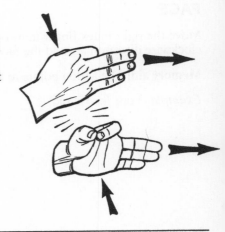

FALL, AUTUMN

Hold the left arm upright with a slight lean to the right. Move the right index-finger side of the right flat hand downward along the left forearm.

Memory aid: Symbolizes the falling of leaves.

Example: The *fall* weather can be quite cold.

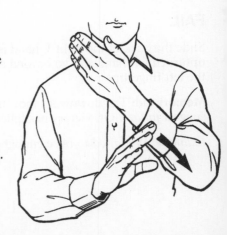

FALL (verb)

Stand the right *V* fingers in the left flat palm. Flip them over so that the backs of the *V* fingers rest on the left palm.

Memory aid: Symbolizes a person *falling* flat on the back.

Example: Don't *fall* down the steps.

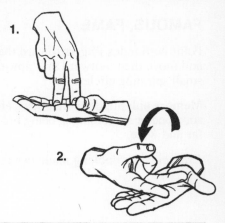

FALSE, ARTIFICIAL, COUNTERFEIT, FAKE, PSEUDO, SHAM

Point the right index finger up and move it across the lips from right to left.

Memory aid: Symbolizes the idea that spoken truth is diverted from its normally straight course.

Examples: He has an *artificial* leg. This is *counterfeit* money.

FAMILY

Place both upright *F* hands to the front with the palms facing each other. Make an outward circular movement with each hand simultaneously until the little fingers touch.

Memory aid: The two *F* hands describe the circle of a *family*.

Example: He comes from a respectable *family*.

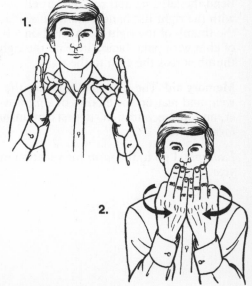

FAMOUS, FAME

Point both index fingers toward the mouth and move them outward and upward in small spiraling circles.

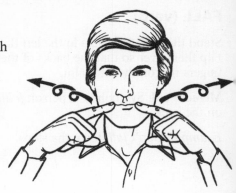

Memory aid: Suggests that news about someone or something is being broadcast far and wide.

Example: Her cooking made her *famous*.

FAR, DISTANT, REMOTE

Move the right *A* hand well forward from an initial position beside the left *A* hand.

Memory aid: Symbolizes the *distance* between two points.

Example: How *far* have you traveled?

FARM, COUNTRY (rural)

Bend the left arm and rub the left elbow with the right flat hand. *Alternative:* Place the thumb of the right open hand on left side of chin with palm facing in. Rub the right thumb across the chin to the right.

Memory aid: The first sign indicates the wear and tear on the elbows of a *farm* worker, and the second sign suggests an unshaven *farm* worker.

Example: I go to the *farm* for vacation every year.

or:

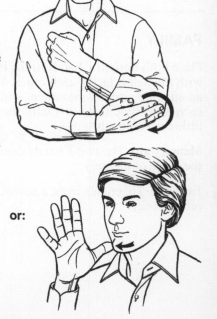

FARMER

Place the thumb of the right open hand on the left side of the chin with the palm facing in. Rub the right thumb across the chin to the right. Add the sign for *person (personalizing word ending)*.

Memory aid: Suggests an unshaven *farmer*.

Example: My best friend's father is a *farmer*.

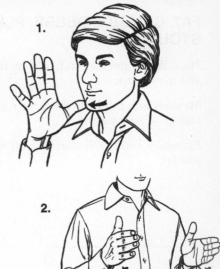

FAST, IMMEDIATELY, QUICK, RAPID, SPEEDY, SUDDENLY, SWIFT

Flick the right thumb from the crooked index finger.

Memory aid: Suggests the *rapid* flicking of a marble from the hand.

Example: He was driving too *fast*.

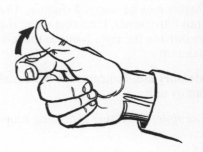

FASTING

Move the right thumb and index side of the F hand across the mouth from left to right. *Note:* Compare *dry*.

Memory aid: The initial indicates the word, and the action suggests dryness of the mouth.

Example: The doctor prescribed a three-day *fast* from solid food.

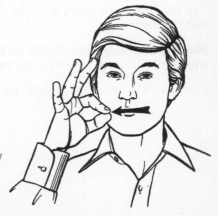

FAT, CHUBBY, OBESE, PLUMP, STOUT

Place both curved open hands by the cheeks and move outward.

Memory aid: Suggests the large round cheeks of a *fat* person.

Example: Too much starchy food will make you *fat*.

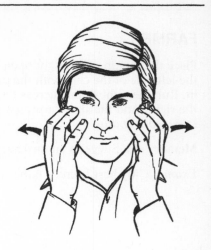

FATHER, DAD

Considered informal but commonly used is the sign made by touching the forehead with the thumb of the right open hand. The fingers may be wiggled slightly. *Alternative* (not illustrated): First sign male; then follow by moving the right hand to the left with palm up.

Memory aid: Indicates the head male of the family unit.

Example: His *father* is coming soon.

FAVORITE

Tap the chin a few times with the right middle finger.

Memory aid: Suggests a dimple on the chin, which is considered cute by many people.

Example: She baked my *favorite* pie.

FEAR, DREAD, TERROR

Hold both open hands to the front with the palms facing forward; then draw them in and down toward the body with a trembling motion. Assume an appropriate facial expression.

Memory aid: Suggests an attempt to ward off something undesirable.

Examples: Sally *fears* heights. He lived in *terror* of being caught.

FEELING, MOTIVE, SENSATION

Move the right middle finger upward on the chest with other fingers extended.

Memory aid: Suggests the direction of inner *feelings.*

Examples: How do you *feel*? My *motive* is right.

FEET

Point first to one foot and then the other.

Memory aid: Both *feet* are identified by pointing to them.

Example: My *feet* are tired.

FEMALE

Trace the right jawbone from ear to chin with the palm side of the right *A* thumb.

Memory aid: The thumb follows the location of the old-fashioned bonnet string.

Example: This cat is *female.*

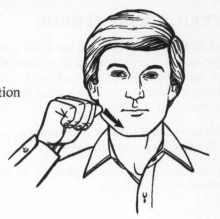

FIND, DISCOVER

Hold the right open hand in front with the palm facing down. Bring the index and thumb together as the hand is raised.

Memory aid: Symbolizes picking something up.

Example: Can you *find* your way home?

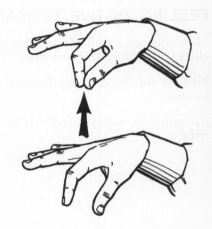

FINE

Place the thumb edge of the right flat open hand at the chest and pivot the hand forward. *Note:* Compare *polite.*

Memory aid: Symbolizes an old-fashioned shirt or blouse with ruffles.

Example: I'm just *fine* today.

FINGERSPELLING, ALPHABET, DACTYLOLOGY, MANUAL ALPHABET, SPELL

With palm facing down, wiggle the fingers of the right flat open hand as the hand moves along a horizontal line to the right.

Memory aid: Emphasizes the use of fingers in *fingerspelling*.

Examples: I can only communicate with the *manual alphabet*. Advanced *dactylology* takes a lot of practice.

FINISH, ALREADY, COMPLETE

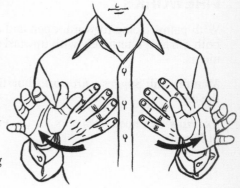

Hold both open hands to the front with palms facing self and fingers pointing up. Shake them quickly outward to the sides a few times. *Note:* This sign is used frequently in everyday conversation. For example: Instead of signing, "I've already been to the store," a deaf person may simply sign, "Store *finished.*"

Memory aid: Symbolizes something being shaken off by the hands.

Example: I have *finished* my college education.

FIRE, BURN, FLAME

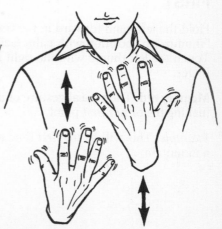

With palms facing in, move both slightly curved open hands up and down alternately in front of the body while wiggling the fingers.

Memory aid: Symbolizes leaping *flames.*

Example: Don't *burn* yourself with that match.

FIRED, DISCHARGED, EXPELLED

Sweep the upturned right flat hand across
the top of the left closed hand from right
to left.

Memory aid: Suggests someone's head being
cut off.

Example: Terry was *fired* last week.

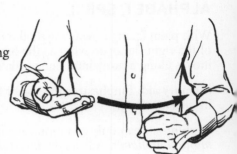

FIREWORKS

With palms facing forward, open and close
both *S* hands alternately with upward movements.

Memory aid: Suggests *fireworks* bursting in
the air.

Example: We need *fireworks* for the Fourth
of July.

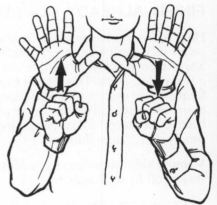

FIRST

Hold the left hand forward in the traditional
"thumbs up" position with palm facing right.
Touch the left thumb with the right index
finger.

Memory aid: The typical gesture of a speaker
making his or her *first* point.

Example: This will be my *first* time to climb
a mountain.

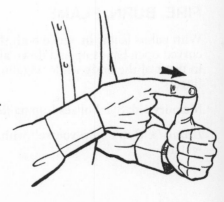

FISH (noun)

Place the fingertips of the left flat hand at the right wrist or elbow. Point the right flat hand forward with palm facing left, and swing from right to left a few times. Most of the movement is at the wrist.

Memory aid: Suggests the swimming motion of a *fish's* tail.

Example: There are plenty of *fish* in this pond.

FISHING

Place both thumb tips in the crooks of their respective index fingers with the other fingers closed. Position the left hand above the right as if holding a *fishing* rod. Pivot the hands quickly up and backward from the wrists.

Memory aid: The action performed when a *fish* is caught.

Example: My uncle loves to go *fishing*.

FLAG, BANNER

Place the right elbow in the left hand and wave the right hand back and forth.

Memory aid: Suggests a *flag* waving on a pole.

Example: Remember to put the *flag* up.

FLIRT, PHILANDERER

With the palms facing down, touch the thumbs of both open hands, leaving the fingers pointing forward. Wiggle the fingers.

Memory aid: Suggests the *flirtatious* batting of the eyelashes.

Example: Ed always was a *philanderer*.

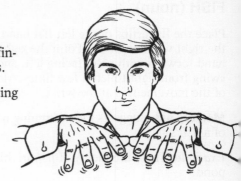

FLOOD

Touch the mouth with the index finger of the right *W* hand a few times (the sign for *water*). Point both palm-down open hands forward and raise them simultaneously while wiggling the fingers.

Memory aid: Suggests rising water.

Example: The heavy rains caused severe *flooding*.

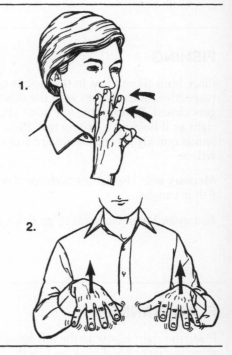

FLOOR

Place the index-finger edge of both flat hands together with palms facing down; then move both hands apart to the sides. The sign can be repeated further to the right.

Memory aid: Symbolizes *flooring* boards placed side by side.

Example: Please sweep the *floor*.

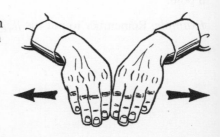

FLORIDA

Fingerspell *F-L*.

Memory aid: The first two letters of the word are initialized. Context and simultaneous lipreading are required for full comprehension.

Example: Florida enjoys a lot of sunshine.

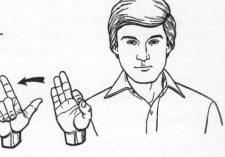

FLOWER

Place the fingertips of the right *and* hand under each nostril separately.

Memory aid: Suggests smelling a *flower*.

Example: Janet was thrilled with the bouquet of *flowers*.

FLY (insect)

Move the right flat hand quickly onto the left forearm. End with the right hand closed.

Memory aid: Symbolizes the act of catching a *fly*.

Example: Keep the *flies* away from my food.

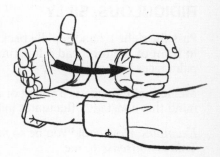

FOLLOW, CHASE, DISCIPLE, PURSUE, SEQUEL

Place both *A* hands to the front with the left one slightly ahead of the right. Move them forward with the right hand following the left. *Note:* Add the sign for *person (personalizing word ending)* when signing *follower, disciple* (can be initialized), or *chaser. Chase* and *pursue* are signed more rapidly than *follow.*

Memory aid: One hand *follows* the other.

Examples: Follow that cab. He's a *disciple* of modern art.

FOOL (verb), JOKE, HOAX

Place the bent index finger across the bridge of the nose and move both head and hand downward simultaneously.

Memory aid: Suggests a person being pulled in a direction he or she did not choose.

Example: He tried to *fool* the authorities.

FOOLISH, NONSENSE, RIDICULOUS, SILLY

Pass the right *Y* hand rapidly back and forth in front of the forehead a few times. The palm faces left.

Memory aid: Suggests a young or childish mind that constantly fluctuates in opinion.

Examples: How could you be so *foolish*? That is *nonsense* to me.

FOOTBALL

Interlock the fingers of both hands vigorously a few times.

Memory aid: Suggests the strong physical contact made in *football.*

Example: When is the next *football* game?

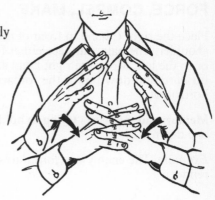

FOR

Touch the right temple with the right index finger; then dip it straight forward until the index finger is pointing forward.

Memory aid: Knowledge is directed outward *for* a particular purpose.

Example: What can you do *for* me?

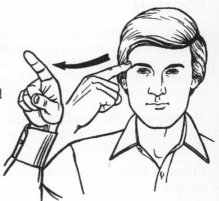

FORBID, BAN, PROHIBIT

Point the fingers of the left flat hand upward with palm facing right. Slap the right *G* hand into the left palm.

Memory aid: Suggests that a person may come up against the strong hand of the law. Note the similarity to the sign for *law.*

Example: They *forbade* our entrance.

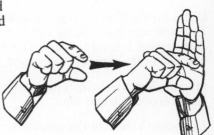

FORCE, COMPEL, MAKE

Place the right *C* hand in front of the right shoulder. The palm can face either forward or to the left. Move the right hand sharply forward and down until the forearm is horizontal.

Memory aid: Suggests trying to hold someone down.

Example: The enemy was *forced* to surrender.

FOREIGN

Rub the index-finger and thumb side of the right *F* hand in a few counterclockwise circles on the underside of the left forearm near the elbow. *Note:* Compare *country* (national territory).

Memory aid: The initial indicates the word, and the action is the same as that for *country*.

Example: Have you ever been to a *foreign* country?

FOREVER, ETERNAL, EVER, EVERLASTING

Circle the right index finger in a clockwise direction with palm facing up; then move the downturned *Y* hand forward. This is a combination of the sign for *always* and *still*.

Memory aid: Symbolizes the continuous progression of clock and time.

Examples: I thought the speaker would go on *forever.* Your effort should have *everlasting* value.

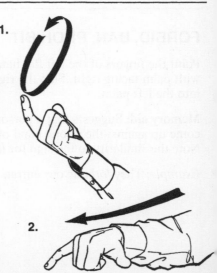

1.

2.

FORGET, FORSAKE

Wipe the palm side of the right open hand across the forehead from left to right. End with the right hand in the *A* position close to the right temple.

Memory aid: Indicates wiping information from the mind.

Example: I will not *forget* you.

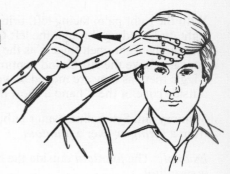

FORK

Move the fingers of the right *V* hand into the left upturned palm a few times. *Note:* Sometimes the three fingers of the right *M* hand are used.

Memory aid: The fingers symbolize the tines of a *fork.*

Example: I would rather use a *fork.*

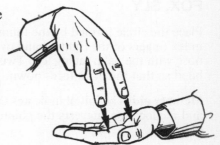

FOUNDATION, SUPPORT

With the palm facing in, hold the left closed hand to the front with the forearm horizontal. Place the right *S* hand first under the left hand, then under the forearm.

Memory aid: Suggests the pillars that *support* a building.

Example: How deep is the *foundation?*

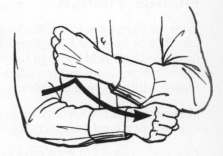

FOUNTAIN, SPRING

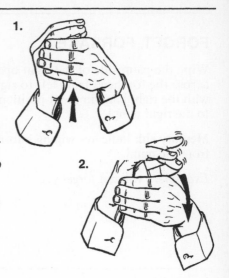

With the right palm facing left, bring the right *and* hand up through the left *C* hand. Wiggle the right open fingers as the hand appears above the left *C*, and continue to wiggle them as they are moved down the outside edge of the *C* hand a short distance.

Memory aid: Symbolizes water bubbling up from a *spring* or over a *fountain*.

Example: The *fountain* outside the hospital is beautiful.

FOX, SLY

Place the circle formed by the thumb and index fingers of the right *F* hand over the nose with the palm facing left. Twist the hand so that the palm faces down.

Memory aid: The initial indicates the word, and the location suggests the pointed nose of a *fox*.

Examples: A *fox* usually keeps itself hidden during daylight. That was a *sly* thing to do.

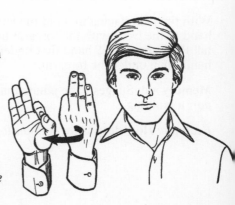

FRANCE, FRENCH

With the right palm facing the right shoulder, flick or twist the *F* hand until the palm faces forward. Add the sign for *person (personalizing word ending)* when signing *French* with reference to a person.

Memory aid: A French chef's sign of approval of a meal well prepared.

Example: Sometimes people try to swim across the English Channel between *France* and England.

FRENCH FRIES

Sign the right *F* hand once, then again a second time slightly to the right.

Memory aid: The two initials are used.

Example: Homemade *french fries* are delicious.

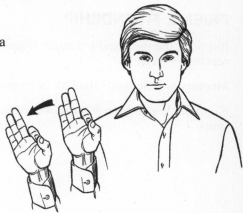

FRESHMAN

Touch the fourth finger of the open left hand with the right index finger. *Note:* Compare *sophomore, junior,* and *senior.*

Memory aid: Counting from the thumb, a *freshman* still has four years of study to complete.

Example: Beth is a *freshman.*

FRIDAY

Make a small clockwise circle with the right *F* hand.

Memory aid: The initial suggests the word, and the circular motion suggests the passing of time.

Example: Come on *Friday.*

FRIEND, FRIENDSHIP

Interlock the right and left index fingers and repeat in reverse.

Memory aid: Suggests the link of *friendship*.

Example: We've been *friends* over twenty years.

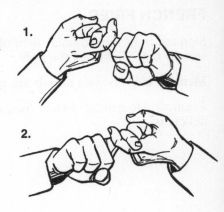

FROG

Hold the closed right hand under the chin with palm facing in. Flick out the right index and middle fingers of the closed right hand.

Memory aid: The flicking fingers picture the jumping nature of a *frog*. The location suggests the expression A *frog* in the throat.

Example: The lake seemed full of *frogs*.

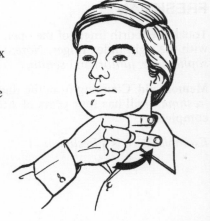

FROM

Touch the upright left index finger with the knuckle of the right *X* index finger; then move the right hand in a slight backward-downward arc. *Note:* Sometimes the left index finger is crooked or pointed forward.

Memory aid: Suggests pulling back *from* something.

Example: I'm leaving *from* the bus terminal.

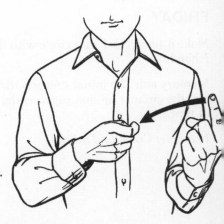

FRUIT

Place the thumb and index fingers of the right *F* hand on the right cheek. Twist forward or backward. *Alternative* (not illustrated): Make the sign for *grow;* then place the right curved open hand over the left *and* hand. Slide the right fingers off the left hand to the right until the right hand also forms an *and* hand.

Memory aid: The basic sign is similar to the one for *apple.* The alternative sign suggests the growth and shape of *fruit.*

Example: Fruit is excellent for one's health.

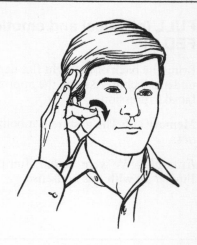

FRUSTRATE

Bring the back of the right flat hand sharply toward the face. The head can also move back slightly.

Memory aid: Suggests a wall of opposition.

Example: Paul's attitude is so *frustrating.*

FULL, FILLED

Move the right flat hand to the left over the thumb edge of the left closed hand.

Memory aid: Indicates that a container is *full* by leveling it off at the brim.

Example: The stadium was *full.*

FULL (physical and emotional), FED UP

Bring the back of the right flat hand up under the chin. Assume the appropriate facial expression.

Memory aid: The gesture symbolizes *fullness.*

Examples: We were so *full* after the meal. I'm *fed up* with this nonsense.

FUN

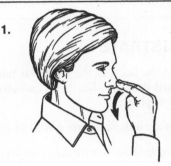

Brush the tip of the nose with the fingers of the right *U* hand. Move the right *U* hand down and brush the left and right *U* fingers up and down against each other a few times.

Memory aid: Suggests that people's noses wrinkle when they laugh.

Example: Skating is *fun.*

FUNERAL, PARADE, PROCESSION

With palms facing forward, hold the right *V* hand up behind the left *V* hand, and move the hands forward with a few short movements.

Memory aid: Suggests people moving in line, as for a *funeral* or *parade.*

Example: How long will the *parade* be?

FUNNY, AMUSING, COMICAL, HILARIOUS, HUMOROUS

Brush the tip of the nose with the fingers of the right *U* hand several times.

Memory aid: Suggests that people's noses wrinkle when they laugh.

Example: The comedian was more *funny* than we expected.

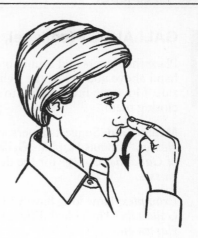

FURNITURE

Shake the *F* hand back and forth near the right shoulder or in front of the chest.

Memory aid: The initialized sign indicates the word.

Example: Our new *furniture* comes this afternoon.

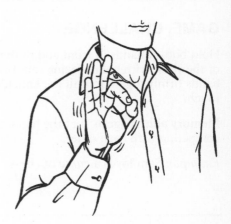

FUTURE, BY AND BY, LATER ON, SOMEDAY

Hold the right flat hand with palm facing left in an upright position close to the right temple. Move it in a forward-upward arc. The greater the arc, the more distant the future that is indicated.

Memory aid: Suggests moving onward into the *future*.

Examples: You have an exciting *future*. Pamela will know more *later on*. The truth will come out *someday*.

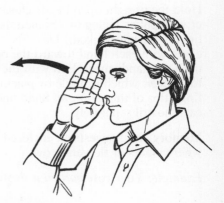

GALLAUDET (college), GLASSES

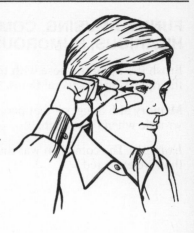

Place the fingers and thumb of the right *G* hand above and below the right eye at the side. Move the fingers back to the ear while closing them.

Memory aid: Suggests a person who wears *glasses.* Thomas Hopkins Gallaudet, founder of *Gallaudet College* for the deaf, wore *glasses.*

Examples: How long have you been at *Gallaudet*? He looked different without his *glasses* on.

GAME, CHALLENGE

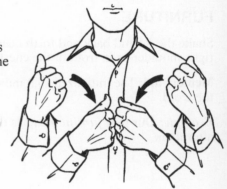

Hold both *A* hands in front and to the sides of the chest with palms facing self. Bring the hands firmly together until the knuckles touch.

Memory aid: Suggests that the hands are competing with each other.

Example: Sam loves a *game* of chess.

GARDEN, YARD

1.

Hold the upright open hands close together with palms facing in. (Sometimes the fingers are interlocked.) Describe a half circle with each hand toward the body until the hands meet. End with the sign for *flower,* which is made by placing the fingertips of the right *and* hand under each nostril separately.

Memory aid: Suggests an enclosed space where plants or flowers grow.

Example: Your rose *garden* is exquisite.

2.

GARDENING, HOEING, RAKING

Place both thumb tips into the crooks of both curved index fingers with the other fingers closed. Hold the left hand in front of the right and pull toward self with both hands in unison. *Note: Raking* can be signed by pulling the right downturned open curved hand toward self.

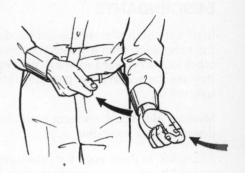

Memory aid: Suggests that the hands are working with a *hoe.*

Example: Mother always looks forward to spring *gardening.*

GASOLINE

Bring the right *A* thumb down into the left *O* hand.

Memory aid: Symbolizes putting *gas* into an automobile tank.

Example: You're almost out of *gas.*

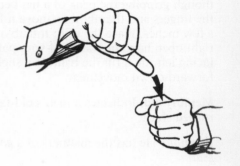

GATE

Point the fingertips of both flat hands together with palms facing in. Move the right hand back and forth a few times.

Memory aid: Symbolizes the action of a *gate.*

Example: Be sure to shut the *gate.*

GENERATION, ANCESTORS, DESCENDANTS

Start with both slightly cupped hands at the right shoulder; then roll them one over the other in a downward-forward movement. Reverse the action if the past generation is referred to.

Memory aid: The movement symbolizes descending or ascending steps.

Examples: Is there hope for future *generations*? My *ancestors* came from Italy.

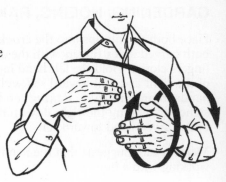

GENTLEMAN

Move the right hand to the forehead as though gripping the peak of a hat between the fingers and thumb; then move it forward a few inches. Place the right thumb of the right open hand on the chest with palm facing left, then tilt the hand in a slight up-forward-down movement.

Memory aid: Indicates a man's old-fashioned ruffled shirt.

Example: He has the manners of a *gentleman*.

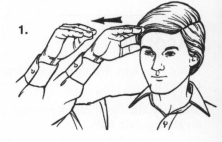

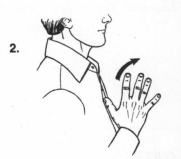

GERMANY, GERMAN

Cross the hands at the wrists with palms facing the body and wiggle the fingers. Add the sign for *person (personalizing word ending)* when signing *German* with reference to a person.

Memory aid: Reminds one of the double eagle emblem of the old German empire.

Example: Sam told us of his visit to the beautiful Black Forest in *Germany*.

GET, ACQUIRE, OBTAIN

Bring both open hands together while simultaneously forming *S* hands and place the right on top of the left.

Memory aid: Suggests taking hold of something and drawing it to oneself.

Example: Did you *get* permission before proceeding?

GET IN

Put the right *V* fingers into the left *O* to sign *get in*.

Memory aid: Suggests a person's legs getting into a hole.

Example: Go ahead and *get in* the car.

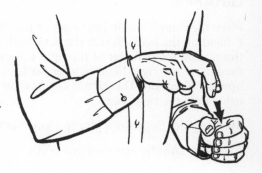

GET OUT, GET OFF

Pull the right *V* fingers out of the left *O* hand.

Memory aid: Suggests a person's legs being pulled out of a hole.

Example: Get out of this building immediately.

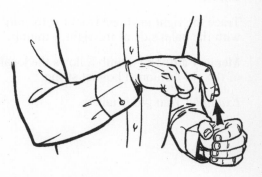

GIFT, AWARD, BESTOW, CONFER, CONTRIBUTE, PRESENT, REWARD

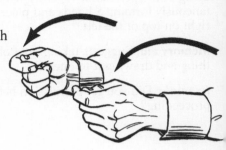

With the palms facing each other, place both closed hands to the front with the thumb tips touching the inside of their respective crooked index fingers. Move both hands forward simultaneously in an arc.

Memory aid: A natural gesture of *giving* something to someone.

Examples: Please accept this small *gift*. I'd like to make a *contribution*.

GIRAFFE

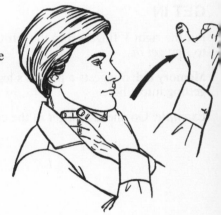

Place the thumb and index finger of the left *C* hand on the neck. Touch the neck with the thumb and index finger of the right *C* hand, then move the right hand in a forward-upward direction. This sign is often made using only the right hand.

Memory aid: Suggests a *giraffe's* long neck.

Example: Giraffes run very gracefully.

GIRL

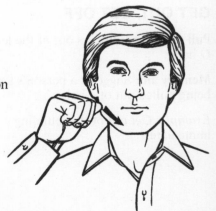

Trace the right jawbone from ear to chin with the palm side of the right *A* thumb.

Memory aid: The thumb follows the location of the old-fashioned bonnet string.

Example: That *girl* is tall.

GIVE, DISTRIBUTE

Hold both *and* hands to the front with palms facing down. Move them forward simultaneously while forming flat hands with fingers pointing forward and palms facing up.

Memory aid: Suggests the act of *giving*.

Example: I want to *give* you a present.

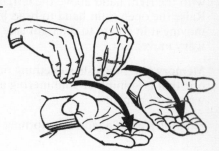

GLASS (drinking)

Place the little-finger edge of the right *C* hand on the left flat palm and raise the right hand a short distance.

Memory aid: Indicates the size and shape of a *glass*.

Example: She bought a pretty set of *glasses*.

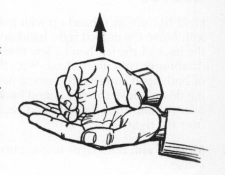

GLASS (substance), CHINA, DISH, PORCELAIN

Touch the teeth with the right index finger.

Memory aid: The teeth are breakable, just like *glass*.

Example: You have fine *china*.

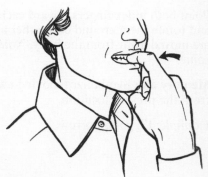

GLORY, GLORIOUS

Holding the hands in the horizontal position with the right hand above the left, clap once. Raise the open right hand to head level while moving it in an arc to the right side with a wavy movement.

Memory aid: Suggests something or someone that is shining or shimmering and worthy of applause.

Example: What a *glorious* morning this is.

GLOVES

Hold the left open hand up with palm facing self. Move the curved right hand down over the back of the left hand a few times. *Alternative* (not illustrated): With the palms of both open and slightly curved hands facing down, move the right hand backward over the left; then the left hand backward over the right.

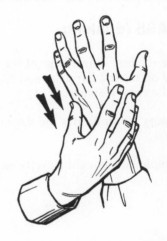

Memory aid: Both signs mimic putting on *gloves*.

Example: These are the strongest *gloves* I have ever owned.

GO

Point both index fingers toward each other and rotate them around each other as they are moved away from the body. *Note:* See *come*.

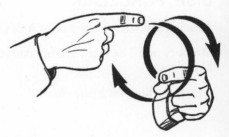

Memory aid: Symbolizes moving away from the present location.

Example: I'll *go* tomorrow.

GOAT

Place the thumb side of the right *S* hand on the point of the chin. Move the right hand up to the forehead while changing to a *V* hand with palm facing left.

Memory aid: Suggests the beard and horns of a *goat*.

Example: Goat's milk is easy to digest.

GOD

Point the right *G* finger in a forward-upward direction at head level. (Some signers use the whole flat hand with the palm facing left). Move the right hand in a backward-downward arc toward self, ending with a *B* hand in front of the upper chest with palm still facing left.

Memory aid: The finger or hand pointing upward suggests *God* is above all. The *B* hand in the position for *be* can suggest the eternal existence of *God*.

Example: God is omniscient.

GOLD

Touch the right ear with the right index finger, or grasp the right earlobe between the right index finger and thumb. Shake the right *Y* hand as it moves down and forward.

Memory aid: Suggests both the idea of earrings and the color of *gold*.

Example: Gold is considered to be the most attractive metal by many people.

GOLF

Point the right *A* hand down at waist level with the thumb side of the left *A* hand touching the little-finger side of the right hand. Swing both hands from right to left.

Memory aid: The position and action of a *golf* player.

Example: How much time do you spend playing *golf*?

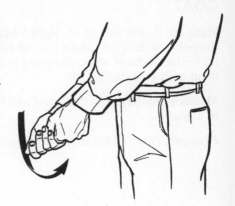

GONE, ABSENT

Draw the right open hand down through the left *C* hand and end with the right hand in the *and* position below the left hand.

Memory aid: Suggests something disappearing down a hole.

Example: My money is *gone*.

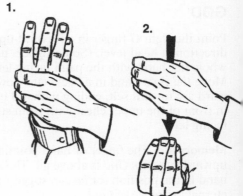

GOOD, WELL

Place the fingers of the right flat hand at the lips; then move the hand down into the palm of the left hand with both palms facing up. *Alternative* (not illustrated): Raise the right thumb in the "thumbs up" position for informal use.

Memory aid: Suggests something that has been tasted, approved, and offered to another.

Example: We have found their merchandise to be of *good* quality.

GOSPEL

Slide the little-finger edge of the right *G* hand across the flat left hand from fingertips to heel a few times.

Memory aid: The initial indicates the word, and the action is similar to the sign for *new*. Thus something new is "news," and the meaning of *gospel* is "good news."

Example: Please read to me from the *Gospel* of John.

GOSSIP

Open and close the *Q* fingers and thumbs several times in front of the mouth.

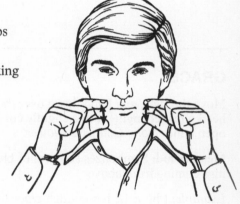

Memory aid: The fingers seem to be talking rapidly to each other.

Example: I'm sick of *gossip*.

GOVERNMENT, CAPITAL, FEDERAL, POLITICS

With the right index finger at the right temple, make a small forward circle; then place the index finger on the temple. An initialized hand may be used for *capital*, *federal*, and *politics*.

Memory aid: Pointing to the head symbolizes the authority of *government*.

Example: Allen has great faith in the *government*.

GOVERNOR

With the right index finger at the right temple, make a small counterclockwise circle; then place the index finger on the temple. Add the sign for *person (personalizing word ending).*

Memory aid: Pointing to the head symbolizes the authority of *government.*

Example: The *governor* listened to our suggestions with interest and respect.

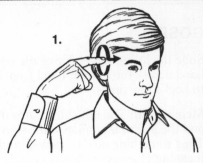

1.

2.

GRACE

Move the right *and* hand down over the head while changing it to a slightly curved open hand. *Note:* Compare *shower.*

Memory aid: Symbolizes showers of blessings coming from above.

Example: I hope he has enough *grace* to accept me.

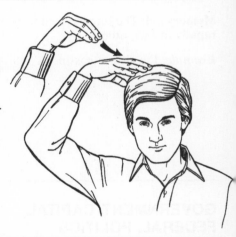

GRADUATE

Make a small clockwise circle with the right *G* hand and bring it down onto the left flat palm.

Memory aid: The initial indicates the word, and the action is similar to that for *seal.* Therefore, a *graduate's* education is sealed.

Example: What year did you *graduate?*

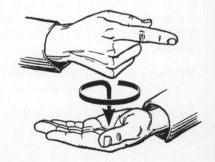

GRANDFATHER

Touch the forehead with the thumb of the right open hand, which has its palm facing left. Move the right hand in two forward arcs. *Alternative* (not illustrated): Begin with the informal sign for *father;* then hold both open hands to the front with palms up and move twice toward the left shoulder.

Memory aid: The combination of the sign for *father* and the double hand movements of both signs suggest the reference to someone of the older generation.

Example: My *grandfather* is ninety.

GRANDMOTHER

Touch the chin with the thumb of the right open hand, which has its palm facing left. Move the right hand in two forward arcs. *Alternative* (not illustrated): Begin with the informal sign for *mother;* then hold both open hands to the front with palms up and move twice toward the left shoulder.

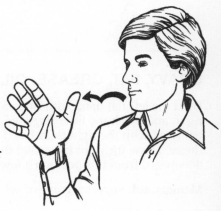

Memory aid: The combination of the sign for *mother* and the double hand movements of both signs suggest the reference to someone of the older generation.

Example: We will see *grandmother* today.

GRAPES

Place the fingertips of the right curved hand on the back of the closed left hand. Move the right hand down on the left hand with several small hops.

Memory aid: Can suggest the number of *grapes* in a bunch.

Example: The *grapes* are ripe.

GRASS

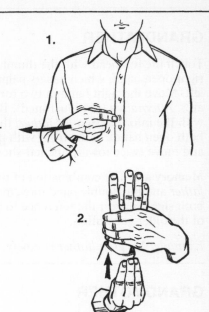

Move the right *G* hand to the right while shaking it from the wrist, then open the fingers of the right *and* hand as they pass up through the left *C* hand. These are the signs for *green* and *grow*. *Alternative* (not illustrated): Pivot the right *G* hand from the wrist as it moves from left to right in front of the chest.

Memory aid: Both signs suggest that something green is growing.

Example: Michael cuts our *grass* for us.

GRAVY, FAT, GREASE, OIL

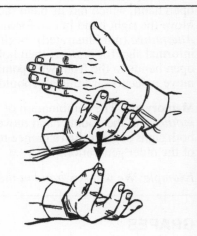

Hold the left flat hand with fingers pointing right, and pinch the little-finger edge of the left hand with the right thumb and index finger. Draw the right index and thumb downward from this position a few times.

Memory aid: Suggests *gravy* or *oil* dripping.

Examples: Do you want *gravy* on your potato? The *fat* dripped from the fried chicken.

GRAY

Pass the fingers of both open hands back and forth through the open spaces between the fingers.

Memory aid: The merging fingers suggest the mixture of black and white to produce *gray*.

Example: Paint your equipment *gray*.

GREEN

Move the right *G* hand to the right while shaking it from the wrist.

Memory aid: The initial indicates the word, which requires context and simultaneous lipreading for full comprehension.

Example: My grass is not very *green.*

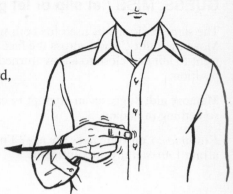

GRIEF, MOURN

Bring the palm sides of both *A* hands together in front of the heart and rotate them back and forth as though crushing something between the hands.

Memory aid: Suggests that the heart is crushed with the weight of *grief.*

Example: His faithful dog *mourned* him for weeks.

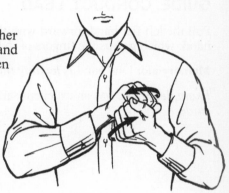

GROUP, ASSOCIATION, AUDIENCE, CLASS, COMPANY, DEPARTMENT, ORGANIZATION, SOCIETY, TEAM

Hold both *C* hands upright before the chest with palms facing. Move the hands outward in a circle until the little fingers touch. The basic sign may be utilized for all the key words, but sometimes the signer will prefer to initialize the sign.

Memory aid: The circle suggests an area encompassing several people.

Examples: My *group* was unsuccessful. The *audience* applauded enthusiastically.

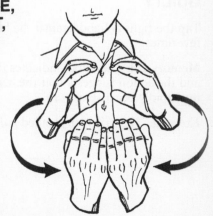

GUESS, MISS (let slip or let go)

The same basic sign is used for both words. Move the right *C* hand across the face from right to left and close to a downturned *S* position.

Memory aid: Suggests an attempt to catch something in midair.

Examples: Can you *guess* my age? I'm afraid I *missed* my appointment.

GUIDE, CONDUCT, LEAD

Pull the left flat hand forward with the right hand, which grasps the fingers of the left.

Memory aid: One hand is *leading* the other.

Example: Frank was an excellent safari *guide*.

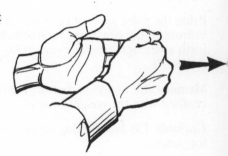

GUILTY

Tap the right *G* hand against the heart area a few times.

Memory aid: The initial indicates the word, and the action suggests that the heart is beating rapidly because of *guilt*.

Example: The prisoner pleaded *guilty*.

GUITAR

Hold the left hand forward and to the left with thumb extended and fingers partially curled. Place the thumb of the right *A* hand in the crook of the index finger and pivot the hand up and down in front of the chest.

Memory aid: The position and movement for playing a *guitar.*

Example: Do you take *guitar* lessons?

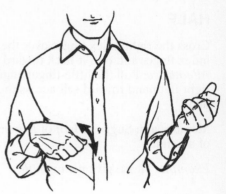

HABIT, CUSTOM, PRACTICE

Touch the forehead with the right index finger. Change the right hand to an *S* hand as it is brought down and crosses the left *S* hand at the wrist. Push both hands down slightly.

Memory aid: Suggests that the mind is bound by *habit.*

Examples: His *habit* is to shout when he is nervous. It is my *practice* to retire to bed early.

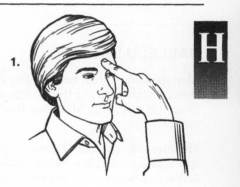

1.

2.

HAIRCUT

Open and close the right *H* fingers near the hair several times.

Memory aid: The action of cutting hair.

Example: He needs a *haircut.*

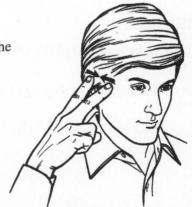

HALF

Cross the right index finger over the left index finger and pull it back toward self. *Alternative:* Pull the little-finger edge of the right flat hand toward self across the left flat hand.

Memory aid: Suggests *half* of a finger or *half* of a hand.

Example: Please give me my *half*.

or:

HALLELUJAH

Clap the hands; then hold up one or both closed hands with the thumb tips and index fingertips touching. Make small circular movements.

Memory aid: The initial action expresses appreciation, which is then followed by an action symbolizing the waving of small flags.

Example: Hallelujah means "praise the Lord."

1.

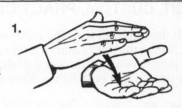

2.

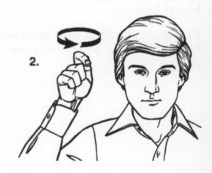

HAMBURGER

Cup the right hand on top of the left cupped hand; then reverse.

Memory aid: Suggests the shaping of *hamburger* patties.

Example: I prefer my *hamburgers* without mustard.

1.

2.

HANDS

Place the downturned right hand over the back of the downturned left hand. Move the right hand toward self, and repeat the action with the left hand over the right.

Memory aid: Each *hand* is referred to individually without reference to the arm.

Example: He washed his *hands* in the sink.

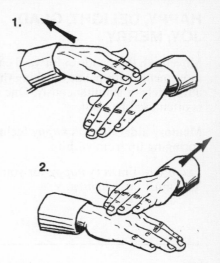

HANG UP, HANGER, SUSPEND

With palm facing forward, move the right *X* hand up and forward a short distance. *Alternative* (not illustrated): Hang the right *X* finger on the left index finger, which is pointing to the right.

Memory aid: Both signs suggest the use of a *hanger* or hook.

Example: Please *hang up* your clothes immediately.

HAPPEN, EVENT, OCCUR

Point both index fingers up with palms facing. Pivot both hands forward from the wrists so that the palms face forward.

Memory aid: Two pointing hands suggest the importance of noticing something.

Example: What *happened* to Nancy's car?

HAPPY, DELIGHT, GLAD, JOY, MERRY

Move both flat hands in forward circular movements with palms touching the chest alternately or simultaneously. One hand is often used by itself.

Memory aid: Suggests *happy* feelings springing up from within.

Examples: I'm very *happy* for you. You must be *delighted*.

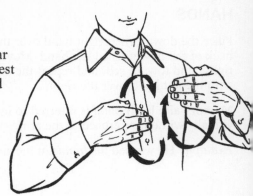

HARD, SOLID

Strike the back of the left closed hand with the middle finger of the right curved *V* hand.

Memory aid: Suggests coming against a firm surface.

Example: The ground was frozen *hard*.

HARD-OF-HEARING

Point the right *H* hand forward and move it in a short arc to the right.

Memory aid: The use of two *H* positions suggests the phrase.

Example: My uncle is *hard-of-hearing*.

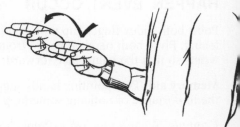

HARP

Place both curved open hands to the front with palms facing. Move the hands backward with slight circular movements while bending and unbending the fingers. Both hands may also move toward the body at the same time.

Memory aid: The movement of playing the *harp*.

Example: Lynn plays the *harp* beautifully.

HAT

Pat the top of the head with the right flat hand.

Memory aid: The location of a *hat*.

Example: Do you wear a *hat*?

HATE, ABHOR, DESPISE, DETEST, LOATHE

Hold both open hands in front of the chest with palms facing down, and flick both middle fingers outward simultaneously.

Memory aid: Symbolizes the desire to get rid of something.

Examples: I *hate* mathematics. Corine *loathes* insects of all kinds.

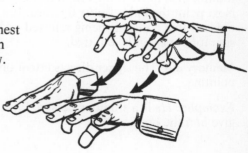

HAVE, HAD, HAS, OWN, POSSESS

Place the fingertips of both bent hands on the chest.

Memory aid: Symbolizes pointing out personal *ownership*.

Examples: Kevin *has* measles. We *possess* two cars.

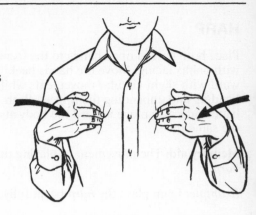

HAWAII

Make a counterclockwise circle with the right *H* hand in front of the face with the palm facing self.

Memory aid: The initial suggests the word, which requires context and simultaneous lipreading for full comprehension.

Example: The islands of *Hawaii* are beautiful.

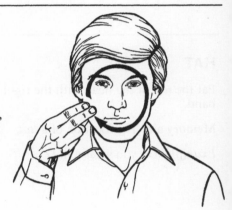

HE, HIM

Move right hand to forehead as though gripping the peak of a hat between fingers and thumb; then move it forward a few inches. Next point the index finger forward. If it is obvious that a male is being referred to, the sign for *male* can be omitted.

Memory aid: The signer directs attention by pointing.

Examples: *He* is a studious person. Please give *him* the book.

1.

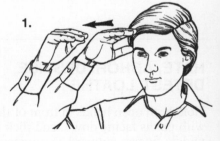

2.

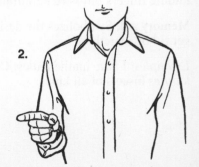

HEAD

Place the fingertips of the right bent hand against the right temple and move the right hand downward in an arc until the fingertips touch the jaw.

Memory aid: The fingers feel the side of the *head*.

Example: My *head* aches.

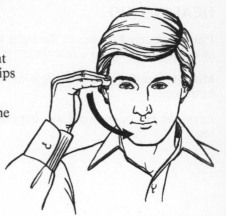

HEALTHY, ROBUST, WELL, WHOLESOME

Place the fingertips and thumbs of both curved open hands on the chest, then move them forward while forming S hands. *Note:* Compare *strong*.

Memory aid: Suggests that the body has strength.

Examples: I'm thankful for a *healthy* family. I feel *well* now.

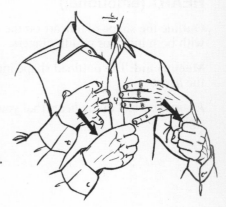

HEARING (person)

Place the right index finger in front of the mouth and make a few small forward circular movements. *Note:* Compare *say*.

Memory aid: The sign is similar to the one for *say* and indicates that a *hearing* person can learn to speak easily.

Example: Is your friend a *hearing person* or deaf?

HEARING AID

Place the curved fingers of the right *V* hand at the right ear. Twist a few times.

Memory aid: Suggests placing a *hearing aid* in the ear.

Example: His *hearing aid* was impossible to see.

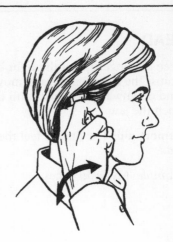

HEART (emotional)

Outline the shape of a heart on the chest with both index or middle fingers.

Memory aid: The outlined shape indicates the *heart.*

Example: I feel in my *heart* that you are right.

HEART (physical)

Place the right middle finger over the heart with the other fingers extended.

Memory aid: The right hand feels for a heartbeat.

Example: He ran until his *heart* was beating rapidly.

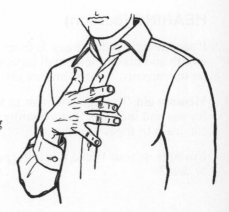

HEART ATTACK

Place the right middle finger over the heart with the other fingers extended. Close the right hand and strike the left palm sharply.

Memory aid: Suggests that the heart has suffered a blow.

Example: The risk of *heart attacks* can sometimes be reduced by proper diet and exercise.

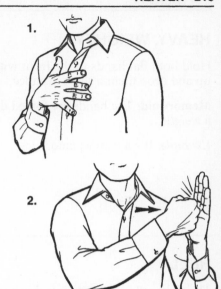

HEARTBEAT

Strike the chest with the right *A* hand several times. The palm faces self.

Memory aid: The action represents the *heartbeat*.

Example: The nurse could not detect Cindy's *heartbeat*.

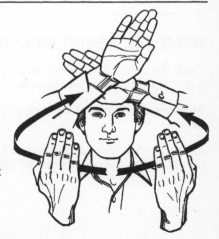

HEAVEN, CELESTIAL

Hold both flat hands out in the front with fingers pointing up and palms facing self. Make a circle with both hands toward self; then pass the right hand under the left palm and up as the hands are crossed at forehead level.

Memory aid: The circle suggests that *heaven* is a perfect place, and the upward movement indicates that *heaven* is above.

Example: Little David was told that his mother had gone to *heaven*.

HEAVY, WEIGHTY

Hold both flat hands to the front with palms up and drop them a short distance.

Memory aid: The hands are forced down by a *weight*.

Example: It's a *heavy* piano.

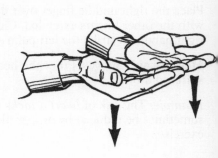

HELL

The right index finger points down, then with palms facing the body, move both slightly curved open hands up and down alternately in front of the body while wiggling the fingers.

Memory aid: Symbolizes leaping flames.

Example: Jesus Christ had more to say about *hell* than heaven.

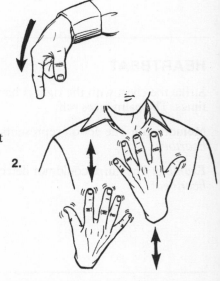

HELP, AID, ASSIST, BOOST

Place the closed right hand on the flat left palm and lift both hands together.

Memory aid: Suggests the giving of a *helping* hand.

Examples: His *aid* was appreciated. Their donation was a real *boost* to the fund.

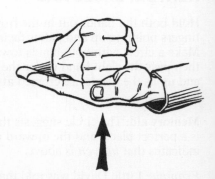

HERE

Hold both flat hands to the front with palms facing up. Make forward semicircles in opposite directions.

Memory aid: A natural gesture.

Example: I'm glad that Jack is *here.*

HI, HELLO

Move the right *B* hand in a small arc to the right from the forehead.

Memory aid: Similar to a salute.

Example: Don't forget to say "*Hi*" to your aunt.

HIDE

Touch the lips with the right *A* thumb; then move the right *A* hand forward under the left curved hand, which has its palm facing down.

Memory aid: The right hand *hides* under the left.

Example: The deer remained *hidden* from view.

HIGH, ADVANCED, PROMOTION

Point the fingertips of both bent hands toward each other and raise both hands simultaneously. *Alternative* (not illustrated): Sometimes the right *H* hand is raised upward.

Memory aid: Suggests going up to a *higher* level.

Example: Paul has a *high* position in his company.

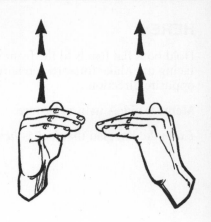

HIRE, EMPLOY, INVITE

Swing the right *H* or flat hand in toward the right side with palm facing up.

Memory aid: Suggests the idea of pulling someone in to oneself and supporting the person.

Example: I got *hired* today.

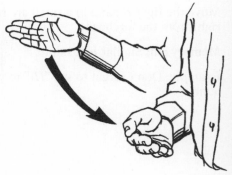

HIS, HER, THEIR, YOUR, YOURS (singular)

Push the right flat hand forward with palm facing out toward the person or persons being referred to. The signs for *male* and *female* can precede *his* and *her* if it is not obvious from the context.

Memory aid: Suggests the idea of something separate or apart from the signer.

Examples: His desk is cluttered. Have you visited *their* home?

HISTORY

Shake the right *H* hand up and down a short distance.

Memory aid: The initial indicates the word, and the action can suggest the up-and-down experiences of *history*.

Example: My favorite subject is *history*.

HIT

Strike the knuckles of the right closed hand against the left upright index finger.

Memory aid: Symbolizes aggressive contact.

Example: Don't *hit* your brother Allen with that toy.

HOCKEY

Brush the knuckles of the right *X* finger across the left flat palm a few times.

Memory aid: Suggests the shape and action of a *hockey* stick.

Example: Ice *hockey* is a very fast sport.

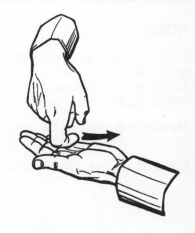

HOLD

Place both *S* hands in front of the body, palms in, right hand over left hand, and move them a short distance toward the body.

Memory aid: Suggests *holding* an object and pulling it to oneself.

Example: Please *hold* this package while I unlock the door.

HOLY, DIVINE, HALLOWED, RIGHTEOUS, SANCTIFIED

Make a right *H* hand; then move the right flat palm across the left flat palm from heel to fingertips. *Note:* Initialize each word individually. Some signers maintain the initialized hand shapes instead of the right flat hand when moving across the left hand.

Memory aid: The initials indicate the words, and the movement is the same as that for *clean.*

Example: He felt a *holy* and *divine* presence.

HOME

Place the fingertips of the right *and* hand first at the mouth, then at the right cheek. Sometimes the position at the cheek is made with a slightly curved hand.

Memory aid: Suggests the place where one eats and sleeps.

Example: I'm going *home* tomorrow.

HONEST

Move the middle finger of the right *H* hand along the left upturned flat hand from palm to fingertips.

Memory aid: The initial *H* makes a straight and *honest* line.

Example: Please be *honest* with me.

HONOR, HONORARY

With the palm facing left, move the right *H* hand in a backward arc toward the face. The head is often bowed simultaneously. *Alternative:* Start with the *H* hand at the forehead and swing in a downward and forward arc.

Memory aid: The initial *H* and the bowed head symbolize the meaning.

Example: He did the *honorable* thing.

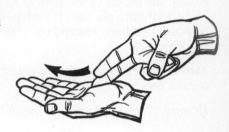

HOPE, ANTICIPATE, EXPECT

Touch the forehead with the right index finger; then bring both flat hands before the chest or head with palms facing. Bend and unbend them simultaneously a few times.

Memory aid: Suggests that the mind *anticipates* something while the hands nod in agreement.

Examples: I *hope* you are right. Geoffrey is fully *expecting* success.

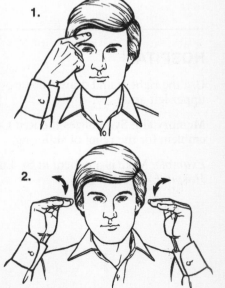

1.

2.

HORSE

Extend the thumb of the right *U* hand and place it on the right temple with palm facing forward. Bend and unbend the *U* fingers a few times.

Memory aid: Suggests the movement of a *horse's* ears.

Example: Melanie wants a *horse* of her own.

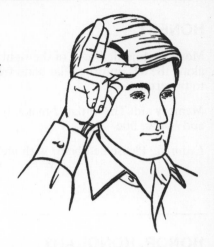

HORSEBACK RIDING

Point the fingers of the left *B* hand to the front with palm facing right. Straddle the inverted right *V* fingers over the left hand. Move the hands with a forward-up-down movement.

Memory aid: The right hand rides the left hand.

Example: I began *horseback riding* lessons one year ago.

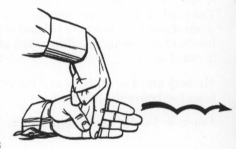

HOSPITAL

Use the right *H* and draw a cross on the upper left arm.

Memory aid: Symbolizes the Red Cross emblem for the relief of suffering.

Example: Mike is a patient at St. Luke's *Hospital.*

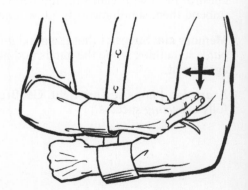

HOT, HEAT

Place the fingers and thumb of the right *C* hand at the sides of the mouth, then quickly pivot the hand forward to the right.

Memory aid: Suggests removing *hot* food from the mouth.

Example: It's too *hot* to work.

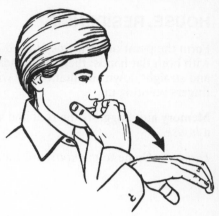

HOTEL

Rest the little-finger edge of the right *H* hand on the left vertical index finger while moving the *H* fingers back and forth.

Memory aid: The initialized right hand indicates the word, and the movement can suggest a *hotel* sign revolving on a pole.

Example: Which *hotel* did Brenda recommend?

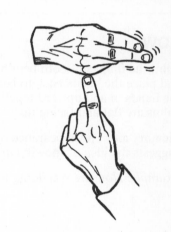

HOUR

Point the fingers of the left flat hand either up or forward with palm facing right. Move the index finger of the right *D* hand in a complete circle by rotating the wrist. Keep the right index finger in constant contact with the left hand.

Memory aid: Follows the movement of a minute hand on a clock.

Example: I will be gone for one *hour*.

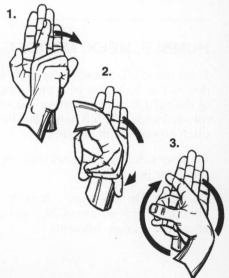

HOUSE, RESIDENCE

Form the point of a triangle at head level with both flat hands; then move them apart and straight down simultaneously with the fingers pointing up.

Memory aid: Suggests the roof and walls of a *house*.

Example: Come to my *house* for lunch.

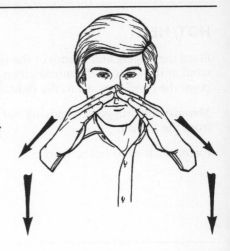

HOW

Point the fingers of both bent hands down and place the hands back to back. Revolve the hands in and upward together until the palms are flat and facing up.

Memory aid: The appearance of the palms suggests the idea of showing *how*.

Example: How are you doing today?

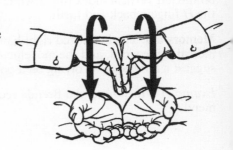

HUMBLE, MEEK, MODEST

Point the left flat hand to the right with palm down. Touch the lips with the index finger of the right *B* hand and move it down and forward under the left hand. The head is often bowed simultaneously.

Memory aid: Suggests a willingness to take the lower position.

Examples: Dr. Johns was a *humble* man, although highly educated. She was *modest* about her accomplishments.

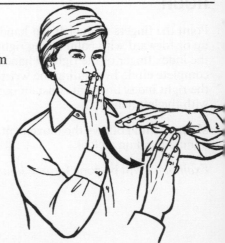

HUNGRY, APPETITE, CRAVE, FAMINE, HUNGER, STARVE

Move the thumb and fingers of the right *C* hand down the center of the chest from just below the throat. *Note:* Compare *wish.*

Memory aid: Suggests the direction that food travels to the stomach.

Examples: I'm *hungry.* He has an enormous *appetite.*

HUNT, GUN, RIFLE, SHOOT

Hold the left *A* hand out to the front at shoulder level, with the palm facing up and the thumb slightly extended. Place the right hand just below the chin with the palm facing in. Jerk both hands backward slightly as the right index finger is crooked.

Memory aid: Symbolizes the use of a *rifle.*

Example: When is deer-*hunting* season?

HURRY, HUSTLE, RUSH

Move one or both *H* hands quickly forward in short arcs. *Note:* If two hands are used, they can be quickly raised up and down alternately.

Memory aid: Suggests someone walking rapidly.

Examples: What's your *hurry?* It's a *rush* job.

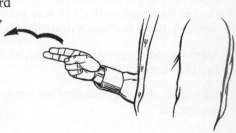

HURT (emotion)

Place the right middle finger on the heart with other fingers extended; then twist the hand quickly forward and outward from the wrist.

Memory aid: Suggests that the feelings of the heart have been wrenched from the chest.

Example: I felt *hurt* by her words.

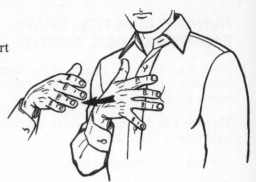

HUSBAND

Move the right hand to the forehead as though gripping the peak of a hat between the fingers and thumb; then move it forward a few inches. Clasp the hands with the right hand above the left. The latter position is the sign for *marriage.*

Memory aid: Indicates a married male.

Example: She has a handsome *husband.*

1.

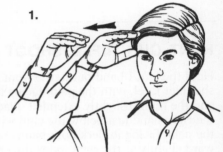

2.

HYPOCRITE, FAKE, IMPOSTER

Place the right flat hand over the back of the left flat hand, with all fingers pointing forward. Bend the hands downward as one.

Memory aid: Suggests a covering, as in the use of a mask.

Example: That organization has plenty of *hypocrites.*

1.

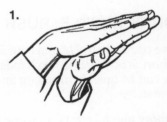

2.

I

Position the right *I* hand with palm facing left and thumb touching the chest.

Memory aid: The initial *I* in close proximity to the body suggests the individual.

Example: Do you know what *I* want?

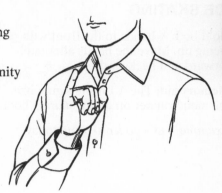

ICE, FREEZE, RIGID

Hold both open hands to the front with palms facing down. Curve the fingers and make them *rigid* while simultaneously moving the hands down a short distance.

Memory aid: The fingers become stiff and contract with cold.

Example: The wind is *icy* cold.

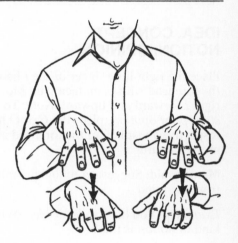

ICE CREAM, LOLLIPOP

Pull the right *S* hand toward the mouth with a downward twist a few times. The tongue may also be shown.

Memory aid: The action of licking an *ice cream* cone.

Example: Paul dropped his *ice cream* on the ground.

ICE SKATING

Hold both *X* hands to the front with palms facing up. Move the hands alternately forward and backward.

Memory aid: The *X* fingers symbolize the metal runner on an *ice-skating* boot.

Example: Let's go *ice skating* today.

IDEA, CONCEPT, NOTION, OPINION

Place the right little finger of the *I* hand on the forehead with palm facing in. Move the right *I* forward and upward. *Note:* To sign *concept* or *opinion,* place the *C* or *O* hand respectively just before the forehead and move forward.

Memory aid: Suggests a thought coming from the mind.

Examples: You have a clever *idea.* What kind of *notion* is that?

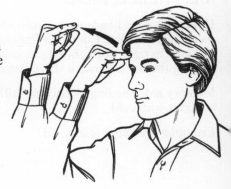

IF

Point the two *F* hands forward and move them up and down alternately with palms facing each other.

Memory aid: The movement suggests scales that may tip one way or the other.

Example: If you go, I will also.

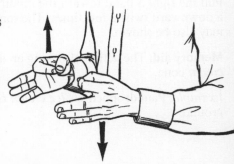

IGNORANT

Place the back of the right *V* hand on the forehead. It can tap the forehead a few times if emphasis is required.

Memory aid: The *V* hand could suggest a mind void of knowledge.

Example: Don't be *ignorant* of Jim's intention.

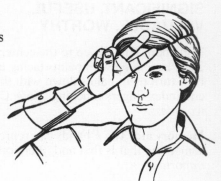

I LOVE YOU

Hold the right hand up with palm facing forward. The thumb, index, and little fingers are extended.

Memory aid: The letters *I*, *L*, and *Y* are combined.

Example: Your script says, *"I love you."*

IMAGINATION, FANTASY, FICTION, THEORY

Hold right *I* hand near forehead with palm facing in. Move the *I* hand forward and upward in a few rolling circles. *Note:* To sign *fiction* or *fantasy,* use an *F* hand and to sign *theory,* use a *T* hand.

Memory aid: Suggests futuristic thoughts coming from the mind.

Example: What a vivid *imagination* you have.

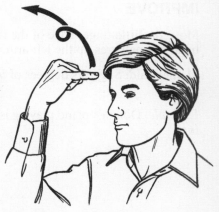

IMPORTANT, MERIT, PRECIOUS, SIGNIFICANT, USEFUL, VALUABLE, WORTHY

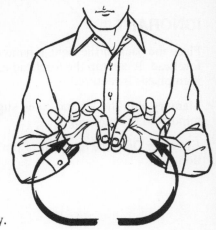

Bring both *F* hands up to the center of the chest beginning with palms facing up, and then turn them palms down with the thumbs and index fingers touching. *Note:* Compare *worthless.*

Memory aid: The *F* hands can represent something that is first and, therefore, *important.*

Example: She has an *important* responsibility.

IMPRESS, EMPHASIZE, STRESS

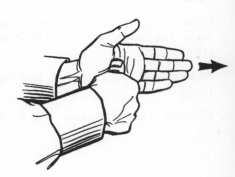

Press the right thumb into the palm of the left flat hand. Sometimes the right hand is rotated forward slightly while the thumb is being pressed into the left palm, and sometimes both hands are moved forward slightly.

Memory aid: An *impression* is made in the left palm.

Example: His writing style *impresses* me.

IMPROVE

Move the little-finger edge of the right flat hand in small arcs up the left arm.

Memory aid: Suggests degrees of *improvement.*

Example: Donna's piano playing is *improving.*

IN

Move the closed fingers of the right *and* hand into the left *C* hand.

Memory aid: The right hand is going *in* through an opening.

Example: Paula hung her dress *in* the closet.

INCLUDE, INVOLVE

Hold the left *C* hand to the front with palm facing right. Make a sweeping circular movement from right to left (or left to right) with the right open hand; then form the *and* position and place it in the left *C* hand.

Memory aid: The movement suggests a gathering together into one.

Example: Let's *include* Linda in this activity.

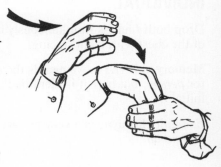

INCREASE, ADD, GAIN WEIGHT, LOSE WEIGHT

Move the right *H* fingers from a palm-up position to a palm-down position and place them on the left palm-down *H* fingers. Repeat a few times. To sign *lose weight,* reverse the action.

Memory aid: Weight is either added to or removed from the left *H* fingers.

Examples: I expect an *increase* in attendance this year. The teacher *added* more rules this semester. I can tell that you have *lost weight.*

INDIA, INDIAN

With palm facing left, place the tip of the
A thumb on the center of the forehead and
twist slightly. Add the sign for *person
(personalizing word ending)* when signing
Indian with reference to a person.

Memory aid: Touching the forehead
reminds one of the red dot some *Indian*
women wear.

Example: Allen has been to *India* three
times.

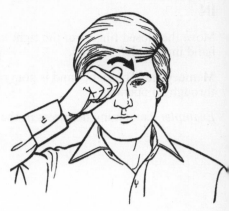

INDIVIDUAL

Drop both *I* hands simultaneously in front
of the chest with palms facing.

Memory aid: The movement is the same as
for *person,* but here it is identified by the
initial *I.*

Example: Dwayne is a very private
individual.

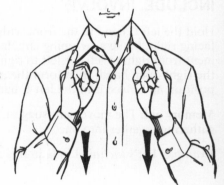

INFLUENCE

Hold the left flat or curved hand with palm
down and fingers facing right. Place the fingers of the right *and* hand on the back of the
left hand and move the right hand forward
and to the right while opening the fingers.

Memory aid: Suggests an area of *influence.*

Example: Tom had little *influence,* I'm
afraid.

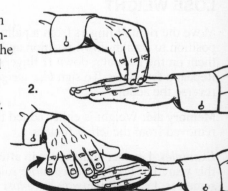

INFORM, INFORMATION, NOTIFY

Place the fingers of both *and* hands on each side of the forehead, then move them in a downward forward arc to an open hand position with palms facing up.

Memory aid: Suggests offering *information* from the mind.

Example: Please keep me *informed* of the facts.

INJECTION, SHOT, SYRINGE, VACCINATION

Place the curved thumb, index, and middle fingers of the right hand at the upper left arm and move the thumb toward the curved fingers. *Vaccination* can also be signed by thrusting the bunched fingertips of the right thumb, index, and middle fingers into the upper left arm with several short movements.

Memory aid: Symbolizes the use of a hypodermic *syringe* or needle.

Example: Polio *shots* are very successful.

IN-LAW

Place the index and thumb side of the right *L* hand on the front of the palm-forward left hand. Begin near the top; then move the right hand downward in a small arc to the base of the left hand. Some prefer to sign *in* first.

Memory aid: This is the sign for *law.*

Example: It is a good thing when *in-laws* get along well with each other.

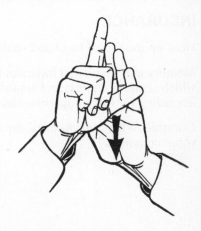

INNOCENT

Place the fingers of both *H* hands at the mouth and move both hands out and down until the palms face up. *Alternative:* Sign *not* and *blame.*

Memory aid: Suggests that the lips have spoken honestly and *innocently.*

Example: Everyone thinks he is *innocent.*

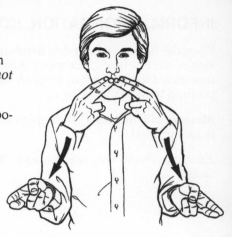

INSULT

Move the right index finger forward and up with a slight twist.

Memory aid: The hand symbolizes a sword that is used to injure an opponent.

Example: I don't want to *insult* your intelligence.

INSURANCE

Hold up the right *I* hand and shake it.

Memory aid: The initial indicates the word, which requires context and simultaneous lipreading for full comprehension.

Example: Which *insurance* company would you recommend?

INTEREST

Place the thumb and index finger of each hand on the chest, with one hand above the other. Bring the index fingers and thumbs together as the hands are moved forward. Keep the other fingers extended.

Memory aid: Suggests that a person's inner feelings are being drawn toward something.

Example: I found our conversation *interesting.*

INTERNATIONAL

Point the little finger of the left *I* hand forward with the palm facing down. With the palm facing down, rotate the right *I* hand forward around the left *I* hand.

Memory aid: The initial indicates the word, and the action suggests the idea of something that goes around the world.

Example: Steve travels *internationally* for his company.

INTERPRET, REVERSE INTERPRET, TRANSLATE

Hold the *F* hands with palms facing and the left palm facing forward; then rotate positions so that the right palm faces forward. To sign *reverse interpret* use the *R* hands with the reverse action of *interpret,* and follow with the regular sign for *interpret.* To sign *translate* use *T* hands and make the same movement as for *interpret.*

Memory aid: The changing positions of the hands suggest the idea of changing from one language to another.

Example: Will you *interpret* for me?

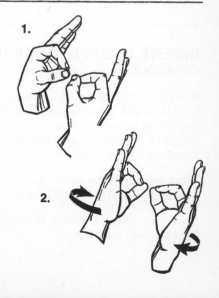

INTO, ENTER

Push the right fingers down through the left C hand.

Memory aid: Symbolizes going *into* a hole.

Example: Why did she *enter* the kitchen?

INTRODUCE

Move both flat hands in from the sides with palms up until the fingertips almost touch.

Memory aid: Suggests bringing two people together.

Example: I'll *introduce* you to my mother.

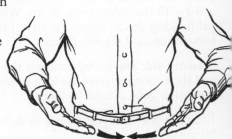

INVENT, CREATE, MAKE UP, ORIGINATE

With the palm facing left, touch the forehead with the right index finger of the 4 hand. Beginning with the fingertips, push the length of the index finger upward on the forehead with a slight forward curve.

Memory aid: The 4 hand suggests lots of new ideas coming from the mind.

Examples: Did you *invent* this gadget? You are very *creative*.

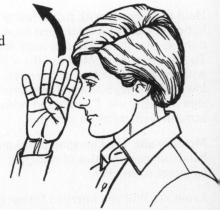

IRONING

Hold the flat left hand in front, palm up, and slide the right *A* hand, palm down, back and forth over the left palm.

Memory aid: Resembles the act of *ironing.*

Example: Jennifer has two hours of *ironing* to do today.

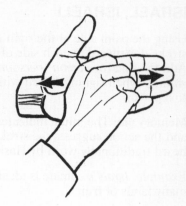

IS

Move the right *I* hand forward from the mouth.

Memory aid: The initial suggests the word, and the action indicates a breathing person and thus a symbolic connection with the verb *to be.*

Example: *Is* my answer correct?

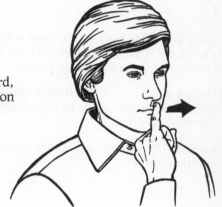

ISLAND

With the palms facing in, touch the *I* fingers and make a circle toward the body until the *I* fingers touch again.

Memory aid: The initial indicates the word, and the movement suggests the shape of an *island.*

Example: This *island* is popular during the summer.

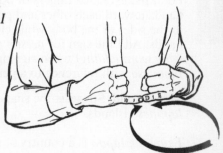

ISRAEL, ISRAELI

Using the palm side of the right *I* finger, stroke downward at each side of the chin. Add the sign for *person (personalizing word ending)* when signing *Israeli* with reference to a person.

Memory aid: The initial indicates the word, and the action suggests the stroking of the beard traditionally worn by Hasidic Jews.

Example: Israel's climate is ideal for growing many kinds of fruit.

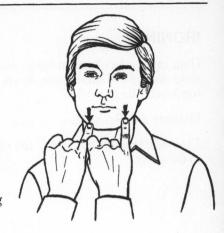

IT

Hold the flat left hand to the front with the palm facing right; then move the little finger of the right *I* hand into the left palm.

Memory aid: The initialized right hand indicates the word and seems to be pointing out something specific.

Example: I've lost my wallet, but *it* must be here somewhere.

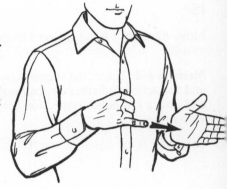

JAPAN, JAPANESE

Point the extended fingers of both *G* hands toward each other and pull them to the sides of the body while closing *G* hands. Add the sign for *person (personalizing word ending)* when signing *Japanese* with reference to a person.

Memory aid: Suggests the shape of the *Japanese* islands.

Example: Japan is a country of many islands.

JEALOUS

Put the right little fingertip at the corner of the mouth and give it a twist.

Memory aid: The little finger suggests the *J*, which causes the mouth to open and drool with *jealousy*.

Example: They both suffer from *jealousy*.

JELLY, JAM

Rub the fingertip of the right *J* across the left palm once or twice.

Memory aid: Suggests spreading *jelly* on bread.

Example: I'd like strawberry *jelly*, please.

JERUSALEM

Fingerspell the word, or sign *J* followed by the sign for *city*. *City* is signed by making the point of a triangle with both flat hands in front of the chest. This is repeated a few times while moving the hands to the right.

Memory aid: The initial followed by the sign for *city* indicates the meaning. The context will often give extra aid.

Example: I found *Jerusalem* fascinating.

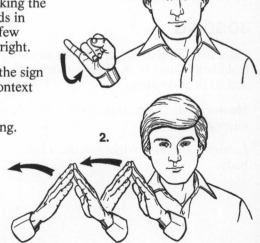

JESUS

Hold both open and slightly curved hands to the front with palms facing. Touch the left palm with the right middle finger; then touch the right palm with the left middle finger.

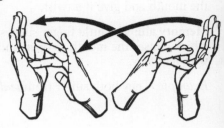

Memory aid: Indicates the nail scars caused by crucifixion.

Example: Jesus died about two thousand years ago.

JEWISH

Place the right open fingers and thumb on the chin with the palm facing self. Draw the hand down below the chin and form an *and* hand.

Memory aid: Symbolizes the beards worn by Hasidic *Jews.*

Example: I love *Jewish* food.

JOGGING

Place both partially open *A* hands to the front with palms facing. Move them back and forth alternately.

Memory aid: The motion of the arms when *jogging.*

Example: Jogging invigorates the whole body.

JOIN, ATTACH, UNITE

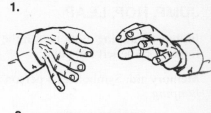

Interlock the index fingers and thumbs of both hands with all other fingers extended.

Memory aid: Suggests two links of a chain.

Examples: Please *join* us for lunch. I am *attached* to a fine company.

JUDGE, COURT, JUDGMENT, JUSTICE, TRIAL

Touch the forehead with the right index finger and form two *F* hands with palms facing. Move the hands up and down alternately. *Note:* Compare *if.*

Memory aid: Suggests that the mind is weighing the evidence.

Example: George goes to *court* next Wednesday.

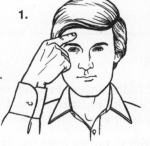

JUICE

Hold the *J* hand at shoulder level, palm forward, and twist at the wrist, two times, so the palm faces self.

Memory aid: The initialized sign suggests the meaning.

Example: Did you have a glass of orange *juice* today?

JUMP, HOP, LEAP

Imitate a jumping motion with the right *V* fingers on the left flat palm.

Memory aid: Symbolizes a person's legs *jumping.*

Example: Dick literally *jumped* for joy.

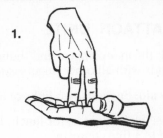

1.

2.

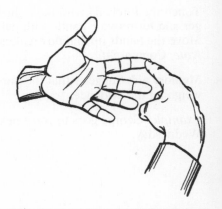

JUNIOR

Touch the index finger of the left open hand with the right index finger. *Note:* Compare *freshman, sophomore,* and *senior.*

Memory aid: Counting from the thumb, a *junior* still has two years of study to complete.

Example: Joe likes the thought of being a *junior.*

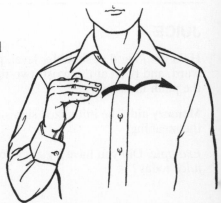

 KANGAROO

Hold the right bent hand to the front with palm facing forward. Move the hand forward with several up and down movements. *Note:* This sign is sometimes done with two hands making identical movements.

Memory aid: Symbolizes the shape and jumping action of a *kangaroo.*

Example: Kangaroos come from Australia.

KEEP

Cross the wrist of the right *V* hand over the wrist of the left *V* hand.

Memory aid: The fingers can symbolize four watchful eyes.

Example: Please *keep* a careful watch on the house.

KEY, LOCK, LOCK UP

Place right crooked index finger into left flat palm and twist right hand. *Alternative* for *lock*, *lock up* (not illustrated): Hold left closed hand to the front with palm down and right closed hand, palm down, above it a short distance. Pivot the right hand around with a short swinging motion until the back of the right wrist rests on the left wrist with right palm up.

Memory aid: The first sign symbolizes the use of a key. The second suggests being locked up by picturing bound hands.

Example: Where is your *key*?

KICK, SOCCER

Sweep the flat index side of the right hand upward to strike the little-finger edge of the flat or closed left hand.

Memory aid: Symbolizes *kicking* a ball.

Example: Let's watch *soccer*.

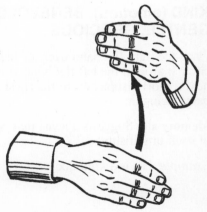

KID

Extend the index and small finger of the right hand. With the palm facing down, put the index finger under the nose. The hand is then pivoted up and down slightly and often moved to the right simultaneously.

Memory aid: Suggests the runny nose of a young child.

Example: Beverly took her *kids* to the pool today.

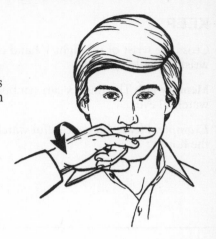

KILL, MURDER, SLAY

Place the slightly curved left hand to the front with palm facing down. Move the right index finger under the left hand while simultaneously giving it a clockwise twist.

Memory aid: Suggests stabbing someone with a knife.

Example: I'm afraid there has been a *murder*.

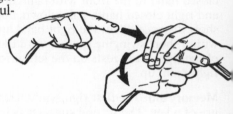

KIND (emotion), BENEVOLENT, GENTLE, GRACIOUS

Place the right flat hand over the heart; then circle it around the left flat hand which is held a short distance from the chest with palm facing in.

Memory aid: Suggests a heart that is giving of itself unselfishly.

Example: His is a *kind* doctor.

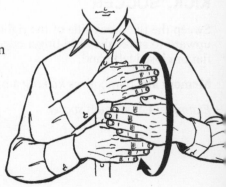

KIND (type), SORT, VARIETY

Point both *K* hands forward and rotate the right *K* forward around the left.

Memory aid: The initials indicate the word, and the circular movement suggests a world full of diversity.

Examples: What *kind* of fish is this? Which *variety* of colors do you prefer?

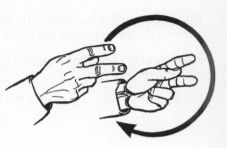

KINGDOM

Move the right *K* hand from the left shoulder to the right waist; then circle the right flat hand over the left flat hand in a counter-clockwise direction.

Memory aid: A combination of the signs for *king* and *over*.

Example: He has created his own little *kingdom*.

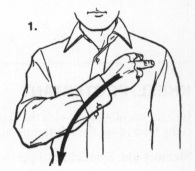

KISS

Place the fingers of the right hand on the lips and then on the cheek.

Memory aid: Suggests two common locations for *kissing*.

Example: They *kissed* when they met.

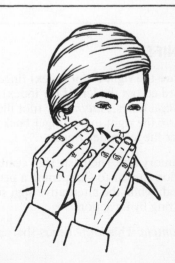

KITCHEN

Place the right *K* hand first palm down, then palm up on the upturned left palm.

Memory aid: The action suggests food being turned over in a pan.

Example: You have a beautiful *kitchen.*

1.

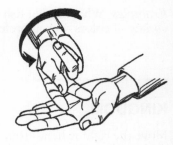

2.

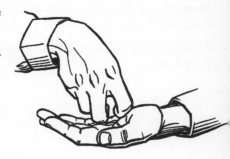

KNEEL, PROTESTANT

Imitate kneeling legs with the fingers of the right *V* hand on the left flat palm.

Memory aid: Symbolizes a person *kneeling.*

Example: June *knelt* down to look.

KNIFE

Move the right *H* (or index) fingers downward across the left *H* (or index) fingers several times. *Alternative* (not illustrated): Move the right index finger back and forth over the left index finger.

Memory aid: The basic sign symbolizes an action similar to sharpening a pencil by hand, while the alternative sign suggests cutting by its action.

Example: This *knife* needs sharpening.

KNOW, INTELLIGENCE, KNOWLEDGE, RECOGNIZE

Tap the fingers of the right slightly curved hand on the forehead a few times. *Note:* Compare *don't know*.

Memory aid: The repository of *knowledge* is considered to be the brain.

Examples: Do you *know* her? Yes, I *recognize* her. Jane does not possess sufficient *knowledge*.

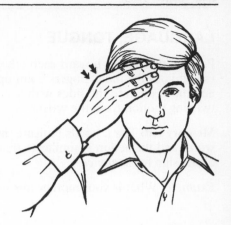

LADY

Trace the right jawbone from ear to chin with the palm side of the right *A* thumb. Then place the right thumb of the right open hand on the chest with palm facing left; then tilt the hand in a slight up-forward-down movement.

Memory aid: Indicates a *lady's* dress or blouse with frilly ruffles.

Example: She must learn to behave like a *lady*.

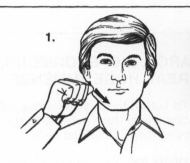

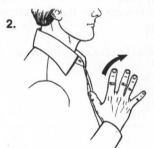

LAND, FIELD

Hold both curved hands to the front with palms facing up and rub the fingertips with the thumbs. Then make circles in opposite directions with both downturned flat hands.

Memory aid: Symbolizes the feeling and leveling of soil.

Example: The soil on the *land* is rich.

LANGUAGE, TONGUE

Point both *L* hands toward each other (sometimes the index fingers point up), and move them to the sides with a twisting motion from the wrists.

Memory aid: The *L* hands indicate the word, and the action is similar to that of the sign for *sentence*.

Example: What is your mother *tongue*?

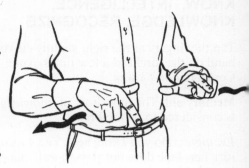

LARGE, BIG, ENORMOUS, GREAT, HUGE, IMMENSE

Hold both *L* hands to the front with palms facing. Move them outward to the sides beyond the width of the body.

Memory aid: The initial and the distance placed between the hands indicate the meaning.

Example: He was carrying an *enormous* box.

LAST, END, FINAL, LASTLY

Hold the left hand to the front with palm facing self and little finger extended. Strike the left little finger with the right index finger as the right hand moves down. Sometimes this sign is made with both little fingers.

Memory aid: The little finger is considered the *last* finger.

Examples: This is my *last* chance. *Lastly,* I thank all of you sincerely.

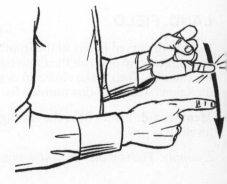

LAST WEEK

Move the right index-finger hand across the left flat palm in a forward movement. Continue the right hand in an upward-backward direction over the right shoulder.

Memory aid: The sign for *week* and pointing to the past.

Example: This is the *last week* for the sale.

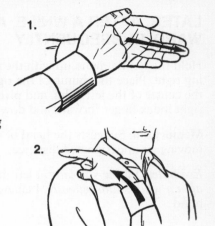

LAST YEAR

Move the right *S* hand in a complete forward circle around the left *S* hand and come to rest with the right *S* hand on top of the left. Then point the right index finger backward over the right shoulder.

Memory aid: The sign for *year* and pointing to the past.

Example: Brian did not take a vacation *last year*.

LATE, BEHIND, NOT DONE, NOT YET, TARDY, TIME

Let the right hand hang loosely in the area between the armpit and waist. Move the hand back and forth from the wrist several times.

Memory aid: Suggests that the action is hanging back.

Examples: You are *late*. You have been *tardy* five times. His stamp collection is *not yet* complete.

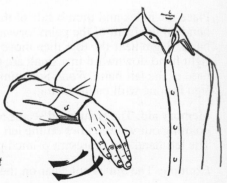

LATER, AFTER A WHILE, AFTER-WARD, SUBSEQUENTLY

Hold the left flat hand up with the palm facing right. Place the thumb of the right *L* in the center of the left palm, and pivot the right index finger forward and down.

Memory aid: Suggests the hand of a clock moving an undesignated distance.

Examples: I'll see you *later*. I left the office *after a while*. *Subsequently,* I changed my mind.

LAUGH, CHUCKLE, GIGGLE

Starting near the corners of the mouth, move both index fingers upward over the cheeks a few times. Assume an appropriate facial expression. *Note:* Compare *smile*.

Memory aid: Suggests the upturned mouth.

Examples: We've never *laughed* so much. Sue *chuckled* at the thought.

LAW

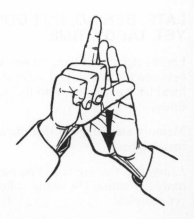

Place the index and thumb side of the right *L* hand on the front of the palm-forward left hand. Begin near the top; then move the right hand downward in a small arc to the base of the left hand. *Note:* Sometimes the sign is done with palms facing.

Memory aid: The right hand seems to be pointing out written *laws* on the left hand. The left hand can represent printed page.

Example: The *law* is not clear on the subject.

LAWYER, ATTORNEY

Place the index and thumb side of the right *L* hand on the front of the palm-forward left hand. Begin near the top; then move the right hand downward in a small arc to the base of the left hand. *Note:* Sometimes the sign is done with palms facing. Add the sign for *person (personalizing word ending).*

Memory aid: The right hand seems to be pointing out written *laws* on a printed page.

Example: Scott's *lawyer* won the case.

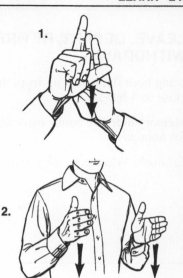

1.

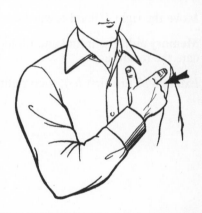

2.

LAZY, SLOTHFUL

Tap the palm of the right *L* hand at the left shoulder several times.

Memory aid: Suggests that a person needs to shoulder his or her load of the work.

Example: He's the *laziest* individual I know.

LEARN

Place the fingers of the right open hand on the upturned left palm. Close the right fingers as the hand is moved to the forehead. The fingertips are then placed on the forehead.

Memory aid: The right hand seems to be taking information from the left hand and putting it into the mind. The left hand can represent a book.

Example: How can you *learn* with all this noise?

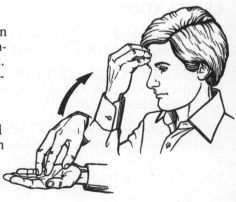

LEAVE, DEPART, RETIRE, WITHDRAW

Bring both flat hands up from the right and close to *A* hands.

Memory aid: The hands *leave* one position for another.

Example: What time are you *leaving*?

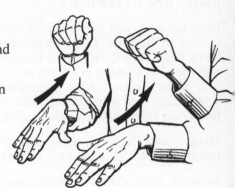

LEFT (direction)

Move the right *L* hand toward the left.

Memory aid: The initial and direction indicate the meaning.

Example: Turn first *left*, then right.

LEGISLATION

Place the thumb of the right *L* hand first on the left shoulder and then on the right.

Memory aid: Can suggest the idea that when *legislation* is passed, the weight of government's shoulders is behind it.

Example: The senator proposed new *legislation* that was extremely controversial.

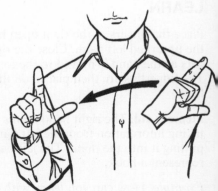

LEMON

Hold the thumb of the right *L* hand at the lips. Assume an expression indicating sourness.

Memory aid: The initial *L* and the facial expression indicate the meaning.

Example: He grimaced as he tasted the *lemon*.

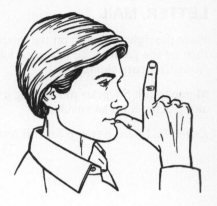

LEND, LOAN

Cross the *V* hands (the sign for *keep*) at the wrists and move them away from the body. *Note:* Compare *borrow*.

Memory aid: The outward action suggests that something is being offered to another.

Example: I will gladly *lend* you what you need.

LESSON, EXERCISE (mental)

Place the little-finger edge of the right flat hand across the fingers of the left flat hand. Move the right hand in a small arc so that it rests at the base of the left hand.

Memory aid: Suggests a section of a page to be studied.

Example: The correspondence course has ten *lessons*.

LETTER, MAIL

Place the right *A* thumb on the mouth and
then on the palm of the upturned left hand.
Note: Compare *stamp*.

Memory aid: Suggests moistening a stamp
and placing it on an envelope.

Example: I need a stamp for this *letter*.

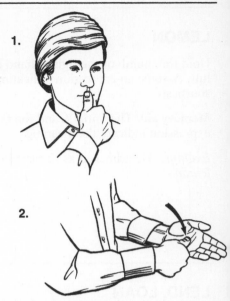

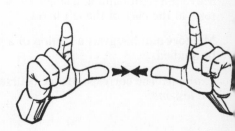

LIBRARY

Make a small clockwise circle with the right
L hand.

Memory aid: The initial indicates the word,
which requires context and simultaneous
lipreading for full comprehension.

Example: Jennifer's interest in *libraries*
began at an early age.

LICENSE, CERTIFICATE

Touch the thumb tips of both *L* hands
together a few times with palms facing
forward. The *C* hands may be used for
certificate.

Memory aid: Uses both the initial and the
shape.

Example: Be sure to get your marriage
license before Saturday.

LIE, FALSEHOOD

Point the right index finger to the left and move it horizontally across the lips from right to left.

Memory aid: Symbolizes the idea that spoken truth is diverted from its normally straight course.

Example: Don't *lie* to me.

LIE DOWN, RECLINE

Place the back of the right *V* fingers on the left flat palm.

Memory aid: Symbolizes a person in the *reclining* position.

Examples: Grandfather *lies down* for a nap every afternoon. My sister is *reclining* on the couch.

LIFE, EXISTENCE

Put palm sides of both flat open hands on abdomen and raise them up to the chest while wiggling fingers. *Existence* may be signed with *E* hands. *Note:* Compare *live*. *Alternative* (not illustrated): Perform the same movement with *L* hands.

Memory aid: The first sign suggests that where there is movement there is *life*, and the second suggests the same with the additional indication of initials.

Example: My *life* is exciting.

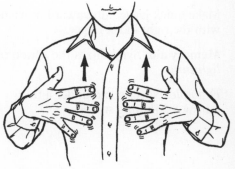

LIGHT, BRIGHT, CLEAR, LUMINOUS, OBVIOUS

Hold both *and* hands at chest level with palms down. Open the hands as they are moved up and to the sides with palms facing forward.

Memory aid: Suggests sunbeams shining over the horizon.

Example: The sky was *bright* with morning sunlight.

LIGHT (weight)

Hold both flat hands to the front with palms up and raise them up slightly a few times.

Memory aid: The hands appear to be bouncing a light object up and down.

Example: Your sister is *light* to carry.

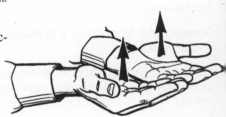

LIGHTNING

Make quick jagged downward movements with the right index finger.

Memory aid: Symbolizes the action of *lightning*.

Example: Never stand under a tree during a *lightning* storm.

LIKE, ADMIRE

Place the right thumb and index finger against the chest, with the other fingers extended. Bring the thumb and index finger together as the hand is moved a short distance forward. *Note:* Compare *please.*

Memory aid: Symbolizes the inner feelings going out to someone or something.

Examples: I *like* pears. I *admire* his artistic ability.

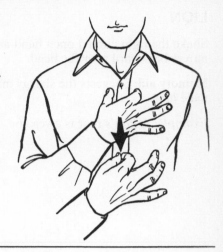

LIMIT, CAPACITY, RESTRICT

Place both bent hands in front with the thumb sides closest to the chest and the right hand a short distance above the left. Move both hands forward a short distance.

Memory aid: The space between the hands can suggest a *limited* area.

Example: We need to know our financial *limit.*

LINE

Trace a line down the center of the left flat hand with the right little finger.

Memory aid: Illustrates a straight *line.*

Example: They're painting *lines* on the parking lot.

LION

Shake the right curved open hand as it moves backward over the head.

Memory aid: Suggests the shaggy mane of a male *lion.*

Example: A *lion's* roar is awesome.

LIPREADING, ORAL, SPEECHREADING

Hold the right curved *V* fingers at the mouth. Move around the mouth in a counterclockwise direction.

Memory aid: The initial indicates the voice, and the movement draws attention to the movement of the lips when using the voice.

Example: How good are you at *lipreading*?

LIPS

Outline the lips with the right index finger.

Memory aid: The *lips* are emphasized.

Example: His *lips* turned blue with cold.

LIQUOR, WHISKEY

Strike the back of the closed left hand with the extended little finger of the right hand a few times while keeping the right index finger extended.

Memory aid: Suggests the size of the small glass used for a shot of *whiskey*.

Example: Joe shouldn't drink so much *whiskey*.

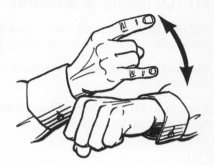

LIST

Place the little-finger edge of the bent right hand on the fingers of the left flat hand. Move the right hand down the left hand in several short arcs.

Memory aid: The right hand seems to be pointing out items on a *list* in the left hand.

Example: Is Sam on your *list*?

LISTEN, HEAR

Place the cupped right hand behind the right ear and turn the head a little to the left. *Alternative* (not illustrated): Point to the right ear with the right index finger.

Memory aid: The first sign is a natural gesture, and the alternative directs attention to the ear.

Example: Can you *hear* the train in the distance?

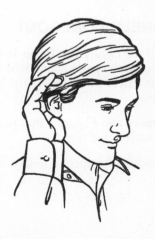

LITTLE (quantity, amount)

Rub the tip of the right thumb and index finger together. *Note:* Compare *small.*

Memory aid: The slight movement indicates the meaning.

Examples: I'll come for a *little* while. I take a *little* sugar in my coffee.

LIVE, ADDRESS, DWELL, RESIDE

Move the palm sides of both *L* (or *A*) hands up from the abdomen to the chest. *Note:* Compare *life.*

Memory aid: The initials indicate the word, and the action suggests that just as life *lives* within the body, so the body *resides* at a particular address.

Example: Where do you *live*?

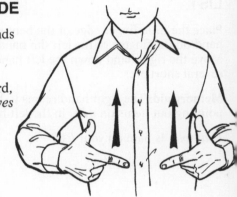

LONELY, LONESOME

Hold the right index finger in front of the lips with the palm facing left. Move the index finger down across the lips a few times.

Memory aid: Suggests that persons by themselves are silent.

Example: She spent a *lonely* summer.

LONG

Extend the left flat hand to the front with palm facing down. Run the right index finger up the left arm, beginning at the fingertips.

Memory aid: Suggests the length of the arm.

Example: He read a *long* poem.

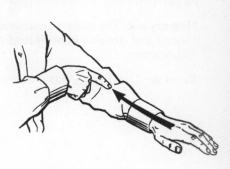

LOOK, GAZE, LOOK AT, LOOK AT ME, LOOK BACK, LOOK DOWN, OBSERVE, WATCH

Point the fingers of the right *V* hand at the eyes and then in the particular direction desired. *Note:* Compare *see*.

Memory aid: The two fingers represent the two eyes.

Example: *Look* carefully while you drive.

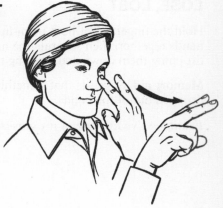

LORD, CHRIST, KING, QUEEN, ROYAL

Move the right *L* hand from the left shoulder to the right waist. Initialize the other words with the same basic movement.

Memory aid: Suggests the sash sometimes worn by *royalty*.

Example: *Christ* was crucified.

LOS ANGELES

Fingerspell *L-A*.

Memory aid: The initials combined with the context and simultaneous lipreading indicate the meaning.

Example: Los Angeles has a warm climate.

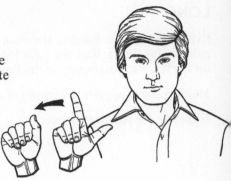

LOSE, LOST

Hold the fingertips of both palm-up *and* hands together; then separate the hands by dropping them down and opening them.

Memory aid: Suggests that something has dropped out of the hands.

Example: I've *lost* one of my gloves.

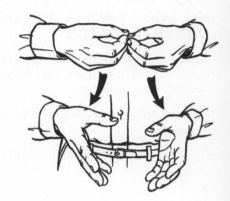

LOUSY, ROTTEN

Place the thumb of the right 3 hand on the nose, then pivot the hand sharply downward. Assume an appropriate facial expression.

Memory aid: Can suggest a person suffering from a head cold with a streaming nose.

Example: This is a *lousy* job.

LOVE

Cross either the closed or flat hands over the heart with palms facing in.

Memory aid: Symbolizes the *love* of the heart.

Example: He *loved* her dearly.

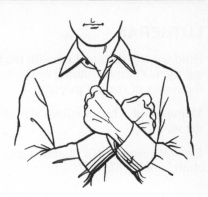

LUCKY

Touch the chin with the right middle finger; then flip the hand around so that the palm faces forward.

Memory aid: Some people consider themselves *lucky* to have a dimple on the chin.

Example: Jean considered herself *lucky* to have won the prize.

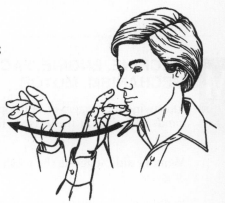

LUNCH

Move the fingers of the right closed *and* hand to the mouth a few times. Place the left flat hand at the outer bend of the right elbow, and raise the right forearm to an upright position with palm facing left. *Note:* This sign is a combination of *eat* and *noon*.

Memory aid: Suggests the meal eaten when the sun is overhead.

Example: She cooked *lunch* for us.

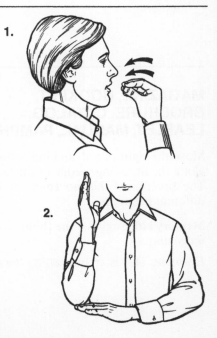

LUTHERAN

Hold the left flat hand up with the palm facing right. Place the thumb of the right *L* in the center of the left palm.

Memory aid: The initialized sign indicates the word.

Example: Robert has attended a *Lutheran* church all his life.

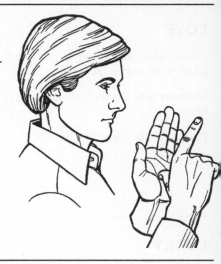

M MACHINE, ENGINE, FACTORY, MECHANISM, MOTOR

Intertwine the fingers of both open hands and pivot at the wrists a few times.

Memory aid: Suggests the meshing of gears.

Examples: You have complicated *machinery* here. This is a powerful *motor*.

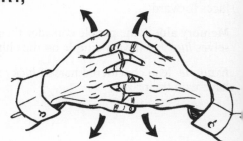

MAGAZINE, BOOKLET, BROCHURE, CATALOG, LEAFLET, MANUAL, PAMPHLET

Move the right thumb and index finger along the little-finger edge of the left hand. The direction of this movement varies in different locations.

Memory aid: Suggests the thinness of a *magazine*.

Example: This is an interesting *booklet*.

MAGIC

Hold both closed hands to the front and open them suddenly with a forward movement. Repeat a few times.

Memory aid: Suggests a magician's hands when performing a trick.

Example: He disappeared like *magic*.

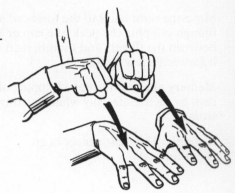

MAJOR, AREA, FIELD, SPECIALTY

Point the fingers of the left hand forward with the palm facing right. Move the little-finger edge of the right flat hand forward along the left index finger.

Memory aid: Suggests the idea of going in a definite direction.

Example: What is your *major*?

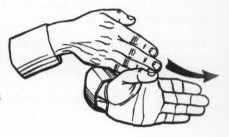

MAKE, FASHION, FIX

Strike the right *S* hand on the top of the left *S* hand and twist the hands slightly inward. Repeat for emphasis as needed.

Memory aid: Suggests the action of unscrewing something.

Examples: He *fashioned* the sculpture with great care. Mother *fixed* a fine meal.

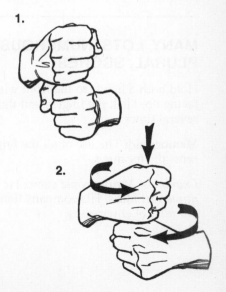

MALE

Move the right hand to the forehead as though gripping the peak of a cap or hat between the fingers and thumb; then move it forward a few inches.

Memory aid: Old-fashioned tipping of caps by men, especially when greeting women.

Example: The *male* peacocks are beautiful.

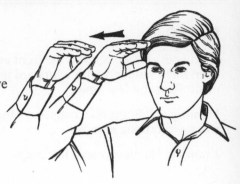

MAN

Touch the thumb of the right open hand on the forehead, then on the chest.

Memory aid: This sign is a combination of *father* and *fine.* It suggests that it is a fine thing to have a father who is a real *man.*

Example: Is your teacher a *man* or a woman?

MANY, LOTS, NUMEROUS, PLURAL, SCORES

Hold both *S* hands to the front with palms facing up. Flick the fingers and thumbs open several times.

Memory aid: The use of all the fingers represents the meaning.

Examples: Many people came. He presented *numerous* ideas. His company finances a *plurality* of enterprises.

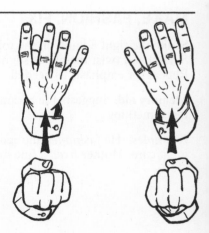

MARRY, MARRIAGE

Clasp the hands in a natural position with the right hand above the left.

Memory aid: A couple joins hands during their wedding ceremony.

Examples: They will be *married* in three weeks. Their *marriage* is successful.

MATCH, FIT, COMBINE

Hold both curved open hands to the front with palms facing self. Move the hands together until the fingers interlock.

Memory aid: Suggests two gears coming together.

Example: We need to paint the walls to *match* the carpet.

MATHEMATICS, ALGEBRA, CALCULUS, GEOMETRY, STATISTICS, TRIGONOMETRY

Make an upward and inward motion with both *M* hands so that the right *M* hand crosses inside the left. Use *A* hands for *algebra*, *C* hands for *calculus*, and so on.

Memory aid: The X-shaped movement suggests the multiplication symbol.

Example: Christine made good grades in *algebra*.

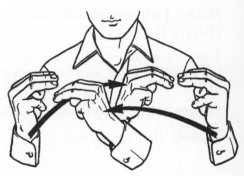

MAY, MAYBE, PERHAPS, POSSIBLY, PROBABLY

Hold both flat hands to the front and move them up and down alternately.

Memory aid: Symbolizes the weighing of one thing against another.

Examples: Maybe I should go. *Perhaps* she should resign.

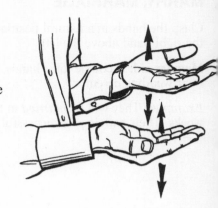

ME

Point the right index finger toward the chest.

Memory aid: The signer directs attention to himself.

Example: Can you understand *me?*

MEAN (adjective), CRUEL, HURTFUL

Strike the right bent *V* knuckles against the left bent *V* knuckles with a downward movement.

Memory aid: Suggests unpleasant contact.

Example: He's a *mean* boss.

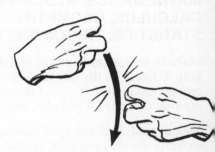

MEAN (verb), INTEND, PURPOSE

Place the fingertips of the right *V* hand in the palm of the left flat hand, which has its palm facing either to the right or upward. Draw the right hand away slightly; rotate it in a clockwise direction and rethrust the *V* fingers into the left palm.

1.

2.

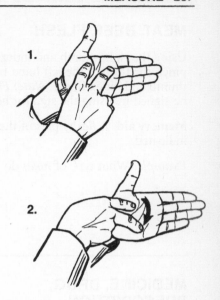

Memory aid: Suggests the *intention* to go from one situation to another.

Examples: Do you understand what I *mean*? My *purpose* should be clear.

MEASLES

Tap the right side of the face in several places with the fingertips of the right curved open hand.

Memory aid: Suggests the spots produced by *measles*.

Example: All my brothers have had *measles*.

MEASURE

Touch the thumb tips of both *Y* hands together a few times.

Memory aid: Indicates *measuring* by using the extended thumbs and little fingers.

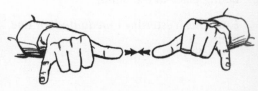

Example: Please *measure* the table.

MEAT, BEEF, FLESH

Using the right thumb and index finger, pinch the flesh of the left hand between the thumb and index finger. *Note: Flesh* can also be signed by using the sign for *body*.

Memory aid: A *fleshy* part of the hand is indicated.

Example: What type of *meat* do you prefer?

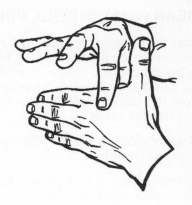

MEDICINE, DRUG, PRESCRIPTION

Make small circles on the left palm with the right middle finger.

Memory aid: Suggests the grinding of herbs or elements used in making *medicine.*

Example: This *medicine* tastes awful.

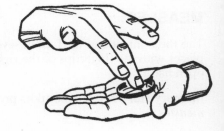

MEDITATE

Make forward circles with the right *M* hand near the right temple.

Memory aid: The *M* hand indicates the word, and the movement suggests action taking place in the mind.

Example: Yesterday I *meditated* for one hour.

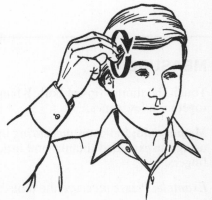

MEET, ENCOUNTER

Bring both extended index finger hands together from the sides with palms facing.

Memory aid: Suggests two persons *meeting*.

Example: I *met* Ruth only yesterday.

MEETING, ASSEMBLE

Bring both open hands in from the sides while forming *and* hands, and let the fingertips touch.

Memory aid: The fingers symbolize individuals coming together.

Example: The people *assembled* eagerly.

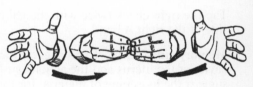

MEMBER, BOARD, CONGRESS, LEGISLATURE, SENATE

Place the right extended *M* fingers at the left shoulder and move them across to the right shoulder. Initialize each word.

Memory aid: The initial suggests the word, and the shoulders symbolize authority.

Example: Don's been a *member* of the *board* for three years.

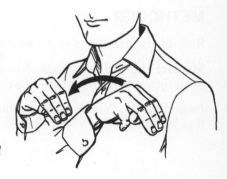

MEMORIZE

Place the right index finger on the center of the forehead; then move the right hand forward from the forehead to an *S* position, with the palm facing in.

Memory aid: Represents a firm grip on information.

Example: Please *memorize* this phone number.

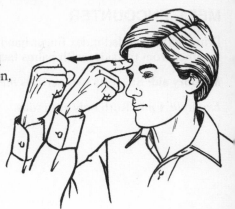

MENSTRUATION, PERIOD

Tap the right cheek twice with the palm side of the right *A* hand.

Memory aid: The cheek can suggest the cavity of the uterus and the action can suggest the loosening of material for the discharge of the menses.

Example: Her *period* stopped two months ago.

METHODIST

Rub the flat hands together enthusiastically.

Memory aid: The early *Methodists* were particularly noted for their enthusiastic worship.

Example: John Wesley began the movement that became the *Methodist* Church.

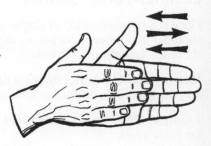

MEXICO, MEXICAN

Draw the right extended *M* fingertips downward over the right cheek a few times. *Alternative* (not illustrated): Place the *H* fingers of both hands above the mouth with the palms facing self. Draw the hands out to the cheeks with a slight downward movement.

Memory aid: The initial of the first sign indicates the word, and the actions of this sign and of the second sign suggest *Pancho Villa's* whiskers.

Example: Tom went to *Mexico* for a vacation.

MIDNIGHT

Hold the left arm in a horizontal position pointing right with flat or curved hand facing down. Move the right hand over and below the wrist of the left with fingers pointing down.

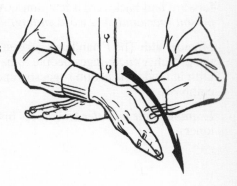

Memory aid: Symbolizes the sun being below the horizon on the opposite side of the earth.

Example: Don woke at *midnight*.

MILK

Squeeze one or both slightly open *S* hands with a downward motion. Do it alternately if two hands are used.

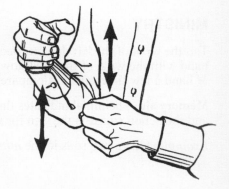

Memory aid: Symbolizes the act of *milking* a cow.

Example: I'd like some cold *milk*, please.

MIND, BRAIN, INTELLECT, MENTAL

Tap the right index finger on the forehead a few times.

Memory aid: The *mind* is related to the brain.

Examples: George has a brilliant *intellect*. My *mind* is tired.

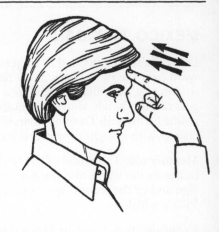

MINISTER, PASTOR

Place the right *F* hand in front of the right shoulder with palm facing forward. Move it forward and backward a few times. Add the *person (personalizing word ending)* sign.

Memory aid: The *F* hand can suggest that the preacher encourages people to have faith in God. The action suggests repeated emphasis.

Example: Our *minister* truly loves his parishioners.

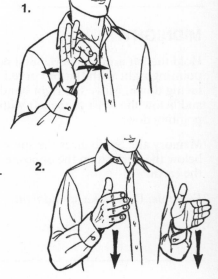

MINISTRY

Tap the wrist of the left downturned closed hand with the wrist of the right downturned *M* hand a few times. *Note:* Compare *work*.

Memory aid: The initial indicates the word, and the action suggests the sign for *work*.

Example: I have two sons in the *ministry*.

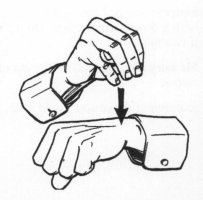

MINUTE

Hold the flat left hand vertically with palm facing right. Let the index finger of the right *D* hand touch the left palm with the index finger pointing up. Move the right index finger past the little-finger edge of the left hand.

Memory aid: Follows the movement of a *minute* hand on a clock.

Example: I will be one *minute*.

MIRACLE, MARVEL

Move the open hands up and forward a few times with palms facing out. Tap the wrist of the right *S* hand on the wrist of the left *S* hand a few times. This sign is a combination of the signs for *wonderful* and *work*.

Memory aid: Suggests an attitude of awe while beholding the work of a *miracle*.

Example: It will take a *miracle* to solve this problem.

MIRROR

Hold up the slightly curved right hand at eye level, and look at the palm while pivoting the hand slightly from the wrist.

Memory aid: Suggests looking at one's reflection in a *mirror*.

Example: She constantly looks at herself in a *mirror*.

MISSION

Make a circle with the right *M* hand over the heart.

Memory aid: The initial indicates the word, and the action suggests that one's heart must be in it to be successful.

Example: Where is your *mission* headquarters?

MISSIONARY

Make a counterclockwise circle with the right *M* hand over the heart. Add the *person (personalizing word ending)* sign.

Memory aid: The initial indicates the word, and the action suggests that one's heart must be in it to be successful.

Example: The Apostle Paul was the first known Christian *missionary* to Europe.

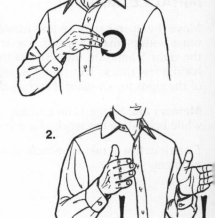

MISUNDERSTAND

Put the right *V* hand to the forehead, touching first with the middle finger, then twisting the hand and touching with the index finger.

Memory aid: The twisting motion and the use of two fingers suggest uncertainty in the mind.

Example: Phyllis *misunderstood* the instructions.

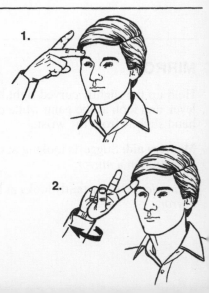

MONDAY

Make a small clockwise circle with the right *M* hand.

Memory aid: The initial suggests the word, and the circular motion suggests the passing of time.

Example: Come on *Monday*.

MONEY, CAPITAL, FINANCES, FUNDS

Strike the back of the right *and* hand into the left upturned palm a few times.

Memory aid: Suggests a person showing another how much *money* is in the hand.

Examples: The project requires a lot of *money*. Do you have the *capital*?

MONKEY, APE

Scratch the sides of the chest with both claw-shaped hands.

Memory aid: The scratching of a *monkey* to relieve pest infestation in its fur.

Example: The *ape* is quite clever.

MONTH, MONTHLY

Point the left index finger up with palm facing right. Move the right index finger from the top to the base of the left index finger. Repeat a few times to sign *monthly*.

Memory aid: The left index finger's three joints and tip represent the four weeks of a *month*.

Examples: The project will take two *months*. Have you continued with your *monthly* report?

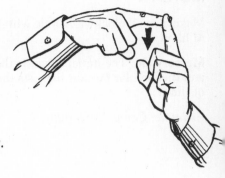

MOON

Hold the shape of the right *C* hand around the right eye.

Memory aid: The initial shape represents the shape of the *moon,* and the locality of the eye suggests that people can see by the *moon's* light.

Example: The *moon* affects the ocean tides.

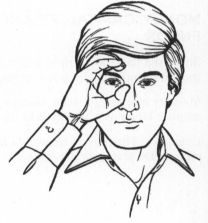

MORE

Touch the fingertips of both *and* hands before the chest with palms facing down. The right hand can be brought up to meet the left from a slightly lower position.

Memory aid: Adding one *and* to another suggests the meaning.

Example: There were *more* people than expected.

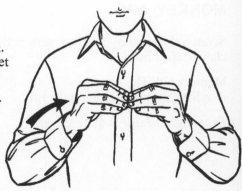

MORNING

Place the left flat hand with palm facing the body in the bend of the right elbow. Bring the right flat hand toward self until the arm is upright with the palm facing the body.

Memory aid: The left arm indicates the horizon, while the right hand symbolizes the rising of the sun.

Example: Good *morning*.

MOSES

Place the *Q* fingers of both hands at the temples with the palms facing each other. Close the fingers as the hands are moved to the sides.

Memory aid: Suggests the pulling of the veil over *Moses'* face after his conversation with God. The Bible records that *Moses'* face shone to the extent that people could not look at him.

Example: Moses was a prophet.

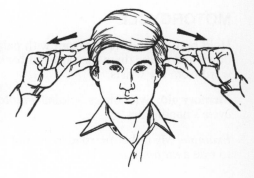

MOST

Touch the fingertips of both *and* hands together before the chest with palms facing down (the sign for *more*). Move the right hand up while forming the *A* hand. *Alternative* (not illustrated): Place both *A* hands together in front of the chest with palms facing, and raise the right hand.

Memory aid: Raising the right hand higher suggests the meaning.

Example: Most people there are friendly.

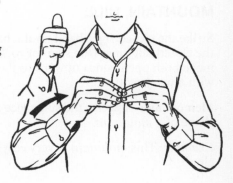

MOTHER, MOM, MAMA

Considered informal but commonly used is the sign made by touching the right chin or cheek with the thumb of the right open hand. The fingers may be wiggled slightly. The sign for *mama* is similar except that the thumb touches the cheek several times. *Alternative* (not illustrated): First sign *female;* then move the right hand to the left with palm facing up.

Memory aid: Indicates the head female of the family unit.

Examples: My *mother* is always cheerful. *Mama,* I love you.

MOTORCYCLE

Hold both *S* hands to the front with palms down and rotate them forward and backward from the wrists.

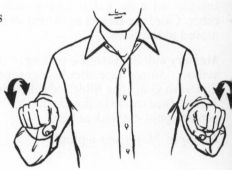

Memory aid: Symbolizes holding a *motorcycle's* handlebars.

Example: My father persuaded me not to ride a *motorcycle*.

MOUNTAIN, HILL

Strike the closed right hand on the back of the closed left hand (the sign for *rock*), then move both open hands upward to the front with a wavy motion.

Memory aid: Suggests the substance and shape of a *mountain*.

Example: This *mountain* is very easy to climb.

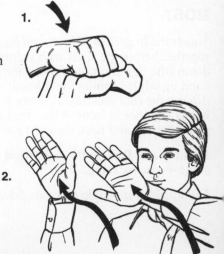

1.

2.

MOUSE

Brush the right index finger to the left across the nose tip a few times.

Memory aid: Suggests the twitching nose of a *mouse.*

Example: I saw a *mouse* run under the cabinet.

MOUTH

Point to the mouth with the right index finger.

Memory aid: The *mouth* is identified by pointing to it.

Example: The baby opened its *mouth* for the bottle.

MOVIE, CINEMA, FILM

Place both flat open hands palm to palm with the left palm facing somewhat forward. Slide the right hand back and forth over the left hand a few times. Most of the movement is from the right wrist.

Memory aid: Symbolizes the rapidly moving *film* frames.

Example: What's showing at the *movies* tonight?

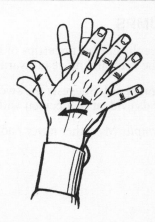

MUCH, LOT

Place both open and slightly curved hands to the front with palms facing; then draw them apart to the sides.

Memory aid: The hands seem to be holding something that is expanding.

Examples: His decision created *much* happiness. There are a *lot* of sheep in that field.

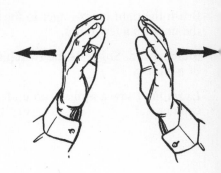

MULTIPLY, ARITHMETIC, CALCULATE, ESTIMATE, FIGURE, WORSE

Make an upward and inward motion with both *V* hands so that the right *V* crosses inside the left.

Memory aid: The X-shaped movement suggests the *multiplication* symbol.

Examples: Judy never learned her *multiplication* tables. The distance must be *calculated* carefully. Their financial situation is *worse*.

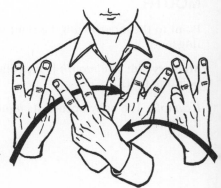

MUMPS

Place the curved fingertips of both hands at the neck and move outward slightly.

Memory aid: Suggests the swollen neck glands evident in a person with *mumps*.

Example: My father never had *mumps*.

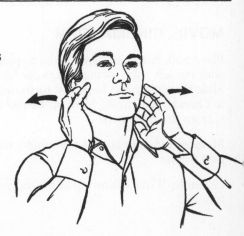

MUST, HAVE TO, IMPERATIVE, NEED, NECESSARY, OUGHT TO, SHOULD, VITAL

Move the right bent index finger firmly downward a few times.

Memory aid: Suggests the idea of standing with determination on a chosen position.

Examples: I *must* have the list by Monday. You *should* never let your guard down.

MY, MINE, OWN, PERSONAL

Place the palm of the right flat hand on the chest.

Memory aid: The hand over the heart suggests protection of *personal* belongings.

Examples: This is *my* book. Voting is a *personal* right I exercise.

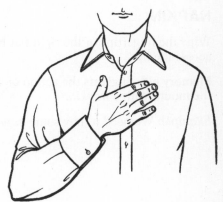

MYSELF, SELF

Bring the *A* hand against the center of the chest with palm facing left.

Memory aid: The thumb can be thought of as representing *self*.

Example: I bought *myself* a present today.

NAME, CALLED, NAMED

Cross the middle-finger edge of the right *H* fingers over the index-finger edge of the left *H* fingers. To sign *called* or *named,* move the crossed *H* hands in a small forward arc together.

Memory aid: Reminds one that those who cannot write have to sign their *name* with an *X.*

Example: Please spell your *name* for me.

NAPKIN

Wipe the fingertips of the right flat hand across the lips.

Memory aid: Suggests the action of wiping the mouth with a *napkin.*

Example: We need to buy some *napkins.*

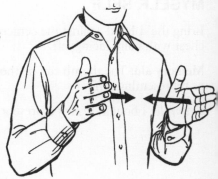

NARROW

Place both flat hands to the front with palms facing and move them closer together.

Memory aid: The decreasing distance indicates the meaning.

Example: It was a *narrow* canal.

NARROW-MINDED

Hold both flat hands near the sides of the forehead with palms facing and fingers pointing forward. Move both hands forward and inward until the fingertips meet.

Memory aid: Suggests a mind that is closed.

Example: Some people are so *narrow-minded.*

NATION, NATIONAL, NATURE, NATURAL

Make a clockwise circle above the back of the left *S* hand with the right extended *N* fingers; then bring the *N* fingers down on the back of the left hand.

Memory aid: The initial indicates the word, and the action suggests something that is established on a solid foundation.

Examples: Nations must learn to live at peace with one another. It's *natural* to want to be accepted.

NEAR, ADJACENT, BY, CLOSE TO

Hold the left curved hand away from the body with palm facing in. Move the back of the right curved hand from a position close to the body to one near the palm of the left hand.

Memory aid: The proximity of the hands suggests the meaning.

Example: The dog obediently came *near.*

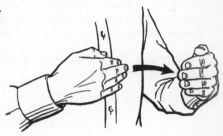

NECKTIE

Hold both extended *N* fingers in front of the neck. Rotate the right *N* fingers forward around the left *N* fingers; then move the right hand down a short distance with palm facing up.

Memory aid: Symbolizes the movements necessary in hand-tying a *necktie*.

Example: I can't find my blue *tie*.

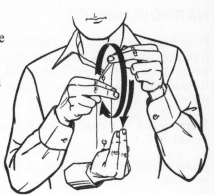

NEGATIVE

Place the right index finger horizontally across the left palm, which is facing out.

Memory aid: Symbolizes a minus sign.

Example: Don't be so *negative*.

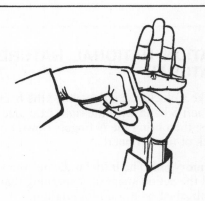

NEIGHBOR

Hold the left curved hand away from the body with palm facing in. Move the back of the right curved hand close to the palm of the left. Bring both flat hands down simultaneously with palms facing each other. This is a combination of *near* and *person* (*personalizing word ending*).

Memory aid: The proximity of the hands suggests the meaning.

Example: Jerry is my *neighbor*.

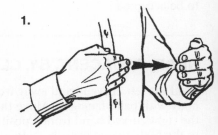

1.

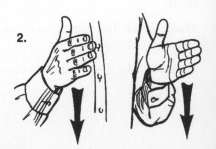

2.

NEPHEW

Place the right extended *N* fingers close to the right temple and shake back and forth from the wrist.

Memory aid: The initial *N* is placed near the male sign position.

Example: How many *nephews* do you have?

NERVOUS, JITTERY, JUMPY

Hold both open hands to the front with palms facing down and make the hands tremble.

Memory aid: Suggests the physical expression of *nervousness*.

Example: Joan gets so *nervous* before an examination.

NEVER

Trace a half circle in the air to the right with the right flat hand; then drop the hand away to the right.

Memory aid: Suggests a circle that can *never* be completed because the hand has dropped away.

Example: I'll *never* shop there again.

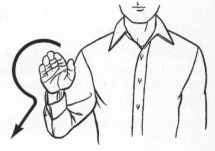

NEW

Pass the back of the slightly curved right hand across the left flat palm from fingers to heel. Continue the movement of the right hand in a slight upward direction.

Memory aid: The right hand seems to be suggesting a *new* direction to the left hand.

Example: Her *new* dress is pretty.

NEWSPAPER, PRINTING, PUBLISHING

Move the right index finger and thumb together as though picking something up; then place them on the left flat palm.

Memory aid: Symbolizes the old-fashioned method of hand-setting type.

Example: We need a *printed* brochure.

NEW YORK

Place the right *Y* hand on the left flat hand and slide it back and forth.

Memory aid: The initial combined with the context indicates the name, and the movement suggests the busy atmosphere of a large city.

Example: There are many tall buildings in *New York.*

NEXT

Hold both flat hands to the front with palms facing in and the right hand behind the left. Move the right hand over to the front of the left hand. *Note:* Compare *beyond*.

Memory aid: Suggests overcoming an obstacle and proceeding to whatever is *next*.

Example: What is *next*?

NEXT YEAR

Move the right *S* hand in a complete forward circle around the left *S* hand and come to rest with the right *S* hand on top of the left. Then point the right index finger forward.

Memory aid: The sign for *year* and pointing to the future.

Example: Next year we plan to visit the west coast of America.

NIECE

Place the right extended *N* fingers close to the right side of the chin and shake back and forth from the wrist.

Memory aid: The initial *N* is placed near the *female* sign position.

Example: You are my favorite *niece*.

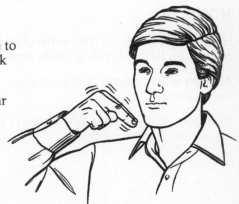

NIGHT, EVENING

Hold the left arm in a horizontal position
with the fingers of the left downturned flat
hand pointing right. Place the right forearm
on the back of the left hand and point the
right curved hand downward.

Memory aid: The right hand symbolizes
the sun going below the horizon.

Example: It's a rainy *night*.

NO

Bring the right thumb, index, and middle
fingers together.

Memory aid: Suggests a combination of the
signs for *N* and *O*.

Example: My answer is *no*.

NONE, NO

Hold both *O* hands in front of the chest and
move them to the side in opposite directions.

Memory aid: A double zero emphasizes
the meaning.

Examples: There is *none* left. We carry *no*
spare parts for that model.

NOON, MIDDAY

Point the left flat hand to the right with palm facing down. Rest the right elbow on the back of the left hand with the right arm in a vertical position and the palm facing left.

Memory aid: The left arm indicates the horizon, and the right hand symbolizes the position of the sun at *midday*.

Example: Lunch will be at *noon*.

NORTH

Move the *N* hand upward.

Memory aid: Indicates the direction on a compass.

Example: The *north* wind is blowing.

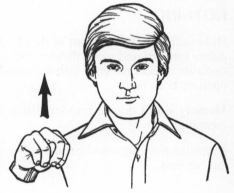

NOSE

Touch the tip of the nose with the right index finger.

Memory aid: The *nose* is identified by pointing to it.

Example: Some people have had cosmetic *nose* surgery.

NOT, DO NOT

Place the right *A* thumb, palm left, under the chin and move it forward and away from the chin. *Alternative* (not illustrated): Cross both flat hands with palms down: then uncross them by moving both hands out sideways. The head can also be shaken to emphasize the negative.

Memory aid: The thumb moving out from under the chin suggests something that cannot be swallowed. The uncrossing of the hands is a natural negative sign.

Example: I'll *not* be a part of it.

NOTHING

Hold both *O* hands in front of the chest with palms forward and move them to the sides in opposite directions while simultaneously opening both hands.

Memory aid: A double zero emphasizes the meaning.

Example: Nothing could persuade Nicole to cut her hair.

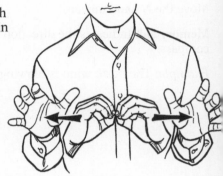

NOTICE, NOTE, OBSERVE

Point toward the right eye with the right index finger; then place it in the palm of the left flat hand.

Memory aid: Suggests directing the attention to a particular point.

Example: Please *note* the new instructions.

1.

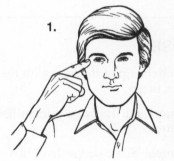

2.

NOW, CURRENT, IMMEDIATE, PRESENT

Hold both bent (or *Y*) hands to the front at waist level with palms facing up. Drop both hands sharply a short distance.

Memory aid: Suggests that the hands feel the weight of something *now*.

Examples: Do it *now*. It is a *current* problem. My pain was *immediate*. I predict the *present* situation will not last long.

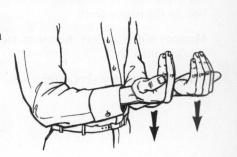

NUN

Outline a semi-circle with the right *N* hand by going up the left side, across the forehead, then down the right side of the face.

Memory aid: The outline resembles a veil.

Example: Stacey's aunt, Mary, decided to become a *nun* when she was only fifteen years old.

NURSE

Place the right extended *N* fingertips on the upturned left wrist.

Memory aid: The initial indicates the word, and the action suggests the taking of a person's pulse rate.

Example: Julia says she wants to be a *nurse* when she grows up.

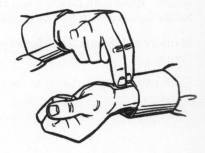

NUTS, PEANUTS

Move the right *A* thumb forward from behind the upper teeth.

Memory aid: Suggests the use of teeth to break a *nut's* shell.

Example: *Nuts* are very nutritious.

OBEY, OBEDIENCE

Hold both *A* hands close to the forehead with palms facing in. Bring them down and forward, ending in the flat-hand position with palms facing up.

Memory aid: Suggests a mind offering to cooperate.

Example: Please *obey* all traffic rules.

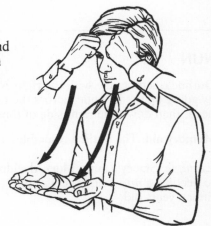

OCEAN, SEA

Touch the mouth with the index finger of the right *W* hand a few times (the sign for *water*). Move both downturned curved hands forward with a wavy motion.

Memory aid: Symbolizes the waves of the *ocean*.

Example: It's fun to swim in the *ocean*.

1.

2.

ODD, PECULIAR, STRANGE, WEIRD

Give the right *C* hand a quick downward twist in front of the eyes.

Memory aid: Suggests distorted vision.

Examples: What an *odd* person Jack is. He found himself in *strange* circumstances.

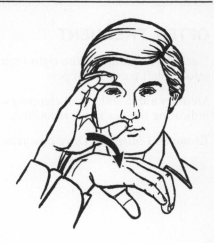

OFF

Move the flat downturned right hand upward a few inches, *off* the back of the flat downturned left hand.

Memory aid: Moving one item *off* another.

Example: Make sure the oven is *off* before leaving the house.

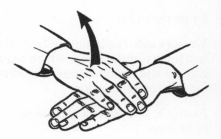

OFFER, PRESENT, PROPOSE, SUGGEST

Move both flat hands in an upward-forward movement with palms facing up.

Memory aid: The gesture represents giving a gift to someone.

Examples: Jane was *offered* an excellent opportunity. We *presented* the idea to Ron.

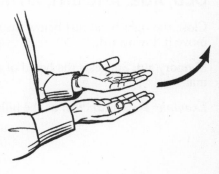

OFTEN, FREQUENT

Place the fingertips of the right bent hand into the left palm and repeat.

Memory aid: Similar to a clapping action, indicating the desire for *repetition*.

Example: I *often* see Dave downtown.

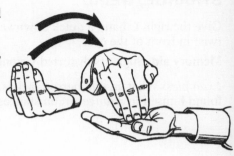

OHIO

Fingerspell *O-H.*

Memory aid: The initials indicate the first two letters of the word, which requires context and simultaneous lipreading for full comprehension.

Example: The state of *Ohio* is east of Indiana.

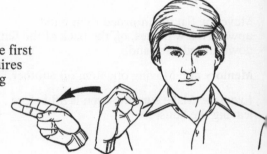

OLD, AGE, ANCIENT, ANTIQUE

Close the right hand just below the chin and move it downward.

Memory aid: Suggests the beard of an *old* man.

Example: He's as *ancient* as the hills.

OLYMPICS

Form *F* hands and interlock the thumbs and index fingers a few times as the hands move to the right.

Memory aid: Represents the five Olympic rings.

Example: This year's *Olympics* were more spectacular than last year's.

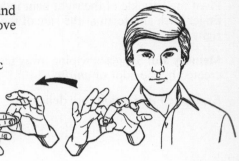

ON

With both palms facing down, place the right flat hand on the back of the left flat hand.

Memory aid: Indicates something *on* top of something else.

Example: The typewriter is *on* the desk.

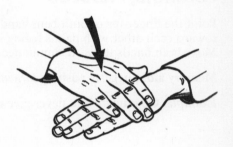

ONCE

Hold the left flat hand at chest level with the palm facing right. Touch the left palm with the right index (or *L* hand), which is then moved sharply upward to a vertical position.

Memory aid: The single finger indicates the meaning.

Example: The teacher gave her instructions only *once*.

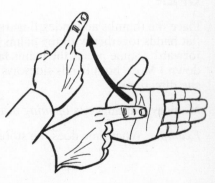

ONION

Pivot the knuckle of the right bent index finger back and forth at the side of the right eye.

Memory aid: Suggests wiping away tears created by the odor of *onions.*

Example: Fried *onions* are delicious.

ONWARD, ADVANCE, FORWARD, PROCEED

Point the fingertips of both bent hands toward each other with palms facing in. Move both hands forward simultaneously.

Memory aid: Suggests pushing *forward.*

Example: Go *onward* and never give up.

OPEN

Place the thumbs and index fingers of both flat hands together with the palms facing forward. (Some prefer the palms facing down.) Move both hands sideways in opposite directions.

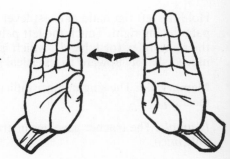

Memory aid: Suggests *opening* drapes.

Example: What time does the store *open*?

OPERATION, INCISION, SURGERY

Move the right *A* thumbnail down (or across) the chest or abdomen.

Memory aid: Symbolizes the use of a *surgical* knife.

Example: Where was the *incision* made?

OPPORTUNITY

Hold both *O* hands to the front with palms down. Move both hands forward and up while forming *P* hands.

Memory aid: The first two letters of *opportunity* are signed.

Example: Carl gave me my first *opportunity*.

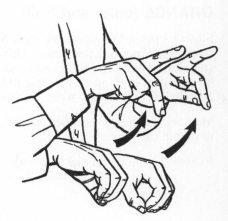

OPPOSITE, CONTRARY, CONTRAST

Point both index fingers toward each other and move them away from each other in opposite directions.

Memory aid: Suggests the idea of separation.

Example: This information is *contrary* to what I received.

OR, EITHER

Point the index finger of the left *L* hand forward with palm facing right. Move the right index finger from the tip of the left thumb to the top of the left index finger a few times.

Memory aid: The back-and-forth movement suggests one finger *or* the other.

Example: We could leave now, *or* we could wait one hour.

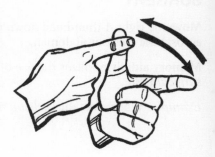

ORANGE (color and fruit)

Slightly open and squeeze the right *S* hand in front of the mouth a few times. *Alternative* (not illustrated): The color *orange* can also be signed by holding up the right *O* hand and shaking it from the wrist.

Memory aid: Suggests squeezing an *orange* to obtain the juice.

Example: Would you like an *orange*?

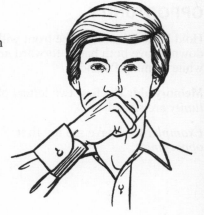

ORBIT

Make a forward circle around the left closed hand with the right index-finger hand. End with the right index resting on top of the left hand.

Memory aid: Suggests a spacecraft which *orbits* around the earth before landing.

Example: How long has the space station been in *orbit*?

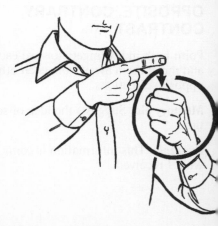

OUR

Place the slightly cupped right hand on the right side of the chest with palm facing left. Move the right hand forward in a circular motion, bringing it to rest near the left shoulder with the palm facing right.

Memory aid: The circular movement suggests the inclusion of others.

Example: Our team is winning.

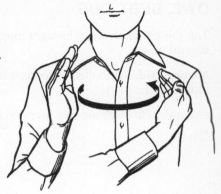

OURSELVES

This sign is a combination of *our* and *self*. *Our* is signed by placing the slightly cupped right hand on the right side of the chest with the palm facing left. Move the right hand forward in a circular motion, bringing it to rest near the left shoulder with the palm facing right. *Self* is signed by placing the right *A* hand against the center of the chest with palm facing left.

Memory aid: The circular movement suggests the inclusion of others, and the thumb of the *A* hand can represent the self.

Example: We will paint the house *ourselves*.

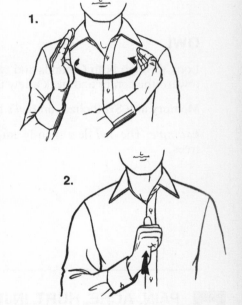

OUT

Place the downturned fingers of the open right hand in the left *C* hand with the right fingers protruding below the left *C*. Draw the right hand up and *out*.

Memory aid: Symbolizes coming up *out* of a hole.

Example: They came *out* of the house slowly.

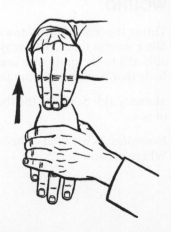

OWE, DEBT, DUE

Tap the left palm with the right index finger several times.

Memory aid: Symbolizes a request to put money in the palm.

Example: He *owes* me two months' rent.

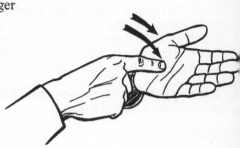

OWL

Look through both *O* hands and twist them toward the center and back a few times.

Memory aid: Symbolizes an *owl's* large eyes.

Example: The *owl* flew silently among the trees.

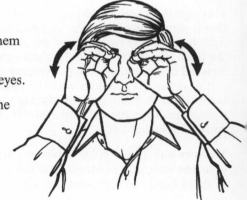

PAIN, ACHE, HURT, INJURY, WOUND

Thrust the index fingers toward each other several times. This may be done adjacent to the particular area of the body that is suffering from *pain*.

Memory aid: Suggests the throbbing of *pain*.

Examples: What kind of *pain* is it? Where are you *hurt*?

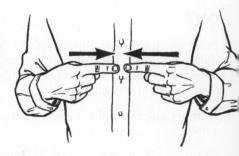

PAINT

Brush the fingertips of the right hand back and forth on the left palm.

Memory aid: Symbolizes *painting* with a brush.

Example: Let's *paint* this room.

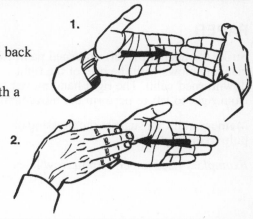

PAJAMAS

Place the palm side of the right open hand in front of the face and move it down to chin level while forming an *and* hand; then brush the fingertips of both flat open hands down the chest a few times.

Memory aid: A combination of the signs for *sleep* and *clothes*.

Example: Betty has been invited to a girl's *pajama* party.

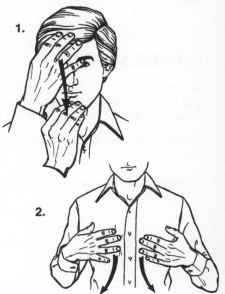

PANTS, SLACKS, TROUSERS

Place the curved open hands just below the waist and move them up to the waist while simultaneously forming *and* hands. *Alternative* (not illustrated): Outline first the left leg and then the right by using both flat hands that point down with palms facing.

Memory aid: The first sign symbolizes pulling up *pants* and the second outlines each *pant* leg separately.

Example: Your *pants* are baggy.

PAPER

Strike the heel of the left upturned palm two glancing blows with the heel of the right downturned palm. The right hand moves from right to left to perform the movement.

Memory aid: Can suggest the pressing of pulp to make *paper*.

Example: I need *paper* with narrow lines.

PARADE, MARCH

Swing the fingers of both bent hands back and forth sideways as they are moved forward with one hand behind the other.

Memory aid: Symbolizes organized *marching*.

Example: Let's watch the *parade* from here.

PARAGRAPH

Place the thumb and fingertips of the right *C* hand against the left flat palm.

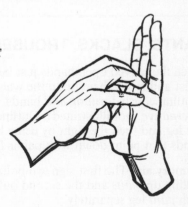

Memory aid: The space between the right thumb and fingers can indicate the depth of a *paragraph* on a page.

Example: Please write two or three *paragraphs*.

PARALLEL

With palms facing down, move both extended index fingers forward simultaneously. Fingers do not touch.

Memory aid: Two items moving in *parallel*.

Example: The parade musicians marched in *parallel* rows.

PARENTS

Place the middle finger of the right *P* hand at the right temple, then at the right side of the chin. *Note:* Compare *adult*.

Memory aid: The initial indicates the word, and the two locations refer to the basic male and female positions.

Example: She respected her *parents'* wishes.

PARK (a vehicle)

Bring the right 3 hand down onto the left flat palm. Movements suggesting the parking of a vehicle can also be made with the right 3 hand on the left palm.

Memory aid: The 3 hand symbolizes a person in a car.

Example: Where did you *park*?

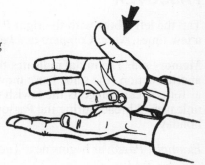

PARTY

Hold both *P* hands in front and swing them back and forth from left to right.

Memory aid: The initial indicates the word, and the movement indicates lively action.

Example: They decided to plan a *party* for Don.

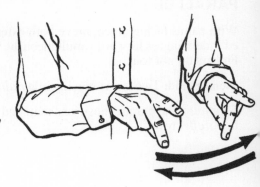

PASS

Pass the right *A* hand forward from behind the left *A* hand.

Memory aid: Represents the action of *passing*.

Example: The truck *passed* me quickly.

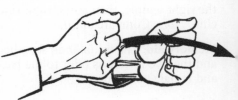

PASSOVER

Tap the left elbow with the right *P* fingers a few times. *Note:* Compare *cracker*.

Memory aid: The initial indicates the word, and the action (the same basic movement as for *cracker*) suggests the Jewish use of unleavened bread during the Passover holiday.

Example: *Passover* begins next Tuesday.

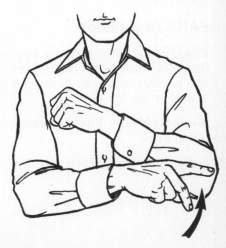

PAST, AGO, FORMERLY, LAST, ONCE UPON A TIME, USED TO, PREVIOUSLY

Move the right upraised flat hand backward over the right shoulder with palm facing the body. The amount of emphasis with which sign is made can vary depending on the length of time involved. *Note:* See *was* and *were* for alternative signs.

Memory aid: Indicates that which is behind.

Examples: The *past* is forgiven. Richard was *formerly* a lawyer. The prizes were *previously* awarded annually.

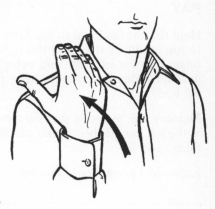

PATIENT, PATIENCE, BEAR

Move the right *A* thumb downward over the lips.

Memory aid: Suggests a person experiencing difficulties or frustrations without talking about it.

Example: Please be *patient* with me.

PATIENT (noun)

Use the right *P* fingers and draw a cross on the upper left arm.

Memory aid: The initial *P* combined with the sign for *hospital* indicate the word.

Example: The hospital *patient* was happy with her doctor's care.

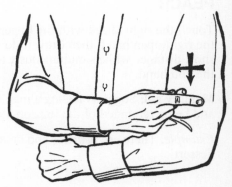

PAY

Hold the left flat hand to the front with palm facing up. Place the tip of the right index finger into the left palm and swing it forward until the index finger points away from the body.

Memory aid: Suggests that the money held in the left hand is being *paid* out for something.

Example: I know I *paid* that bill.

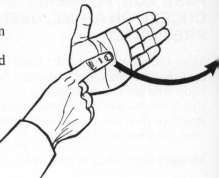

PEACE

Place the right flat hand on the left flat hand at chest level; then place the left on the right. Now move both flat hands down and to the sides with palms down. Pass from one position to another smoothly and continuously.

Memory aid: Symbolizes hands grasping in agreement followed by harmonious continuance with individual plans.

Example: The *peace* agreement was signed today.

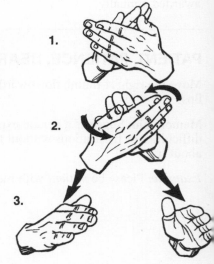

PEACH

Touch the right cheek with the fingertips of the right open hand; then draw it down a short distance while simultaneously forming the *and* hand.

Memory aid: Suggests feeling a man's beard and being reminded of the fuzz on a *peach*.

Example: There are *peaches* and cream for dessert.

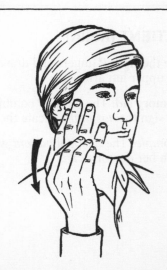

PEAR

Hold the left *and* hand in front with the palm facing in. Place the right thumb and fingers over the left hand; then slide the right fingers off to the right until they also form an *and* hand.

Memory aid: Suggests the broad-to-narrow shape of a *pear*.

Example: I can only enjoy ripe *pears*.

PEOPLE

Make inward circles alternately from the sides with both *P* hands. *Note:* Some signers prefer to direct the circles forward.

Memory aid: The *P* hands suggest the word, and the action suggests people milling around.

Example: Many *people* came to the meeting.

PEPPER

Hold the right *O* hand to the front with the *O* pointing down to the left. Shake down to the left a few times.

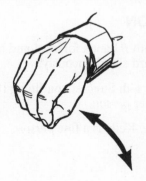

Memory aid: Symbolizes the use of a *pepper* shaker.

Example: He likes a lot of *pepper* on his food.

PERFECT

Move the middle fingertips of both *P* hands together so that they touch. *Note:* Sometimes this sign can be used interchangeably with the sign for *exact*.

Memory aid: The letter *P*s meet perfectly.

Example: He plays the piano with *perfect* precision.

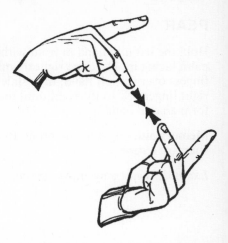

PERIOD, APOSTROPHE, COLON, COMMA, EXCLAMATION POINT, SEMICOLON

Draw the shape of the appropriate punctuation mark in the air with the right index finger or with the right index finger and thumb, which touch at the tips. The other fingers are closed.

Memory aid: The natural shape.

Example: Don't use too many *exclamation points*.

PERSON

Place both *P* hands forward and move them downward simultaneously.

Memory aid: Suggests outlining the form of another *person*.

Example: Kelly is a fine *person*.

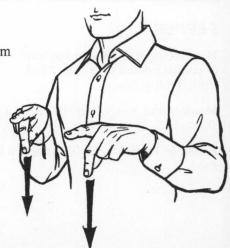

PERSON (personalizing word ending)

Hold both flat open hands to the front with palms facing; then move them down simultaneously.

Memory aid: Suggests outlining the form of another *person*.

Examples: John is our official welcom*er* (sign *welcome* and *person*). There are many Americ*ans* (sign *America* and *person*) who are Christi*ans* (sign *Christ* or *Jesus* and per*son*). Malcolm is a clever invent*or* (sign *invent* and *person*).

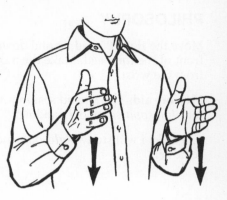

PERSONALITY, ATTITUDE, CHARACTER

Move the right *P* hand in a circle over the heart. To sign *attitude* and *character,* initialize the same action with an *A* and *C* hand respectively.

Memory aid: The letter signed over the heart suggests the meaning.

Example: She has a sweet *personality*.

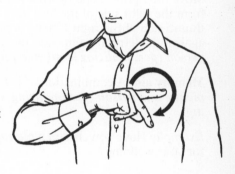

PERSUADE, COAX, PROD, URGE

Place both closed hands to the front with palms facing and both thumb tips in the crook of the respective bent index fingers. Position the left hand slightly in front of the right; then move both hands firmly toward the body in short back-and-forth stages.

Memory aid: Can symbolize the pulling action required to lead an unwilling mule.

Example: Maybe I can *persuade* him to try his hand at gardening.

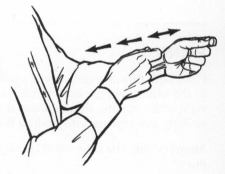

PHILOSOPHY

Move the right *P* hand up and down just in front of the forehead. Make the movement from the wrist.

Memory aid: The *P* hand searches the mind for *philosophical* understanding.

Example: I will study *philosophy* next semester.

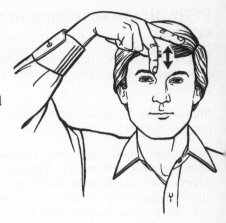

PHOTOGRAPHER

Move the right *C* hand down and forward from the right side of the face until the thumb side of the right *C* hand is placed against the left flat palm. Add the sign for *person (personalizing word ending)*.

Memory aid: A combination of the signs for *picture* and *person (personalizing word ending)*.

Example: Have you chosen a *photographer* for your wedding?

1.

2.

PIANO

Hold both downturned curved open hands to the front; then move them to the left and right while making simultaneous downward striking movements with various fingers.

Memory aid: The movement of playing a *piano*.

Example: This antique *piano* is valuable.

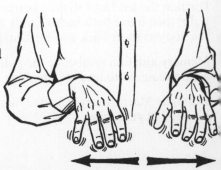

PICTURE, PHOTOGRAPH

Hold the right *C* hand close to the face; then move it forward until the thumb side of the right *C* hand is against the left flat palm. The left palm can face either to the right or to the front.

Memory aid: Suggests that a facial likeness is transferred to the flat surface of a *photograph*.

Example: Let me *photograph* you.

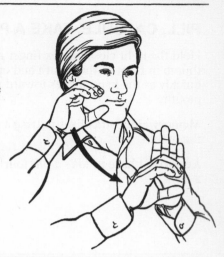

PIE

Pull the little-finger edge of the right flat hand across the palm of the left flat hand twice. Use a different angle the second time.

Memory aid: The movement of cutting a *pie*.

Example: My mother makes the best apple *pie* in town.

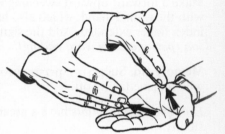

PIG, HOG

Place the back of the right flat hand under the chin with the fingers pointing to the left. Bend and unbend the hand several times from the knuckles.

Memory aid: Can represent the *pig's* snout constantly dipping for more food.

Example: David had chickens, cows, and *hogs*.

PILL, CAPSULE, TAKE A PILL

Hold the right closed index finger and thumb in front of the mouth and open them quickly as the hand moves toward the mouth.

Memory aid: Symbolizes putting a *pill* into the mouth.

Example: I have to *take a pill* four times a day.

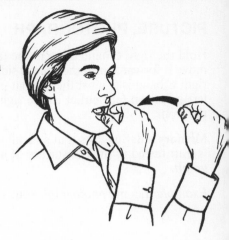

PILOT

Make a forward-upward sweeping motion with the right *Y* hand, which also has its index finger extended. Add the sign for *person (personalizing word ending)*.

Memory aid: Suggests a person involved with a plane taking off.

Example: Airline *pilots* have a great responsibility.

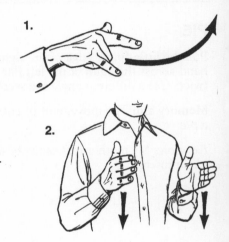

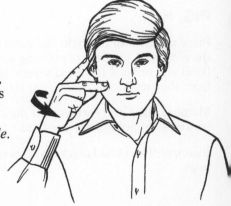

PINEAPPLE

Place the middle finger of the right *P* hand on the cheek and twist forward.

Memory aid: The initial indicates the word, and the sign is made in the same location as the sign for *apple*.

Example: Daniel's favorite fruit is *pineapple*.

PING-PONG, TABLE TENNIS

Place the right thumb tip in the crook of the right index finger with the other fingers closed. Move the hand back and forth, with most of the movement from the wrist.

Memory aid: The action of playing with a *Ping-Pong* paddle.

Example: Many people play *table tennis* for fun.

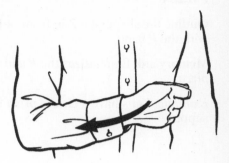

PINK

Stroke the lips downward with the middle finger of the right *P* hand.

Memory aid: Suggests *pink* lips.

Example: The bathroom is *pink*.

PITY, COMPASSION, MERCY, POOR (person or thing), SYMPATHY

Move the right middle finger upward on the chest with other fingers extended; then make forward circular motions in front of the chest with palm down and fingers still in the same position.

Memory aid: Suggests feelings of *compassion* for a person expressed by stroking the person's brow or shoulder.

Examples: Have *pity* on her. He has no *sympathy* for her plight.

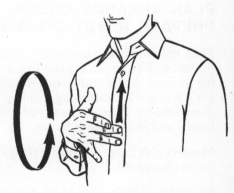

PIZZA

Outline the shape of a *Z* in front of the chest with the *P* hand.

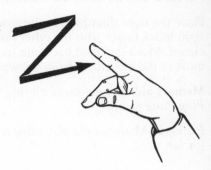

Memory aid: Emphasizes the *P* and *Z*s of *pizza*.

Example: Let's have a cheese *pizza* for supper.

PLACE, AREA, LOCATION, SITE

With the palms facing, hold both *P* hands a short distance in front of the chest and touch the middle fingers. Make a circle toward self with both hands and touch the middle fingertips again. Each word may be initialized in a similar manner.

Memory aid: The initials indicate the word, and the action suggests that the hands are describing the *location* of something within a certain area.

Example: This park covers a large *area*.

PLAN, ARRANGE, ORDER, PREPARE, READY, SYSTEM

Place both flat hands to the front and off to the left with palms facing and fingers pointing forward. Move both hands simultaneously to the right while moving them up and down slightly. *Plan* can be signed with *P* hands, and *ready* with *R* hands.

Memory aid: Suggests placing things in correct sequence.

Examples: What is your *plan*? You need a workable *system*.

PLANT, SOW

Move the right downturned curved hand from left to right while simultaneously moving the right thumb across the inside of the fingers from little finger to index finger.

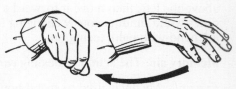

Memory aid: Suggests holding seeds between the fingers and thumb and gradually dropping them into the ground.

Example: When shall we *plant* the potatoes?

PLATE

Make a circle with the thumbs and fingers of both hands. *Alternative* (not illustrated): Touch the teeth with the right index finger and trace a circular outline with both index fingers.

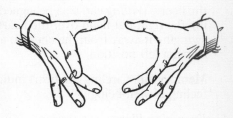

Memory aid: The first sign symbolizes a *plate* by its shape. The alternative sign symbolizes the type of material used in making *plates*.

Example: Your dinner *plates* have a pretty design.

PLAY, RECREATION, ROMP

Hold both *Y* hands in front of the chest and pivot them from the wrists a few times.

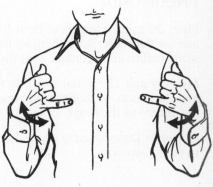

Memory aid: The flexibility of the movement suggests that the hands are free to *play*.

Example: Debbie asked her friend to *play* with her.

PLAYING CARDS

Place both thumb tips in the crooks of their respective index fingers with the other fingers closed. Position the right hand slightly above the left; then move it forward a few times while simultaneously changing it to a 3 hand with palm facing up.

Memory aid: The action of dealing *cards*.

Example: My uncle used to spend hours *playing cards*.

PLEASE, ENJOY, GRATIFY, LIKE, PLEASURE, WILLING

Make a circle with the right flat hand over the heart. *Willing* can also be signed by placing the right flat hand over the heart and swinging it away from the chest to a palm-up or palm-left position.

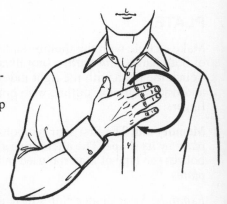

Memory aid: Circling the heart indicates a feeling of well-being.

Examples: Please be my friend. It was a *gratifying* experience. It's a *pleasure* to do it for you. I'd be very *willing* to work for you.

PNEUMONIA

Place the middle fingers of both *P* hands against the chest. Rock them up and down while maintaining contact with the chest.

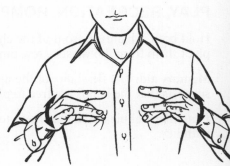

Memory aid: The initial indicates the word, and the action symbolizes the breathing movement of the lungs.

Example: Dress warmly if you don't want to get *pneumonia*.

POETRY, POEM

Move the right *P* hand back and forth with rhythm in front of the left flat hand.

Memory aid: Suggests the rhythmic nature of rhyming *poetry* lines.

Example: Judy likes to write *poetry*.

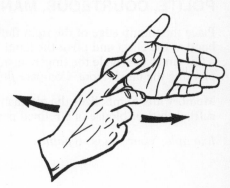

POISON

Make small circles on the left palm with the middle finger of the right *P* hand.

Memory aid: Suggests grinding *poisonous* herbs.

Example: I had a problem with food *poisoning*.

POLICE, COP, SHERIFF

Place the thumb side of the right *C* hand at the left shoulder.

Memory aid: The position at the shoulder indicates those who bear responsibility and authority.

Example: Call the *police*.

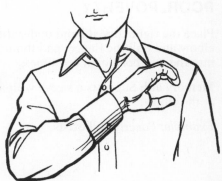

POLITE, COURTEOUS, MANNERS

Place the thumb edge of the right flat open hand at the chest and pivot the hand forward a few times or wiggle the fingers instead of pivoting the hand. *Note:* Compare *fine*.

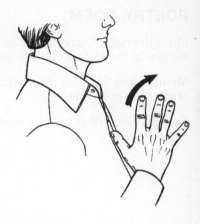

Memory aid: Symbolizes the old-fashioned ruffled shirt or blouse of a refined person.

Example: Your son is so *polite*.

POOL, BILLIARDS, SNOOKER

Hold the left *X* hand forward at waist level with palm facing down and the right *O* hand close to the right side of the waist with the palm facing self. Move the right hand back and forth toward the left hand.

Memory aid: Symbolizes the use of a *billiards* cue.

Example: Will you play *pool* with me?

POOR, POVERTY

Place the right curved hand under the left elbow and pull the fingers and thumb down into the *and* position a few times.

Memory aid: Suggests a sleeve with a hole at the elbow.

Example: Poverty still exists.

POPCORN

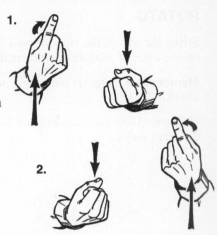

Hold both *S* hands in front with the palms facing up. Flick both index fingers up alternately several times.

Memory aid: Symbolizes the popping of corn kernels.

Example: Please make some *popcorn* for us.

POSITIVE

Cross the right index finger horizontally over the left vertical index finger.

Memory aid: A plus sign.

Example: I believe in being *positive*.

POSTER, SIGN

Hold both index fingers up with palms facing forward and outline a square.

Memory aid: Suggests the shape of a *poster*.

Example: We need an artist to make a *poster* for us.

POTATO

Strike the tips of the right curved *V* fingers on the back of the left downturned *S* hand.

Memory aid: Suggests piercing a *potato* with a fork.

Example: I like *potatoes* cooked in many different ways.

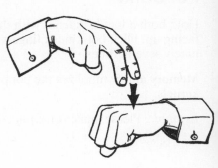

PRACTICE, DISCIPLINE, TRAINING

Rub the knuckles of the right *A* hand back and forth across the left index finger. A *T* hand can be used for *training*.

Memory aid: The right hand seems to be polishing the left index finger to improve the shine, just as *practice* will improve quality.

Example: Practice makes perfect.

PRAY, PRAYER

Place both flat hands to the front with palms touching; then move them toward self while simultaneously inclining the head slightly forward.

Memory aid: A traditional position of the head and hands during *prayer*.

Example: Many have found great comfort in *prayer*.

PREACH, SERMON

Place the right *F* hand in front of the right shoulder with palm facing forward. Move it forward and backward a few times.

Memory aid: The *F* hand can suggest that the preacher encourages people to have faith in God. The action suggests repeated emphasis.

Example: Did you *preach* last Sunday?

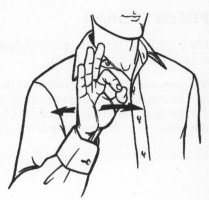

PREFER, RATHER

Place the right flat hand on the chest and move it up toward the right while simultaneously changing to an *A* hand.

Memory aid: The *A* hand seems to suggest an alternative.

Example: I would *prefer* a blue suit.

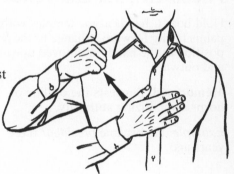

PREGNANT

Interlock the fingers of both hands in front of the abdomen.

Memory aid: Suggests the shape of a *pregnant* woman.

Example: This is my third *pregnancy*.

PRESBYTERIAN

Place (or tap) the right middle finger of the *P* hand on the flat left palm.

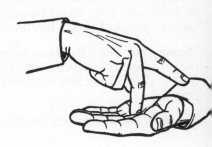

Memory aid: The initial indicates the word, and the standing position can suggest the *Presbyterian* stand for church government by the presbyters (ministers and elders).

Example: The speaker was a *Presbyterian*.

PRESIDENT, SUPERINTENDENT

Hold both *C* hands at the temples with palms facing forward. Change to the *S* position as the hands are moved upward and outward.

Memory aid: Suggests the outline of horns symbolizing authority.

Example: He became *president* three years ago.

PRESSURE

Point the left *G* hand forward; then push down with the right flat hand on the index side of the left *G* hand.

Memory aid: One hand puts *pressure* on the other.

Example: Nadine's boss puts a lot of *pressure* on her.

PREVENT, BLOCK, HINDER, OBSTRUCT

Bring the little-finger edge of the right flat downturned hand against the index finger of the left flat vertical hand. This may be repeated while both hands move forward.

Memory aid: The left hand is *blocking* the right.

Example: The art of *blocking* is vital to football.

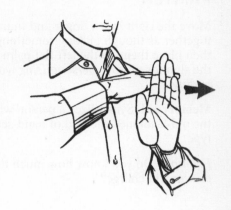

PRIEST, CHAPLAIN, CLERGYMAN, MINISTER

Draw the right *Q* fingertips backward around the right side of the neck.

Memory aid: Suggests the clerical collar.

Example: Our new *priest* will arrive on Tuesday.

PRINCIPAL

Circle the right palm-down *P* hand in a counterclockwise direction over the back of the left flat hand.

Memory aid: This is the basic movement of the sign for *over,* which indicates authority over others.

Example: The new *principal* arrives this coming fall.

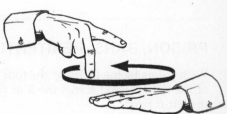

PRINTER

Move the right index finger and thumb together as though picking something up; then place them on the left flat palm. Add the sign for *person (personalizing word ending).*

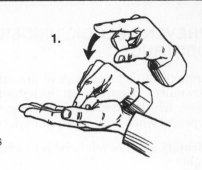

Memory aid: Symbolizes a person who uses the old-fashioned method of hand-setting type.

Example: Do you know how much the *printer* will charge?

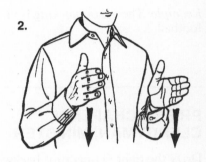

PRINTING, PUBLISHING, NEWSPAPER

Move the right index finger and thumb together as though picking something up; then place them on the left flat palm.

Memory aid: Symbolizes the old-fashioned method of hand-setting type.

Example: We need a *printed* brochure.

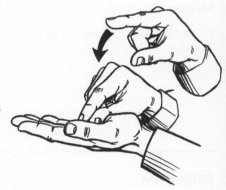

PRISON, BARS, PENITENTIARY

With palms facing in, cross the four fingers of the right *B* hand across the four fingers of the left *B* hand.

Memory aid: Symbolizes the *bars* of a *prison.*

Example: Have you ever been inside a *prison?*

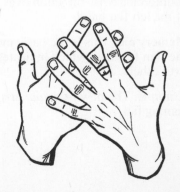

PROBLEM, DIFFICULTY

Touch the bent knuckles of the two *U* (or *V*) hands together and twist in opposite directions while moving downward slightly.

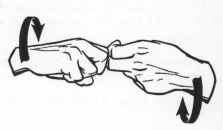

Memory aid: The rubbing knuckles suggest friction.

Example: He faces a difficult *problem.*

PROCESS, PROCEDURE, PROGRESS

With the palms facing in, roll both bent hands over each other a few times with a forward motion.

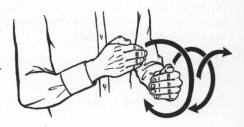

Memory aid: Suggests that action continues while forward *progress* is made.

Example: The *process* of elimination continued.

PROFESSION, PROFESSIONAL

Point the fingers of the left hand forward with the palm facing right. Move the initial *P* sign of the right hand forward along the left index fingers.

Memory aid: Suggests the idea of moving forward in a *profession.*

Example: What is your *profession?*

PROFIT, BENEFIT, GAIN

Place the touching thumb and index finger of the right *F* hand into an imaginary shirt pocket.

Memory aid: Suggests the idea of pocketing the *profit*.

Example: It was a *profitable* venture.

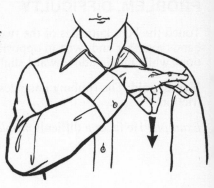

PROGRAM

Move the middle finger of the right *P* hand down the left flat palm; then down the back of the left hand. Twist the left hand slightly between the two phases of this sign so that the observer can see clearly.

Memory aid: Suggests a sheet of paper that is printed on both sides.

Example: Our son's name is on the *program*.

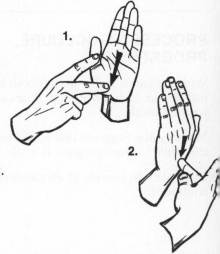

PROJECT

Move the middle finger of the right *P* hand down the left flat palm; then move the little finger of the right *J* hand down the back of the left flat hand. Twist the left hand slightly between the two phases of this sign so that the observer can see clearly.

Memory aid: The initial suggests the word while the action indicates written work that is more than a one-page effort.

Example: Robert accepted the archaeological *project*.

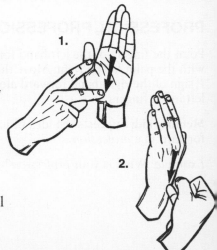

PROMINENT, CHIEF, MAIN

Raise the right *A* hand above head level with the palm facing left.

Memory aid: Points to a high elevation.

Examples: His height makes him *prominent*. He's the *main* coach.

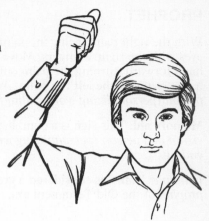

PROMISE

Touch the lips with the right index finger; then move the right flat hand down and slap it against the thumb and index-finger side of the closed left hand. *Alternative* (not illustrated): Touch the lips with the right index finger; then hold the right hand up with palm facing forward and left flat down-turned hand touching right elbow.

Memory aid: The first sign suggests the spoken word is sealed and sure. The second suggest it is backed by an oath.

Example: Paul *promised* he would not tell.

PROOF, EVIDENCE, PROVE

Touch the lips with the right index finger; then bring the right flat hand down onto the palm of the left flat hand. Both hands have palms facing up in the ending position.

Memory aid: Suggests the placing of tangible *proof* in front of a person.

Examples: What *proof* do you have? Please *prove* it.

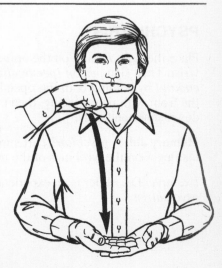

PROPHET

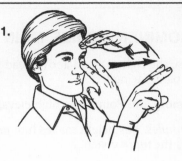

With the right palm facing in, point to the eyes with the right *V* fingers. Move the right hand forward, turning the palm outward as it passes under the left flat palm. Add the *person (personalizing word ending)* sign.

Memory aid: This sign is a combination of *vision* and *person (personalizing word ending)*.

Example: Daniel is considered a great *prophet* of the Old Testament era.

PROUD, ARROGANT, HAUGHTY

With palm facing down, place the thumb of the right *A* hand against the chest and move straight up. The head can be raised slightly with a disdainful facial expression.

Memory aid: Suggests the feelings rising up with *pride*.

Examples: I'm *proud* to be part of the group. Her manner was quite *haughty*.

PSYCHIATRIST

Place the right *P* hand on the upturned left wrist. Then sign *person (personalizing word ending)* by holding both flat open hands to the front with palms facing; then move them down simultaneously.

Memory aid: A *psychiatrist* attempts to put his finger on the workings of the mind.

Example: Dr. Miller is an experienced *psychiatrist*.

PSYCHIATRY

Place the right *P* hand on the upturned left wrist.

Memory aid: As a doctor takes a person's pulse rate, *psychiatry* studies the working of the mind.

Example: Psychiatry deals with the study, treatment, and prevention of disorders of the mind.

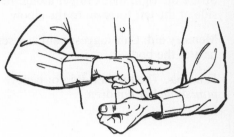

PSYCHOLOGIST

Strike the little-finger edge of the right flat hand on the palm-forward left hand between the thumb and index finger, and repeat. Add the sign for *person (personalizing word ending)*.

Memory aid: The first action of the right hand suggests a division, which can in turn suggest a person who divides and analyzes the mind.

Example: Phil is a fine *psychologist*.

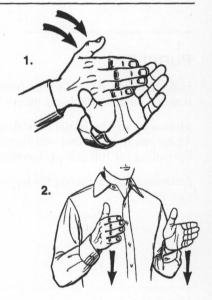

PSYCHOLOGY

Place the little-finger edge of the right flat hand on the palm-forward left hand between the thumb and index finger. The movement is often repeated.

Memory aid: The right hand suggests a dividing line between the left thumb and index finger. *Psychologists* attempt to divide and analyze the mind.

Example: I enjoyed my *psychology* class.

PUNISH

Strike the right index finger along the underside of the left forearm to the elbow.

Memory aid: Can suggest pain at a sensitive part of the body.

Example: The mother did not believe in *punishing* her children.

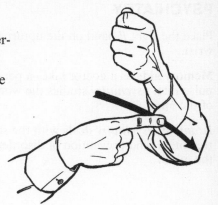

PURPLE

Hold the right *P* hand to the front and shake it at the wrist as the hand moves to the right.

Memory aid: The initial indicates the word, which requires context and simultaneous lipreading for full comprehension.

Example: The bruise on his leg turned *purple*.

PURSE, POCKETBOOK

Place the right *S* hand near the waist with palm facing down.

Memory aid: A common position for holding the strap or handle of a *purse*.

Example: I prefer a black *purse* with this outfit.

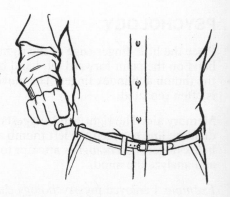

PUSH

Place both open hands to the front with palms facing forward. Push both hands forward with simulated effort.

Memory aid: The act of *pushing*.

Example: Don't *push* me.

PUT, MOVE

Point both curved open hands down to the left. Form *and* hands and move them simultaneously up and over to the right.

Memory aid: Suggests picking something up and changing its location.

Example: Put the flowers on the table.

PUZZLED, PERPLEXED

With the palm facing forward, move the right index finger backward to the forehead, and then crook the finger.

Memory aid: The crooked index finger suggests a question mark, and the location of the implied question is in the mind.

Example: She looked around with a *puzzled* expression on her face.

QUARREL, ROW, SQUABBLE

Point both index fingers toward each other in front of the chest and shake them up and down from the wrists. The hands are often moved parallel to one another, but some move them up and down alternately.

Memory aid: The hands seem to be shooting at each other.

Example: Janet and Susan had a terrible *quarrel* this morning.

QUESTION

Use the right index finger to outline a question mark in the air. Be sure to include the period.

Memory aid: A question mark obviously indicates a *question.*

Example: It is a difficult *question.*

QUIET, CALM, PEACEFUL, SERENE, SILENT, STILL, TRANQUIL

Touch the lips with the right index finger and move both flat hands down and to the sides with palm facing down. *Note:* The right index finger on the lips is often used by itself for the imperative, Be *quiet*!

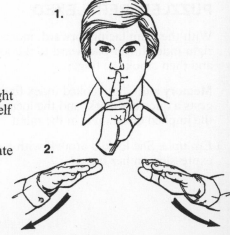

Memory aid: These are gestures that indicate *silence* and *peace.*

Example: The sea was *calm.*

QUOTE, CAPTION, CITE, SUBJECT, THEME, TITLE, TOPIC

Hold both curved *V* hands to the front with palms facing forward. Twist them simultaneously so that the palms face each other.

Memory aid: Symbolizes quotation marks.

Example: The reporter wanted a *quote* from him.

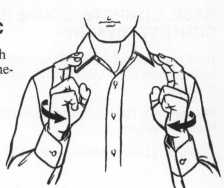

RABBI

With the palms facing in, place the fingertips of the *R* hands on the chest. Move both hands downward simultaneously to the abdomen.

Memory aid: Suggests the rabbinical prayer shawl *(tallit)* that is worn around the neck and covers the shoulders and chest.

Example: Our *rabbi* is a deep thinker.

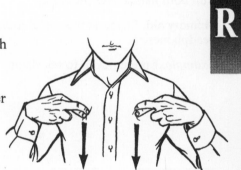

R

RABBIT

Cross the *H* hands at the wrists with the palms facing self. Bend and unbend the *H* fingers a few times. *Alternative* (not illustrated): Place the left *U* hand at the left temple and the right *U* hand at the right temple with palms facing backward. Bend and unbend the *U* fingers a few times.

Memory aid: Both signs suggest a *rabbit's* ears.

Example: She loves white *rabbits*.

RACE, COMPETE, COMPETITION, CONTEST, RIVALRY

Hold both *A* hands to the front with palms facing. Move them quickly back and forth alternately.

Memory aid: The hands can symbolize two runners *competing*.

Example: The *competition* will be strong.

RADIO

Cup both hands over the ears.

Memory aid: Suggests the use of *radio* headphones.

Example: I prefer *radio* to television.

RAIN

Touch the mouth with the index finger of the right *W* hand a few times (the sign for *water*). Move both hands down in short stages with wiggling fingers. *Note:* The first part of this sign–the sign for *water*–is not always included.

Memory aid: Suggests water descending.

Example: You'll need your boots because it's *raining*.

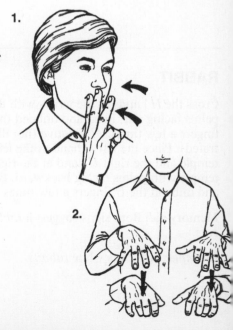

RAINBOW

Point the fingers of the right open hand toward the mouth and wiggle them (the sign for *color*). Move the right open hand over the head from left to right in an arc.

Memory aid: Suggests the colors and shape of a *rainbow*.

Example: Did you see the beautiful *rainbow* this morning?

1.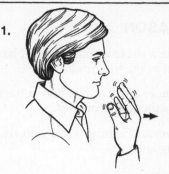

2.

RAT

Brush across the nose tip with the right *R* fingers a few times.

Memory aid: The initial indicates the word, and the action suggests the twitching of a *rat's* nose.

Example: Rats can be difficult to keep under control.

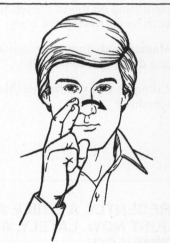

READ

Point the right *V* fingers at the left flat palm and move them downward.

Memory aid: The *V* fingers symbolize two eyes *reading* a book.

Example: Walter can *read* aloud flawlessly.

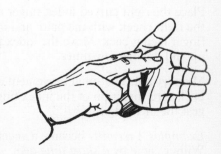

REASON

Make a circle with the right *R* hand just in front of the forehead.

Memory aid: The location at the mind indicates thought processes.

Example: Please give me your *reason* for being late.

RECEIVE

Bring both open hands together while simultaneously forming *S* hands and place the right hand on top of the left hand; then bring both hands toward the body.

Memory aid: Suggests *receiving* something and drawing it to oneself.

Example: Did you *receive* this month's schedule?

RECENTLY, A WHILE AGO, JUST NOW, LATELY, A SHORT TIME AGO

Place the right curved index finger against the right cheek with the palm and index finger facing back. Move the index finger up and down a few times.

Memory aid: The small movement and the backward direction of the index finger suggest the meaning.

Examples: I *recently* became a vegetarian. Wilbur came by *a short time ago*.

RED

Stroke the lips downward with the right index finger (or *R* fingers).

Memory aid: Suggests *red* lips or lipstick.

Example: Susan chose a *red* carpet.

REFRIGERATOR

With palms facing forward, hold both *R* hands up and shake them.

Memory aid: The initial indicates the word, and the action symbolizes coldness.

Example: This *refrigerator* is too expensive.

REFUSE, WON'T

Hold the right *S* (or *A*) hand in a natural position to the front; then move it sharply upward over the right shoulder while simultaneously turning the head to the left at the same time.

Memory aid: Suggests pulling back instead of proceeding in harmony.

Examples: She absolutely *refuses*. He *won't* cooperate.

REGULAR, REGULARLY, CONSISTENT

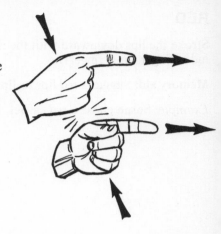

Point both *G* (or *D*) hands forward with the right hand over the left. Move both hands forward while at the same time striking the lower side of the right hand on the upper side of the left a few times.

Memory aid: The repeated striking action indicates *regularity*.

Examples: John visits me *regularly*. Please be *consistent*.

REGULATIONS

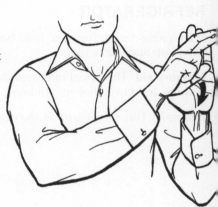

Place the index and thumb side of the right *R* hand on the front of the palm-forward left hand near the top; then move it downward in an arc until it rests at the base of the left hand.

Memory aid: The right hand seems to be pointing out written *rules* on the left hand, which can represent the printed page.

Example: The school's *regulations* seemed fair to Jennifer.

REHABILITATION

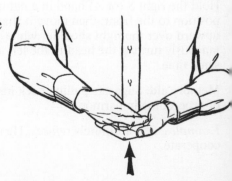

Hold the left flat hand, palm up, to the front. Place the right *R* hand on top of the left hand and lift both hands together.

Memory aid: Initialized sign for *help*.

Example: It is not easy for an alcoholic to *rehabilitate*.

REJECT

Brush the little-finger edge of the right flat hand over and beyond the hand and fingers of the left flat hand, which is palm up.

Memory aid: Suggests pushing something aside.

Example: The proposal was *rejected*.

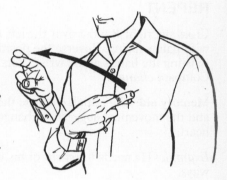

RELIGION, RELIGIOUS

Place the right *R* fingers on the heart and move the hand in a forward-upward arc, leaving the palm facing forward.

Memory aid: The initial indicates the word, and the action suggests that *religion* concerns the heart's relationship with God.

Example: Many American colleges and universities were begun by *religious* groups.

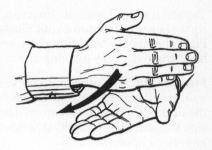

REMEMBER, MEMORY, RECALL, RECOLLECT

Place the thumb of the right *A* hand on the forehead; then place it on top of the left *A*-hand thumb.

Memory aid: Suggests knowledge that a person can keep on top of.

Examples: Do you *remember* his name? I can't *recall* it.

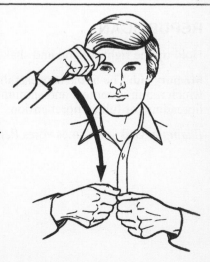

REMIND

Tap the forehead with the fingertips of the right *R* hand. *Alternative* (not illustrated): Place the right *A*-hand thumb tip on the forehead and twist it by pivoting at the wrist.

Memory aid: The initial of the first sign indicates the word, and the action suggests the idea of jogging the memory. The second sign suggests that something needs to be impressed upon the mind.

Example: Please *remind* me when it's time to go.

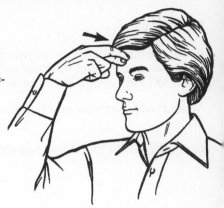

REPENT

Cross the right *R* wrist over the left *R* wrist with palms facing. Reverse the position by twisting the hands at the wrist. *Note:* Compare *change*.

Memory aid: The initials indicate the word, and the movement suggests a change of heart.

Example: He needs to *repent* of his willful ways.

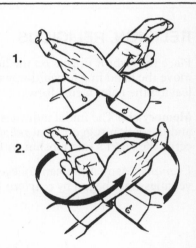

REPUBLICAN

Hold up the right *R* hand and shake it.

Memory aid: The initial suggests the word, which requires context and simultaneous lipreading for full comprehension.

Example: Dad sometimes votes *Republican*.

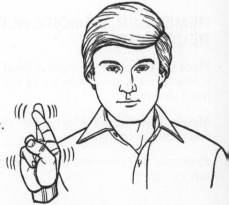

RESCUE, DELIVER, FREE, INDEPENDENT, LIBERTY, REDEEM

Cross the closed hands on the chest with palms facing in; then rotate them to the sides with palms facing forward. Most signers prefer to initialize each word. For example: Use an *R* for rescue; a *D* for deliver, etc. The observer's understanding is aided by the context.

Memory aid: Suggests breaking a rope tied around the wrists.

Examples: The crew were all *rescued.* The eagle gained its *freedom* at last.

RESIGN, QUIT

Position the right *H* fingers in the left *C* hand and pull them out sharply.

Memory aid: Can symbolize jumping out of a hole.

Example: I *resigned* my job today.

RESPECT

Move the right *R* hand in a backward arc toward the face. The head is often bowed simultaneously.

Memory aid: The initial *R* and the bowed head symbolize the meaning.

Example: Jim shows little *respect* for authority.

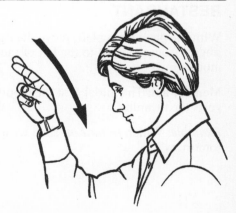

RESPONSIBILITY, BURDEN, OBLIGATION

Place the fingers of both curved hands on the right shoulder. Sometimes both *R* hands are placed on the right shoulder to sign *responsibility*.

Memory aid: Suggests the expression Carrying a load on his shoulders.

Examples: Don't neglect your *responsibility*. It's a heavy *burden* to carry.

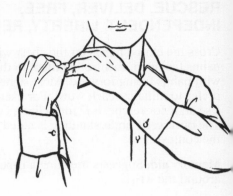

REST, RELAX, UNWIND

Fold the arms in a natural position. Sometimes the *R* hands are used. *Alternative* (not illustrated): Cross the flat (or *R*) hands over the chest.

Memory aid: The sign suggests a natural position of *rest*.

Example: I need to *relax* for a week.

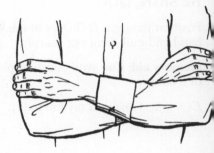

RESTAURANT

With the palm facing left, move the right *R* fingers from the right to the left of the mouth.

Memory aid: The initial *R* at the mouth suggests the meaning.

Example: Which *restaurant* shall we eat at tomorrow?

RESTLESS

Place the back of the right *V* fingers in the left palm and pivot back and forth from the wrist.

Memory aid: Symbolizes a person tossing and turning in bed.

Example: I spent a *restless* night.

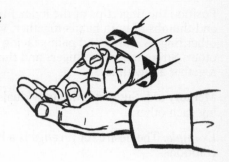

RESTROOM

Move the right *R* hand in a short arc to the right.

Memory aid: The initial indicates the word, and the movement suggests that the direction of the *restroom* is indicated.

Example: Today I wallpapered our *restroom*.

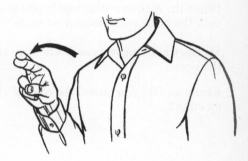

RESURRECTION

Hold the left flat hand to the front with palm facing up. Bring the right *V* hand up from a palm-up position until the *V* fingers stand on the left palm.

Memory aid: The meaning is pictured by the idea of a person rising from a lying position to a standing one.

Example: Christ's *resurrection* is celebrated at Easter.

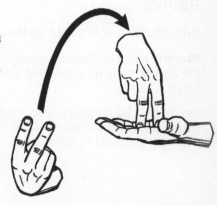

REVENGE

Position the fingertips of the index fingers and thumbs of both hands together, with the other fingers closed and palms facing each other. Strike the index fingers and thumbs together a few times.

Memory aid: Suggests two individuals striking each other.

Example: The desire for *revenge* is a harmful emotion.

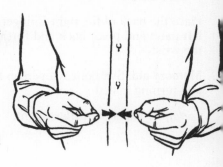

REVIVAL

Brush the *R* fingers alternately upward over the heart with circular motions.

Memory aid: Suggests an excitement of the heart.

Example: Did you attend the *revival* meeting?

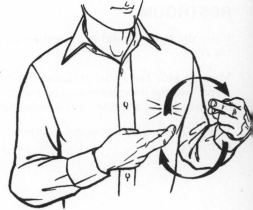

REVIVE

Bring the *R* hands straight up the chest.

Memory aid: The increasing height of the fingers suggests something getting better.

Example: The lifeguard rescued the young girl from the pool and *revived* her with artificial respiration.

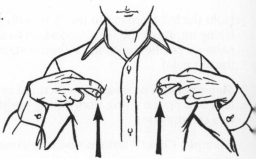

RHYTHM

Move the right *R* hand back and forth with *rhythm* in front of the chest.

Memory aid: The initial and the *rhythmic* movement suggest the meaning.

Example: Michael has an excellent sense of *rhythm*.

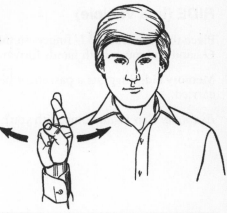

RICH, WEALTHY

Put the back of the right *and* hand in the upturned palm of the left hand; then lift it up above the left hand while simultaneously forming a curved open hand with the palm facing down.

Memory aid: Symbolizes holding a bag of money.

Example: It would be nice to be *wealthy*.

1.
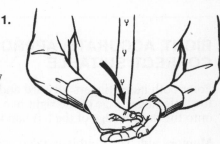

2.
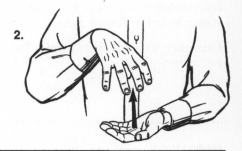

RIDE (on an animal)

Place the right upside-down *V* hand astride the index-finger side of the left flat hand. Move both hands forward together in short arcs.

Memory aid: Symbolizes a horse and its rider.

Example: Joe *rides* rodeo horses.

RIDE (in a vehicle)

Place the right curved *U* fingers in the left *O* hand and move both hands forward.

Memory aid: Suggests a passenger being carried.

Example: Can I *ride* home with you?

RIGHT, ACCURATE, APPROPRIATE, CORRECT, SUITABLE

Point both index fingers forward and bring the little-finger edge of the right hand down onto the thumb edge of the left hand.

Memory aid: The double-handed action can symbolize a person, thing, or circumstance as being doubly *right*.

Examples: You are exactly *right*. The figures are *correct*.

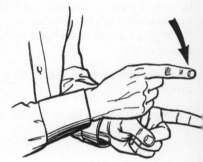

RIGHT (direction)

Move the right *R* hand toward the right.

Memory aid: The initial and direction indicate the meaning.

Example: Turn first *right*, then left.

RISE, ARISE, GET UP

Place both flat hands to the front with palms up, and move them upward once or twice.

Memory aid: Indicates the request for an audience to stand.

Example: Let all in favor please *arise*.

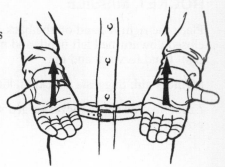

RIVER

Touch the mouth with the index finger of the right *W* hand a few times (the sign for *water*). Place both open hands with palms facing down and wiggle the fingers as both hands move either to the right or to the left. *Alternative* (not illustrated): Sign *water;* then, with palms facing, move both hands in a forward, winding movement.

Memory aid: The first sign suggests the rippling of moving water, and the second suggests the winding course of a *river*.

Example: Marty is fishing down at the *river*.

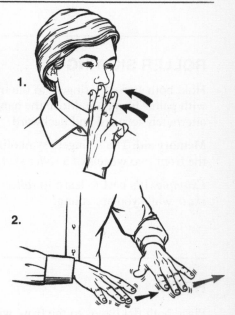

ROCK, STONE

Strike the closed right hand on the back of the closed left hand; then hold both *C* hands slightly apart with palms facing.

Memory aid: Suggests the hardness and size of a *rock*.

Example: The *rocks* are slippery.

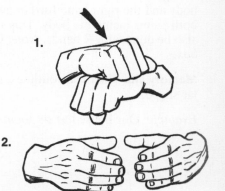

ROCKET, MISSILE

Place the right *R* hand on the back of the closed downturned left hand, and move the right hand forward and up.

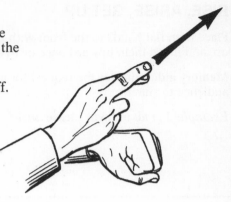

Memory aid: Suggests a *rocket* taking off.

Example: The space *rocket* surged with power.

ROLLER SKATING

Hold both curved *V* fingers to the front with palms facing up. Move the hands alternately forward and backward.

Memory aid: The *V* fingers symbolize the front two wheels of a *roller skate*.

Example: It's best to learn to *roller-skate* while you are young.

ROOM

Place both flat hands to the front with palms facing; then move the left hand close to the body and the right hand further away with both palms facing the body. This sign can also be done with *R* hands. *Note:* Compare *box*.

Memory aid: The hands outline a rectangular shape.

Example: Our house has six *rooms*.

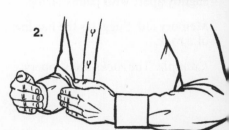

ROOSTER, COCK

Place the right thumb of the 3 hand against the forehead with the palm facing left.

Memory aid: Symbolizes the *rooster's* comb.

Example: The neighbor's *rooster* woke me at dawn.

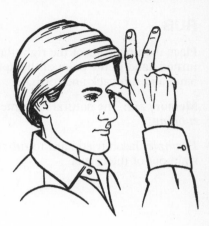

ROPE

Touch the fingertips of both *R* hands; then draw them apart to the sides with a slight wavy motion.

Memory aid: The initial suggests the word, and the movement suggests the twisted strands that make up a *rope*. *Note:* Compare *string*.

Example: Use this *rope* to tie up the boat.

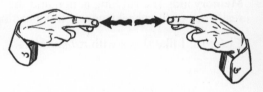

ROWING

Hold both *S* hands to the front with palms facing down. Move them simultaneously in backward circles.

Memory aid: The action of *rowing* a boat with oars.

Example: These hand blisters were caused by *rowing*.

RUB

Place the fingertips of the right flat down-turned hand in the palm of the upturned left hand and *rub* back and forth.

Memory aid: The natural movement of *rubbing*.

Example: Jason tried hard to *rub* the coffee stain out of the carpet.

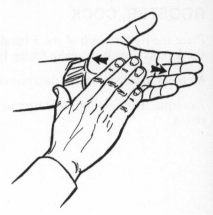

RUBBER

Rub the thumb side of the right *X* hand down the right cheek a few times.

Memory aid: The rubbing action and the resiliency of the cheek suggest the meaning.

Example: I like shoes with *rubber* soles.

RULES

Move the right *R* fingers in a downward arc from the fingertips to the base of the palm of the left flat hand.

Memory aid: The left hand can represent a printed page upon which rules are written.

Example: I think the *rules* are fair.

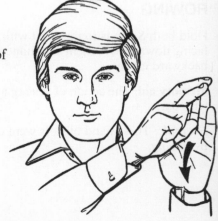

RUN, SPRINT

Place both flat hands palm to palm with the right hand under the left. Slide the right hand quickly forward. *Alternative:* Point both *L* hands forward and hook the right index finger around the left thumb. Wiggle the thumbs and index fingers as both hands move forward quickly.

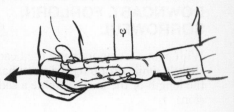

or:

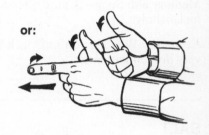

Memory aid: The quick movement of the first sign suggests the meaning. The alternative sign suggests a relay race.

Example: We'll be late if we don't *run*.

RUSSIA, RUSSIAN

Tap the flat open hands, palms down, on the sides of the waist a few times. Add the sign for *person (personalizing word ending)* when signing *Russian* with reference to a person.

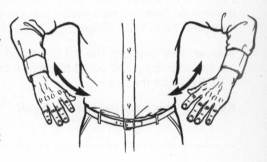

Memory aid: The sign reminds one of a *Russian* dance.

Example: Some of the world's greatest musical composers have come from *Russia*.

SACRIFICE

Place both *S* hands to the front with palms facing up, and move them in a forward-upward direction while simultaneously opening into palm-up flat hands.

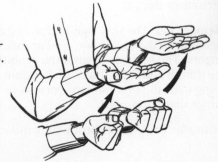

S

Memory aid: The initial indicates the word, and the movement is similar to that of the sign for *offer*. A *sacrifice* is an offering.

Example: He *sacrificed* his life for the cause.

SAD, DEJECTED, DESPONDENT, DOWNCAST, FORLORN, SORROWFUL

With palms facing in, bend the head forward slightly while dropping the open hands down the length of the face. Assume a sad expression.

Memory aid: Suggests an expression of melancholy.

Examples: Why are you *sad*? Jack has been very *despondent* lately.

SALT

Tap the right *V* fingers on the left *H* fingers a few times. Sometimes each of the right *V* fingers is used alternately for the tapping movement. Some signers prefer that the left hand also be in the *V* shape.

Memory aid: Suggests the old-fashioned custom of putting *salt* on a knife and tapping it to distribute the *salt*.

Example: This soup has too much *salt*.

SAME, ALIKE, SIMILAR

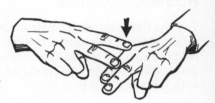

Bring index fingers together with palms facing down. *Alternative:* Move right *Y* hand either back and forth if referring to self or sideways between two similar persons or things.

Memory aid: The first sign indicates the meaning by the use of two *similar* index fingers. The second suggests the meaning by the thumb and little finger of the *same* hand being used to point out two persons or two things that are *similar*.

or:

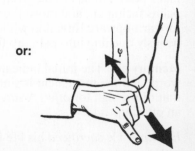

Example: Ted and his brother are *alike*.

SANDWICH

Place the fingertips of both palm-to-palm hands near the mouth.

Memory aid: The two hands suggest two slices of bread.

Example: Do you like cheese *sandwiches*?

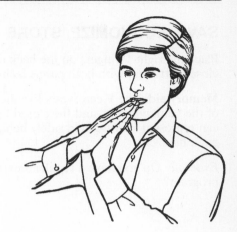

SATISFACTION, CONTENT

Place the right flat hand against the chest a short distance above the left hand in similar position. Simultaneously push both hands down a short distance.

Memory aid: Suggests that the inner feelings are settled.

Example: I'm totally *satisfied* with the result.

SATURDAY

Make a small clockwise circle with the right *S* hand.

Memory aid: The initial suggests the word, and the circular motion suggests the passing of time.

Example: Come on *Saturday*.

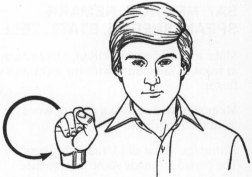

SAVE, ECONOMIZE, STORE

Place the right *V* fingers on the back of the
closed left hand with both palms facing in.

Memory aid: The *V* can symbolize the bars
of the bank window, and the closed left hand
can represent *savings* held safely behind the
bank bars.

Example: Do you have a regular *savings*
program?

SAVIOR, SALVATION, SAVE, SAFE

Cross the *S* hands on the chest with palms
facing in; then rotate them to the sides with
palms facing forward.

Memory aid: Suggests breaking a rope tied
around the wrists.

Example: Jesus Christ is the *savior* of the
Christian faith.

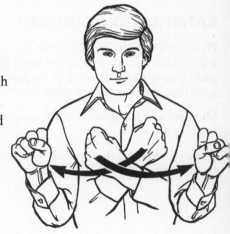

SAY, MENTION, REMARK, SPEAK, SPEECH, STATE, TELL

Make a small forward circular movement
in front of the mouth with the right index
finger.

Memory aid: Suggests a flow of words
from the mouth.

Examples: What did Grady *say* about it?
The president made some appropriate
remarks.

SCATTER, SPREAD

Hold both *and* hands together in front of the body, move them forward and to the sides as they open.

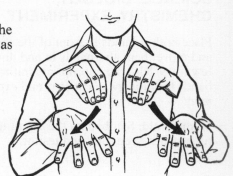

Memory aid: The movement is similar to *scattering* seed.

Example: The chickens *scattered* when the truck sped through the yard.

SCHEDULE

Hold the left open hand to the front with palm facing right. Move the right open hand down across the left hand with palms facing; then move the back of the right hand across the left hand from left to right.

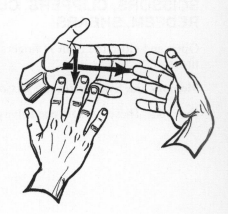

Memory aid: Suggests the vertical and horizontal lines printed on a *schedule* sheet.

Example: Can you fit another lecture into your *schedule*?

SCHOOL

Clap the hands two or three times.

Memory aid: Symbolizes a teacher clapping for attention.

Example: Andrew loves *school*.

SCIENCE, BIOLOGY, CHEMISTRY, EXPERIMENT

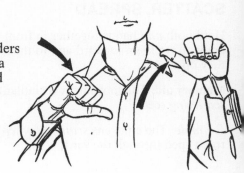

Place both *A* hands in front of the shoulders and move them alternately in and down a few times. Use the appropriate initialized hands for *biology, chemistry,* and *experiment.*

Memory aid: Symbolizes the use of test tubes when preparing and testing a solution.

Example: I found *chemistry* difficult to understand.

SCISSORS, CLIPPERS, CUT, REDEEM, SHEARS

Open and close the right *H* fingers several times.

Memory aid: Symbolizes the *scissor* action.

Example: These *scissors* need sharpening.

SCOLD, REPRIMAND, TELL OFF

Point the right index finger forward and shake it up and down.

Memory aid: A common gesture for *reprimanding* someone.

Example: The boys got a good *telling off.*

SEAL, STAMP

Drop the right *S* hand sharply into the left flat palm and raise it again.

Memory aid: Suggests the use of a rubber *stamp*.

Example: Please *stamp* this application form for me.

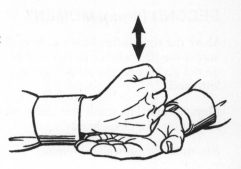

SEARCH, EXAMINE, QUEST, RESEARCH, SEEK

Make a few circular motions across the face from right to left with the right *C* hand. *Note:* Pushing the right index finger or the right *R* hand forward across the flat left palm can also be used for *examine* and *research* respectively. *Note:* Compare *check*.

Memory aid: Can symbolize the use of binoculars to enhance vision.

Example: His eyes *searched* the horizon.

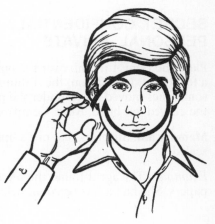

SEASON

Rotate the thumb side of the right *S* hand in a circle on the left flat palm.

Memory aid: The initial indicates the word, and the action symbolizes the fact that the cycle of *seasons* is continuous.

Example: My favorite *season* is spring.

SECOND (time), MOMENT

Move the right index finger a short distance across the flat palm of the left flat hand, but do not go beyond the little-finger edge of the left hand.

Memory aid: The small movement suggests the action of a clock hand.

Example: Please wait a *moment*.

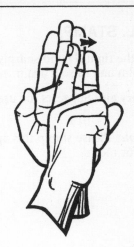

SECRET, CONFIDENTIAL, PERSONAL, PRIVATE

Place the right *A* thumb over the pursed lips a few times. In addition, the *A* thumb is sometimes moved down under the palm of the curved left hand. *Note:* Compare *hide*.

Memory aid: Suggests that one's lips are sealed.

Examples: The agent found the *secret* papers. She had a few *personal* belongings.

SECRETARY

Remove an imaginary pencil from above the right ear, and mimic handwriting action on the left flat hand.

Memory aid: Suggests a *secretary* taking notes on a pad.

Example: Sharon is an excellent *secretary*.

1.

2.

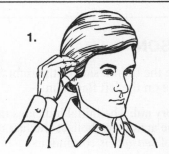

SEE, PERCEIVE, SIGHT, VISION

With the palm facing in, place the fingertips of the right *V* hand near eyes and move the right hand forward.

Memory aid: The *V* fingers suggest eyes that are actively *seeing*.

Examples: I *saw* you at the store. Having good *vision* is a great gift.

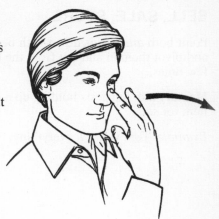

SEEM, APPARENT, APPEAR

Hold the curved right hand up with palm facing left. Turn the hand from the wrist so that the palm faces the head. The signer often glances at the hand to emphasize the meaning.

Memory aid: Suggests that what the eyes see is usually real.

Examples: The new teacher *seems* nice. *Apparently* the snow was predicted.

SELFISH, GREEDY

Point both *V* hands forward with palms facing down; then pull the hands in toward self while simultaneously bending the *V* fingers.

Memory aid: Suggests grabbing everything for oneself.

Example: Don't be so *selfish* with your money.

SELL, SALE, STORE

Point both *and* hands down with bent wrists
and pivot them in and out from the body a
few times.

Memory aid: Suggests holding up a cloth
item for *sale.*

Example: Tom will *sell* everything.

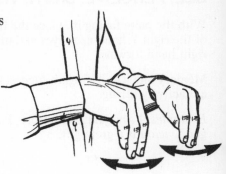

SEND

Touch the back of the left bent hand with
the fingertips of the right bent hand; then
swing the right hand forward.

Memory aid: A common gesture used
when *sending* someone on his way.

Example: I'll *send* Pete right over.

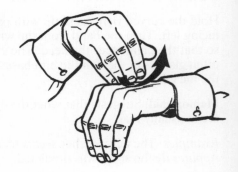

SENIOR

Touch the thumb of the open left hand with
the right index finger. *Note:* Compare *freshman, sophomore,* and *junior.*

Memory aid: Counting from the thumb, a
senior has only one year of study to complete.

Example: Jim felt relieved to be a *senior.*

SENTENCE

Touch the thumb and index fingers of each *F* hand in front of the chest. Pull the hands apart to the sides, either with a straight or wavy motion.

Memory aid: Suggests that words linked together stretch out to form a *sentence.*

Example: Write a practice *sentence.*

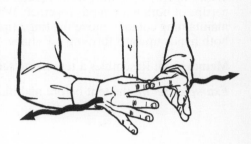

SEPARATE, APART

Place the knuckles of both bent hands together and pull the hands apart.

Memory aid: Suggests a pulling *apart.*

Examples: Keep the blue *separate* from the yellow. They *parted* after many years together. He keeps himself *apart* from others.

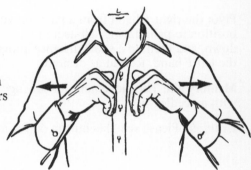

SERVE, SERVICE

Move both upturned flat hands back and forth alternately.

Memory aid: Suggests that something is being offered to another.

Example: The restaurant *service* was excellent.

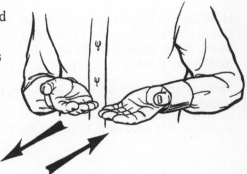

SET UP

With fingertips pointing down, touch the fingertips of both bent hands together. While maintaining contact, move the fingertips of both hands upward forming a V shape.

Memory aid: Resembles a tent being *set up*.

Example: Set up the tent before nightfall.

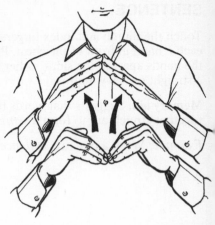

SEW

Pivot the right *F* hand from a palm-down position to palm facing self as it moves down, and then up a short distance above the left *F* hand. Repeat as desired.

Memory aid: The movement for *sewing* with a needle.

Example: Please *sew* this button on for me.

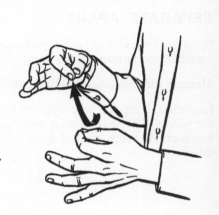

SEX, INTERCOURSE

Hold the left *V* hand to the front with palm facing up. With the palm of the right *V* hand facing down, move it down onto the left *V* hand a few times.

Memory aid: Symbolizes the uniting of two bodies.

Example: Sex education begins at home.

SHADOW

Move the right index finger outward across the right eyebrow (the sign for *black*). Hold the left hand with upturned palm and move the downturned right hand over the left hand from right to left in a partial circle.

Memory aid: Suggests that the black *shadow* of the right hand passes over the left hand.

Example: The *shadows* grew long in the afternoon sun.

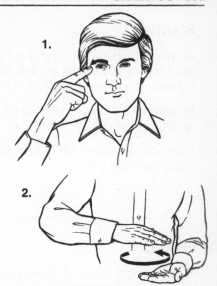

SHAME, ASHAMED

Place the back of the bent right hand against the right cheek with fingers pointing down. Twist the hand so that the fingers point backward. *Alternative* (not illustrated): Place the back of the right bent hand against the right cheek; then move the right hand forward until the palm faces up.

Memory aid: Both signs indicate the blushing of the cheek.

Example: You should be *ashamed* of yourself.

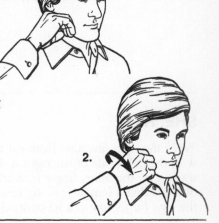

SHAMPOO

Form *A* hands with both hands and rub them on the sides of the head.

Memory aid: The movement suggests the natural action of *shampooing* one's hair.

Example: Tom needed a good *shampoo* to cure his dandruff.

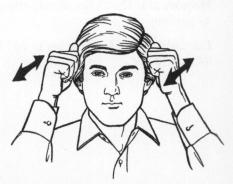

SHARE

Move the little-finger edge of the right flat hand back and forth on the left flat hand between the fingers and wrist.

Memory aid: Suggests *sharing* by separating something into two portions.

Example: Jim asked Bill to help him and *share* the work load.

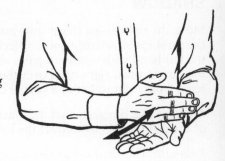

SHAVE

Move the right *Y* thumb downward on the right cheek a few times.

Memory aid: Suggests use of the old-fashioned single-blade straight razor.

Example: He hadn't *shaved* for three days.

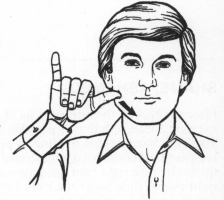

SHE, HER

Trace the right jawbone from ear to chin with the palm side of the right *A* thumb; then point the index finger forward. If it is obvious that a female is being referred to, the sign for *female* can be omitted.

Memory aid: The signer directs attention by pointing.

Examples: What is *she* going to do? Let me talk to *her*.

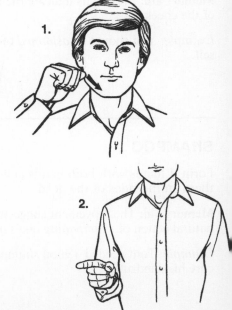

SHEEP, LAMB

Place the back of the right *V* fingers on the left forearm, which is held to the front with its hand closed and palm facing down. Open and close the right *V* fingers as they move up the forearm. To sign *lamb,* add the sign for *small.*

Memory aid: Suggests the shearing of *sheep.*

Example: Sheep are extremely docile creatures.

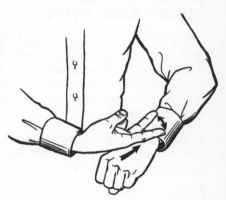

SHIP

Put the right 3 hand on the palm of the left curved hand and move both hands forward simultaneously with a wavy motion.

Memory aid: Suggests a *ship* going over the waves.

Example: Let's go for a cruise on a *ship.*

SHIRT

Grasp the *shirt* between thumb and index and pull slightly. Two hands may be used.

Memory aid: Identifies the *shirt* directly.

Example: I need three white *shirts* for the trip.

SHOCK, BEWILDER, DUMBFOUND, STUN

Circle the eyes with both *C* hands and suddenly open the hands to a wide *C* position. *Alternative* (not illustrated): Move the palm-down open flat hands down sharply from chest to abdomen while jerking the head back slightly.

Memory aid: The first sign suggests the eyes opening wide with *shock*. The second sign suggests that the whole body is jarred.

Examples: John was *shocked* at Claude's appearance. Jill seemed absolutely *stunned*.

SHOES

Strike the thumb sides of both closed hands together a few times.

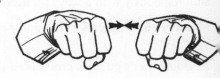

Memory aid: Can suggest the clicking of military heels.

Example: These *shoes* fit perfectly.

SHORT (height), SMALL

Place the right bent hand to the front and push down a few times.

Memory aid: The downward action indicates *shortness*.

Example: Brian is still very *short*.

SHORT (length or time), BRIEF, SOON

Cross the fingers of both *H* hands and rub
the right *H* hand back and forth over the left
index finger from fingertip to knuckle.

Memory aid: The *shortness* of the movement
suggests the meaning.

Examples: We held a *short* conversation.
Please be *brief*. Gerald will arrive *soon*. I
need a *short* piece of wallpaper.

SHOUT, CALL OUT, CRY OUT, ROAR, SCREAM

Place either the right *C* or curved open hand
in front of the mouth and move it forward
and upward with a wavy motion.

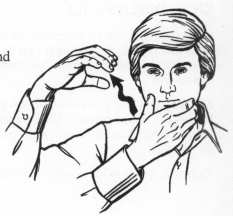

Memory aid: Suggests strong vibrations
coming from the mouth.

Examples: Please *shout* if you need help.
She *cried out* with fear.

SHOW, DEMONSTRATE, EXPRESS, EXAMPLE, REPRESENT, REVEAL

Hold the left flat hand up, with palm facing
forward. Place the tip of the right index
finger in the left palm and move both hands
forward together. All the above words may be
initialized with the right hand, which is placed
in the same position on the left flat palm.

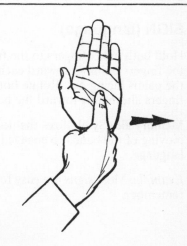

Memory aid: The right hand seems to be *showing* the left hand.

Examples: Sam *demonstrated* his skill at
basketball. How can I *express* my appreciation?

SHOWER

Place the closed *S* (or *and*) hand above the head and thrust downward toward the head while simultaneously opening the hand.

Memory aid: Symbolizes water falling on the head.

Example: I have to take a *shower*.

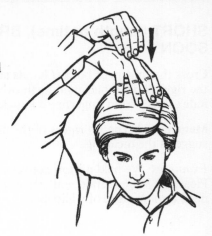

SICK, DISEASE, ILL

Place the right middle finger on the forehead and the left middle finger on the stomach. Assume an appropriate facial expression.

Memory aid: The right hand seems to be feeling the temperature of the forehead, while the left hand indicates an area of discomfort.

Example: What is her *disease* called?

SIGN (language)

Hold both index fingers to the front with the fingers pointing toward each other and the palms facing out. Rotate both index fingers alternately toward the body.

Memory aid: Symbolizes the necessary moving of the hands to engage in *sign* language.

Example: Most *signs* are easy for me to remember.

SIGNATURE, REGISTER

Slap the right *H* fingers down onto the left upturned palm.

Memory aid: The right hand identifies the place for *signing*.

Example: Sign here.

SILVER

Touch the right ear with the right index finger. Move the right hand forward to an *S* position and shake it.

Memory aid: The movement suggests earrings, and the initial indicates the word.

Example: Get the *silver* polish, please.

SINCE, ALL ALONG, SO FAR

Place both index-finger hands before the right shoulder with palms facing in, and index fingers pointing toward the shoulder. Bring both hands down and forward simultaneously until the index fingers are pointing forward with the palms facing up.

Memory aid: Suggests a continuation from a past time to the present.

Examples: Where have you lived *since* graduating? He's been preparing *all along*.

SING, HYMN, MELODY, MUSIC, SONG

Wave the right flat hand from left to right in front of the left flat hand, which has its palm facing right. The *M* hand can be used for *music*.

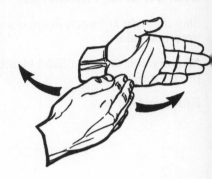

Memory aid: Symbolizes the action of a conductor.

Example: Please *sing* for us.

SISTER

Trace the right jawbone from ear to chin with the palm side of the right *A* thumb. Then point both index fingers forward and bring them together. The latter movement is the sign for *same*.

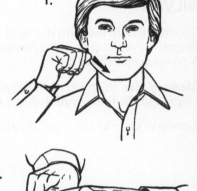

Memory aid: The two signs combined suggest a female of the same family.

Example: She has two *sisters*.

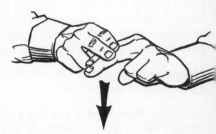

SIT, BE SEATED, SEAT

Place the palm side of the right *H* fingers on the back of the left *H* fingers; then move both hands down slightly. The sign for *be seated* is sometimes the natural one of moving both palm-down flat hands with a downward motion in front of the chest. *Note:* Compare *chair*.

Memory aid: Symbolizes a person *sitting* on a chair.

Example: Please *sit* down.

SKEPTICAL, DISBELIEF, DOUBT, I DOUBT IT, UNSURE

Crook and uncrook the right *V* fingers in front of the eyes several times. Facial expression should be appropriate. *Doubt* and *unsure* can also be signed by raising and lowering both *A* (or *S*) hands alternately at shoulder lever.

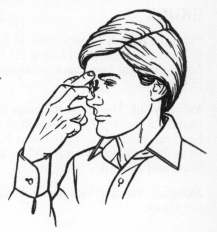

Memory aid: The bent fingers can suggest question marks.

Examples: Larry is *skeptical* about the project. To *doubt* is sometimes wise.

SKIING

Hold both *S* hands to the front and sides. Push down and backward with both hands simultaneously.

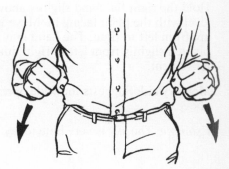

Memory aid: The position for holding and using *ski* poles.

Example: I'd like to learn how to *ski*.

SKIRT

Brush the fingers of both flat open hands downward and outward just below the waist.

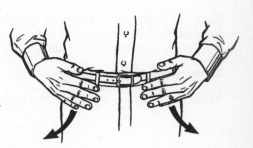

Memory aid: Can suggest the smoothing of a *skirt*.

Example: I like the *skirt* you are wearing.

SKUNK

Point the right *K* fingers down in front of the forehead with the palm facing the head. Move the right hand backward over the top of the head.

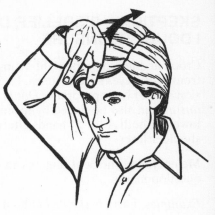

Memory aid: The initial indicates the *K* sounds of the word. The thumb of the *K* hand can also represent the nose being held to avoid smelling a skunk's odor. The action illustrates a skunk's white stripe.

Example: The dog kept a safe distance from the *skunk*.

SKY, HEAVENS, SPACE

Hold the right flat hand slightly above head level with the palm facing in. Move it in an arc from left to right. The hand may also be pivoted slightly from left to right during the movement.

Memory aid: Suggests the wide open *space* above.

Example: The *sky* is very blue today.

SLEEP, DOZE, NAP, SIESTA, SLUMBER

Place the palm side of the right open hand in front of the face and move it down to chin level while forming an *and* hand.

Memory aid: Suggests closing the eyes.

Example: A person can have too much *sleep*.

SLIDE, SLIP

Slide the right downturned *V* fingers across the left flat palm.

Memory aid: Symbolizes a person's feet *sliding*.

Example: Be careful not to *slip* on the ice.

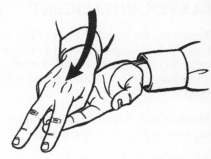

SLOW

Draw the right hand slowly upward over the back of the left hand. Begin near the fingertips and move up to the wrist.

Memory aid: The movement suggests a crawling speed.

Example: Please drive *slowly*.

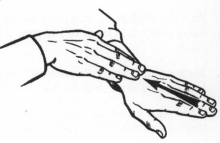

SMALL, LITTLE (measure, size), TINY

Hold both flat hands to the front with palms facing; then move them closer to each other in short stages. *Note:* Compare *little*. *Alternatives* (not illustrated): (1) Extend the right index finger and thumb and slowly close the distance. (2) Place the right bent hand at chest level and move it up and down to indicate a short person.

Memory aid: The first two descriptions suggest decreasing space, while the third suggests a person's height.

Example: She bought a very *small* doll.

SMART, BRIGHT, BRILLIANT, CLEVER, INTELLIGENT

Touch the forehead with the right middle finger while keeping the other fingers extended. Direct the middle finger outward and upward. The index finger can also be used.

Memory aid: Suggests that *brilliant* thoughts are proceeding from the mind.

Examples: Mark is a *smart* boy. It was a *brilliant* speech.

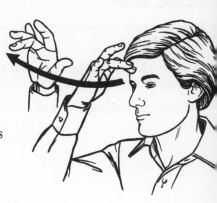

SMELL, FRAGRANCE, FUMES, ODOR, SCENT

Pass the slightly curved palm of the right hand upward in front of the nose a few times.

Memory aid: Suggests passing something in front of the nose in order to *smell* it.

Examples: I love the *smell* of sea air. An unpleasant *odor* filled the room.

SMILE, GRIN

Move the fingers (or just the index fingers) upward and backward across the cheeks from the corners of the mouth. Assume an appropriate facial expression.

Memory aid: The upturned mouth suggests the meaning.

Example: Why are you *grinning*?

SMOKING

Hold the right *V* fingers in front of the lips with palm facing in.

Memory aid: The position for holding a cigarette.

Example: Smoking is recognized as a health hazard.

SNAKE

Move the right index finger forward with a weaving movement as it passes under the downturned palm of the left flat hand. *Alternative* (not illustrated): Move the right *V* fingers forward with circular or winding movements.

Memory aid: The first sign suggests a *snake* slithering out from under a rock. The second sign suggests either the *snake's* V-shape tongue, or the fangs.

Example: It is difficult to see *snakes* that blend in with their background.

SNOW

Place the fingers and thumb of the right curved hand on the chest; then move it forward while simultaneously forming the *and* hand. Next move both palm-down open hands downward while simultaneously wiggling the fingers. *Note:* This is a combination of the signs for *white* and *rain*.

Memory aid: Suggests something white coming down like rain.

Example: It's *snowing*.

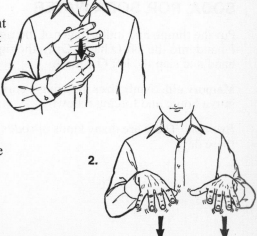

SOAP

Brush the right fingertips across the left palm several times. *Note:* Variations in the direction and manner of rubbing exist for this sign.

Memory aid: The action of rubbing the hands on *soap*.

Example: This *soap* smells refreshing.

SOCKS, HOSE, STOCKINGS

Point both index fingers down. Rub them up and down against each other alternately.

Memory aid: Suggests the use of needles for hand knitting *socks*.

Example: My *sock* has a hole in it.

SODA, POP, SODA WATER

Put the thumb and index finger of the right *F* hand into the left *O* hand. Open the right hand and slap the left *O* with it.

Memory aid: Symbolizes inserting a cork into a bottle and forcing it down.

Example: There are many kinds of *sodas* these days.

1.

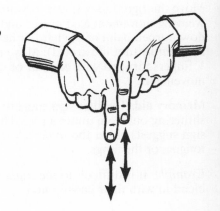

2.

SOFT, RIPE, TENDER

Hold both curved open hands to the front with palms facing up. Move the hands slowly down while forming *and* hands. Repeat a few times.

Memory aid: Suggests squeezing something to test its *softness*.

Example: His head sank into the *soft* pillow.

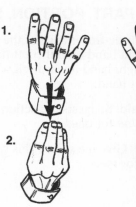

SOIL, DIRT, GROUND

Hold both curved hands to the front with palms facing up and rub the fingertips with the thumbs.

Memory aid: Symbolizes the feeling of *soil*.

Example: The *soil* in the valley is rich and good for growing vegetables.

SOLDIER, ARMS

Place the palm side of the right *A* hand just below the left shoulder and the palm side of the left *A* hand several inches below the right hand.

Memory aid: Symbolizes a *soldier* holding a rifle at the left shoulder.

Example: Mark is a well trained *soldier*.

SOME, PART, PORTION, SECTION

Place the little-finger edge of the slightly curved right hand onto the left flat palm. Pull the right hand toward self while forming a flat right hand.

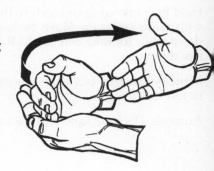

Memory aid: Suggests the action of separating a *portion* for oneself.

Examples: Give me *some*. This *section* is reserved for me.

SOMEONE, SOMEBODY, SOMETHING

Hold the right index finger up with palm facing forward and shake it slightly back and forth from left to right.

Memory aid: The index finger represents *someone* or *something*.

Example: Someone left the front door unlocked.

SOMETIMES, OCCASIONALLY, ONCE IN A WHILE, SELDOM

Hold the left flat hand at chest level with palm facing right. Touch the left palm with the right index fingertip; then move the right index finger upward to a vertical position. Repeat after a slight pause.

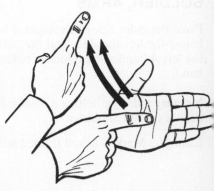

Memory aid: The slow movement indicates irregularity.

Examples: Pete *sometimes* comes early. I travel only *occasionally*. *Once in a while* I create something worthwhile. Jane *seldom* joins in with the group.

SON

Move the right hand to the forehead as though gripping the peak of a hat between the fingers and thumb; then move it forward a few inches. Next move the right flat hand with palm facing up into the crook of the bent left elbow.

Memory aid: Indicates a male baby cradled in the arms.

Example: They have one *son*.

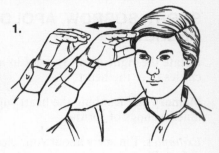

SOPHOMORE

Touch the middle finger of the open left hand with the right index finger. *Note:* Compare *freshman, junior,* and *senior.*

Memory aid: Counting from the thumb, a *sophomore* still has three years of study to complete.

Example: June has begun her *sophomore* year.

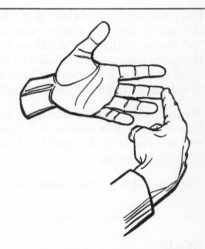

SORE, SORENESS

Put the tip of the *A*-hand thumb on the chin and twist it from side to side.

Memory aid: The action suggests an irritant to the body making one *sore.*

Example: Mike had a *sore* back after shoveling snow.

SORRY, SORROW, APOLOGY, REGRET

Rotate the right *A* (or *S*) hand in a few circles over the heart.

Memory aid: Rubbing the heart suggests inner feelings of *sorrow.*

Examples: I'm *sorry* about your election defeat. Please accept my sincere *apology.*

SOUL

Place the left *O* hand close to the body with the palm facing self. (Some place the fingers and thumb of the left *C* hand on the heart.) Bring the right open hand down over the *O* hand and raise it to shoulder level while simultaneously forming the *F* hand.

Memory aid: Suggests that the *soul* is to be found deep within a person. The position and movement of the right hand are similar to the sign for *find.*

Example: This painting has no *soul.*

SOUP

Hold the left curved hand with palm facing up; then move the slightly curved right *H* fingers into the left palm and upward a few times.

Memory aid: Suggests using a spoon to eat *soup.*

Example: Onion *soup* is my favorite.

SOUR, ACID, BITTER, TART

Place the tip of the right index finger at the corner of the mouth and twist it. It can be twisted back and forth a few times. Assume an appropriate facial expression.

Memory aid: Suggests that the lips resist something *sour* passing through them.

Example: These oranges are *bitter*.

SOUTH

Move the *S* hand downward with palm facing forward.

Memory aid: Indicates direction.

Example: The *south* wind is blowing.

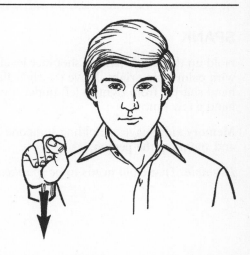

SPAGHETTI, STRING, THREAD, WIRE

Touch the tips of both *I* fingers; then make small spirals as both hands are drawn apart to the sides.

Memory aid: Suggests the length of *spaghetti, string,* or *wire.*

Examples: *Spaghetti* is difficult to eat. I need some thin *wire.*

SPAIN, SPANISH

Move both slightly curved index-finger hands toward the center of the chest from the shoulders, and interlock the index fingers. Add the sign for *person (personalizing word ending)* when signing *Spanish* with reference to a person.

Memory aid: The movement suggests the location of the typical shawl or cape worn by *Spanish* people.

Example: Madrid is the capital of *Spain*.

SPANK

Hold up the left *A* hand at shoulder level with palm facing right. Move the right flat hand sharply from right to left under the left hand a few times.

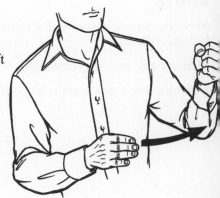

Memory aid: Suggests holding someone and *spanking* the person.

Example: That child needs to be *spanked*.

SPECIAL, EXCEPT, EXCEPTIONAL, EXTRAORDINARY, OUTSTANDING, UNIQUE

Point the left index finger up and take hold of it with the right thumb and index finger. Raise both hands together.

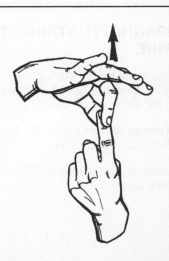

Memory aid: One finger is selected for *special* treatment.

Examples: She's a *special* person. *Except* for the weather, we would have made it.

SPEECH, ADDRESS, LECTURE, TESTIMONY

Pivot the slightly curved right hand forward and backward several times from an upright position at the front and right of the head.

Memory aid: A speaker's common gesture.

Example: The manager will *address* the employees this afternoon.

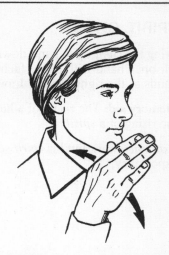

SPEND, SQUANDER, WASTE

Bring the back of the right *and* hand down into the left upturned palm. Open the right hand as it slides off the fingertips of the left hand.

Memory aid: Suggests money slipping away.

Example: Don't *squander* your money.

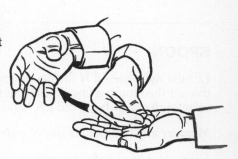

SPIDER

Interlock the little fingers of both curved open hands with the palms facing down. Move the hands forward while simultaneously wiggling the fingers.

Memory aid: Suggests a *spider's* legs in action.

Example: My wife is afraid of *spiders*.

SPIRIT, GHOST

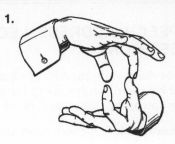

Bring the right open hand down toward the left open hand with palms facing. Create *F* hands as the right hand is drawn upward.

Memory aid: The rising of a hand suggests the rising of a *spirit.*

Example: Mark felt his *spirit* soaring with expectancy.

SPOON

Lift the right curved *H* fingers upward toward the mouth a few times from the palm of the slightly curved left hand.

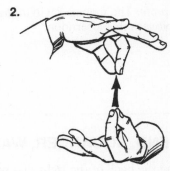

Memory aid: Symbolizes use of a *spoon.*

Example: I need a clean *spoon.*

SPRING, GROW, MATURE

Open the fingers of the right *and* hand as they pass up through the left *C* hand.

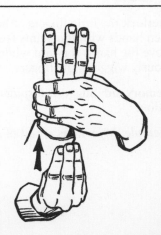

Memory aid: Suggests young shoots coming up out of the ground.

Example: Martha always looked forward to *spring.*

SQUIRREL, CHIPMUNK

Hold the curved fingers of both *V* hands to the front with palms facing. Tap the fingertips of both *V* hands against each other a few times.

Memory aid: Suggests the teeth of a *squirrel* at work on a nut.

Example: There's a *squirrel* living in that tree.

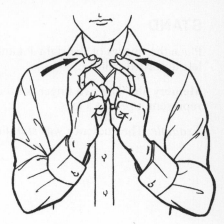

STAGE

Move the right *S* hand across the back of the left downturned flat hand from wrist to fingertips.

Memory aid: The initial indicates the word, and the action suggests someone moving across a *stage*.

Example: Acting on a *stage* always appealed to Julia.

STAMP (postal)

With the palm facing in, touch the lips with the right *U* fingers; then place them with palm facing down on the left palm. *Note:* Compare *letter*.

Memory aid: Symbolizes moistening a *stamp* and sticking it on an envelope.

Example: How many *stamps* do you have?

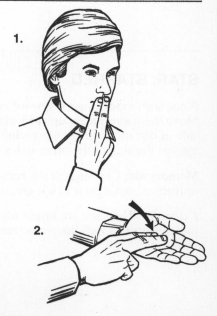

1.

2.

STAND

Place the fingers of the right *V* hand on the left upturned palm.

Memory aid: The two fingers of the *V* hand represent a person's legs.

Example: The audience was *standing*.

STAND UP, ARISE, GET UP, RISE

Begin with the right *V* fingers pointing up and the palm facing in. Make an arc with the *V* fingers until they rest in an upright position on the left upturned palm.

Memory aid: The *V* fingers represent a person's legs, and the movement indicates the meaning.

Examples: Please *stand up*. What time shall we *get up* tomorrow?

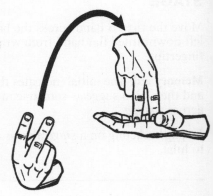

STAR, STARRED

Point both index fingers upward at eye level. Move them alternately upward, striking the side of one index finger a glancing blow against the side of the other index finger.

Memory aid: Can suggest the suns in the universe shooting out newly created *stars*.

Examples: The *stars* are bright tonight. The movie *starred* a well-known actress.

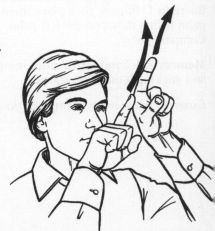

START, BEGIN, COMMENCE, INITIATE

Hold the left flat hand forward with the palm facing right. Place the tip of the right index finger between the left index and middle fingers, then twist in a clockwise direction once or twice.

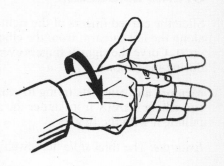

Memory aid: Can symbolize turning the ignition key to *start* a car.

Examples: Her car will not *start*. Let's *begin* the lesson.

STATE (geographical)

Place the index-finger side of the right *S* hand near the top of the left flat hand, which has its palm facing forward. Move the right *S* hand in a downward arc to the base of the left hand.

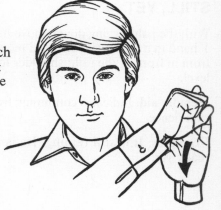

Memory aid: The initial combined with context indicates the word.

Example: What *state* do you live in?

STAY, REMAIN

Place the tip of the right *A* thumb on top of the left *A* thumb and move both hands downward together. *Alternative:* Move either one (or both) *Y* hands firmly downward.

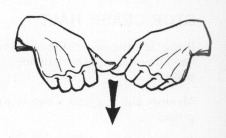

Memory aid: The movement suggests remaining in one spot.

Examples: *Stay* here. The exhilarating feeling *remained* all day.

or:

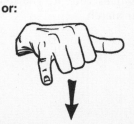

STEAL, EMBEZZLE

Slide the curved fingers of the right *V* hand along the left forearm from the elbow to wrist. Curve the right *V* fingers even more during the action.

Memory aid: Suggests trying to remove something secretly from under the arm by pulling it with the fingers.

Example: The thief *stole* her jewelry.

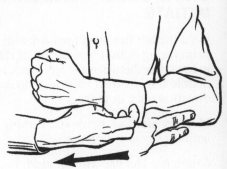

STILL, YET

With the palm facing down, move the right *Y* hand in a downward-forward movement from in front of the right shoulder to waist level.

Memory aid: Indicates continuing from past experience.

Examples: It is *still* raining. He is not ready *yet*.

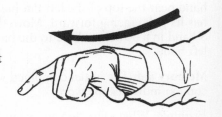

STOP, CEASE, HALT

Bring the little-finger side of the right flat hand down sharply at right angles on the left palm.

Memory aid: Suggests a barrier to *stop* progress.

Examples: Stop it! The soldiers *halted* on their march.

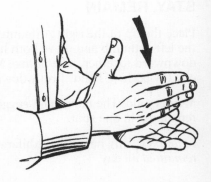

STORY, TALE

Link the thumbs and index fingers of both *F* hands and pull them apart several times. *Note:* Compare *sentence.*

Memory aid: Suggests many sentences linked together to make a *story.*

Example: What is your favorite childhood *story*?

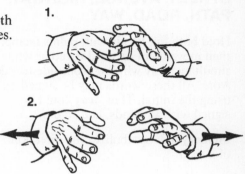

STRAWBERRY

Grasp the left index finger with the right thumb and fingers and twist back and forth. *Alternative* (not illustrated): Pull the right closed thumb and index finger forward from the mouth.

Memory aid: Both signs suggest the removal of the strawberry stem.

Example: Let's have *strawberries* and cream for dessert.

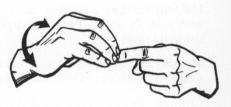

STRAY, DEFLECT, DEVIATE, WANDER

Point both index fingers forward and place them side by side with palms down. Slide the right index finger forward and off to the right.

Memory aid: Suggests the idea of a train leaving the track.

Example: The professor often *strayed* from the subject.

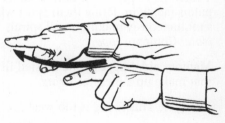

STREET, AVENUE, HIGHWAY, PATH, ROAD, WAY

Hold both flat hands with palms facing; then move them forward together while simultaneously winding from side to side. *Note:* All these words may be signed by using the initial. Thus, *way* could be signed with *W* hands, and so on.

Memory aid: Symbolizes the direction of a *road*.

Example: What *street* do you live on?

STRIKE, REBELLION, REVOLT

Hold up the right *S* hand at the right temple with palm facing in. Twist it sharply so that the palm faces out.

Memory aid: Suggests a mind that is turning away and *striking* out with new thoughts.

Example: The prisoners *rebelled* for three days.

STRING, CORD, THREAD, TWINE

Touch the fingertips of both *I* hands with palms facing in. Draw them apart while simultaneously making small spirals. *Note:* Compare *rope*.

Memory aid: Suggests the twisted fibers that make up a piece of *string*.

Example: This *string* is too weak.

STRONG, MIGHTY, POWERFUL

Move both *S* hands firmly forward and downward. *Alternative:* Describe a downward arc with the right curved hand from the left shoulder to the inside of the left elbow. *Note:* Compare *authority*.

Memory aid: The clenched fists of the first sign suggest *strength,* and the action for the alternative sign suggests a *powerful* biceps muscle.

Example: He gave the ax a *mighty* swing.

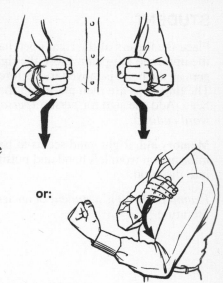

or:

STUBBORN, DONKEY, MULE, OBSTINATE

Place the right flat hand at the temple with the fingers pointing up and palm facing forward. Bend the hand forward. Sometimes two hands are used.

Memory aid: Suggests the downturned ear of an unwilling *donkey* or *mule*.

Example: He is as *stubborn* as a *mule*.

STUCK, CHOKE, TRAPPED

Place the fingertips of the right *V* hand on the neck.

Memory aid: The *V* shape around the neck suggests constriction.

Example: The rear wheels were *stuck*.

STUDENT

Place the fingers of the right open hand on the upturned left palm. Close the right fingers as the hand is moved to the forehead. The fingertips are then placed on the forehead. Add the sign for *person (personalizing word ending).*

Memory aid: Right hand seems to be taking information from left hand and putting it into the mind.

Example: David is a *student* of ancient literature.

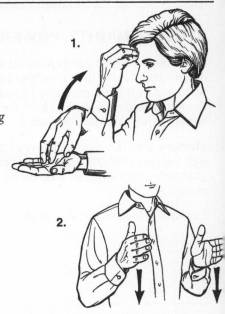

STUDY

Point the right open fingers toward the left flat hand. Move the right hand back and forth a short distance from the left while simultaneously wiggling the right fingers.

Memory aid: The right hand seems to be *studying* the left hand intently. The left hand can represent a book.

Example: How many hours a day do you *study?*

STUPID, DULL, DUMB, DUNCE

Knock the *A* (or *S)* hand against the forehead a few times with the palm facing in.

Memory aid: Knocking on the head can indicate a figuratively hollow interior.

Examples: Some rules seem *stupid.* That's a *dumb* question.

SUBTRACT, ABORTION, DEDUCT, DELETE, ELIMINATE, REMOVE

Move the bent fingers of the right hand downward across the left flat palm.

Memory aid: The right hand seems to be *removing* something from the left.

Example: Remember to *deduct* your expenses.

SUCCESS, ACCOMPLISH, PROSPER, SUCCEED

Point both index fingers toward each other or toward the head; then move them upward while simultaneously making little forward circles. End with both index fingers pointing up and palms facing forward.

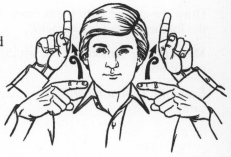

Memory aid: Suggests increasingly higher stages.

Example: He is a *successful* marathon runner.

SUFFER, AGONY, ENDURE

Slowly revolve right *S* hand in a forward circle around left stationary *S* hand. Assume appropriate facial expression. *Alternative* (not illustrated): Place thumb tip of right *A* hand on chin and pivot wrist back and forth a few times. *Note:* The sign for *patient* can combine or interchange with *suffer*.

Memory aid: The *S* hands, facial expression, and cycle action of first sign suggest continuous suffering. The alternative suggests discomforting pressure on the chin.

Example: She has *suffered* much in life.

SUITCASE

Use the right hand to imitate the movement of picking up a *suitcase*.

Memory aid: Symbolizes picking up a *suitcase*.

Example: This *suitcase* is strong.

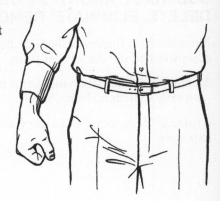

SUMMER

Draw the curved right index finger across the forehead from left to right.

Memory aid: Symbolizes the wiping of perspiration.

Example: This *summer* Bob is going to camp.

SUN

Point the right index finger forward just above head level and make a clockwise circle.

Memory aid: Symbolizes the position and shape of the *sun*.

Example: The *sun* is highest in the sky at noon.

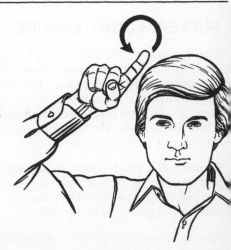

SUNDAY

Place both flat hands to the front with palms facing forward; then move them simultaneously in opposite-direction circles. The circles may be made in either direction.

Memory aid: The hand movements suggest reverential worship.

Example: I usually rest on *Sundays*.

SUNRISE, SUNSET

The flat left hand points to the right hand across the chest with palm facing down. The right *O* hand makes an upward *(sunrise)* or downward *(sunset)* arc in front of the left arm.

Memory aid: The left arm represents the horizon, and the right *O* hand represents the sun rising or setting.

Examples: We will get up at *sunrise*. What a beautiful *sunset*.

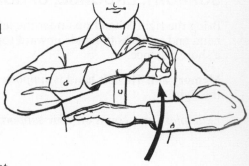

SUNSHINE

Point the right index finger above the head and make a clockwise circle; then sweep the right hand down and to the left, starting with the *and* hand and ending with an open hand.

Memory aid: Symbolizes the sun and its rays.

Example: Plants need *sunshine* to grow.

SUPERVISE, CARE, TAKE CARE OF

Cross the wrist of the right *V* hand over the wrist of the left *V* hand. Move both hands in a counterclockwise circle.

Memory aid: The fingers can symbolize four eyes watchful over all.

Example: We must *take care of* the changes in the will this week.

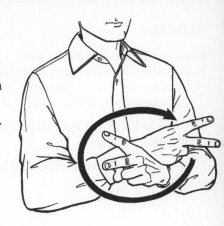

SUPPORT, ENDORSE, UPHOLD

Bring the right *S* hand up under the left *S* hand and move both hands upward together a short distance.

Memory aid: The left hand is *supported* by the right.

Example: Can I count on your *support*?

SURPRISE, AMAZE, ASTONISH, ASTOUND

Place both closed hands at the temples with index fingertips and thumb tips touching. Flick both index fingers up simultaneously.

Memory aid: Suggests wide-eyed *surprise*.

Examples: It was a *surprise* party. The result was *astonishing*.

SURRENDER, FORFEIT, GIVE UP, SUBMIT, YIELD

Hold both *A* hands to the front with palms facing down. Move both hands upward simultaneously while forming open hands with the palms facing forward.

Memory aid: Symbolizes raising hands in *surrender*.

Example: Tom quickly *submitted* to the policeman's request.

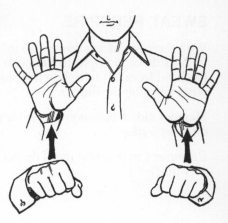

SUSPECT, SUSPICIOUS

With the palm facing in, bend and unbend the right index finger at the temple a few times.

Memory aid: The right index finger seems to be questioning the mind.

Example: I am *suspicious* of his story.

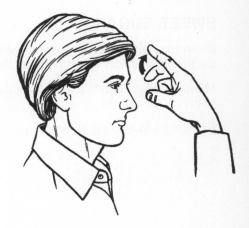

SWALLOW

With the palm facing left, trace a line downward with the right index finger from under the chin to near the base of the neck. *Note:* Compare *thirsty*.

Memory aid: Suggests the direction that liquid flows when *swallowed*.

Example: It hurts me to *swallow*.

SWEAT, PERSPIRE

With the palm facing down, rub the index-finger side of the right hand across the forehead from left to right while simultaneously wiggling the fingers.

Memory aid: A common action for wiping off *perspiration*.

Example: I'm thankful that I do not *sweat* very much.

SWEET, SUGAR

Brush the right fingertips downward over the lips. Sometimes this is done on the chin.

Memory aid: Suggests licking something *sweet* on the fingers.

Example: I love to eat *sweet* things.

SWEETHEART, BEAU, LOVER

Bring the knuckles of both *A* hands together with palms facing inward; then raise and lower both thumbs simultaneously.

Memory aid: Suggests two lovebirds billing and cooing.

Example: She had quite a few *sweethearts*.

SWIMMING

Place the slightly curved hands to the front with the backs of the hands partially facing each other and the fingers pointing forward. Move the hands simultaneously forward and to the sides.

Memory aid: The action simulates the breaststroke.

Example: Swimming regularly will keep your muscles well toned.

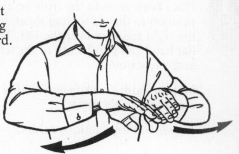

SWITZERLAND

Draw a cross on the chest with the right *C* hand.

Memory aid: Reminds one of the cross on a Swiss flag.

Example: We just returned from *Switzerland*.

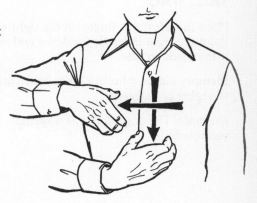

SYRUP, MOLASSES

Move the right index finger across the lips from left to right.

Memory aid: Suggests wiping sticky lips.

Example: I love *syrup* because I have a sweet tooth.

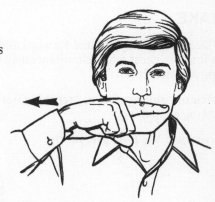

TABLE

Place both arms to the front in a similar position to that of folding them, but put the right forearm over the left. The right flat hand can pat the top of the left forearm a few times.

Memory aid: Can suggest resting the arms on a *table* surface.

Example: I love antique *tables*.

TAIL, WAG

Place the left index finger on the right wrist. Point the right index finger down and swing it from side to side.

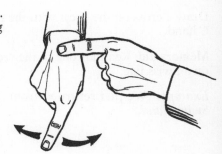

Memory aid: Symbolizes an animal's *tail* swinging or *wagging*.

Example: The dog's *tail* was wagging vigorously.

TAKE

Place the right open hand forward and draw it into the chest while simultaneously forming a closed hand.

Memory aid: Symbolizes reaching out and *taking* something.

Example: We *took* everything.

TALK, COMMUNICATE, CONVERSATION, DIALOGUE, INTERVIEW

Move both index fingers back and forth from the lips alternately. Use *C* hands for *communicate,* and *conversation, D* hands for *dialogue,* and *I* hands for *interview.*

Memory aid: Suggests the words coming and going in a *conversation.*

Example: Our *conversation* was profitable.

TALL

Place the right index finger on the left flat palm and move it straight up.

Memory aid: The upward movement suggests the meaning.

Example: My cousin is very *tall.*

TAN

Move the right *T* hand down the right cheek.

Memory aid: The initial *T* plus the location of the sign suggests the meaning.

Example: I want a good *tan* this summer.

TASTE

Touch the tip of the tongue with the right middle finger. The other fingers of the right open hand are extended.

Memory aid: The finger is giving the tongue a sample *taste*.

Example: What does the flavor *taste* like?

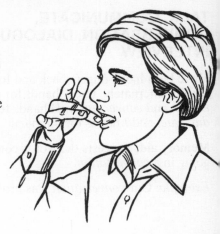

TEA

Rotate the right thumb and index finger over the O shape of the left hand.

Memory aid: Symbolizes stirring *tea* in a cup.

Example: I like a strong cup of *tea*.

TEACH, EDUCATE, INDOCTRINATE, INSTRUCT

Position both open *and* hands at the front and sides of the head, then move them forward while simultaneously forming closed *and* hands.

Memory aid: Suggests pulling out knowledge from the mind and presenting it to others.

Example: Tim will *instruct* you correctly.

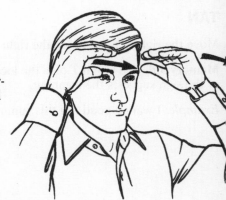

TEACHER

Position both open *and* hands at the front and sides of the head; then move them forward while simultaneously forming closed *and* hands. Add the sign for *person (personalizing word ending)*.

Memory aid: Symbolizes a person who pulls out knowledge from the mind and presents it to others.

Example: A *teacher* can have great influence upon students.

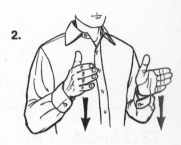

TEAR, RIP, SEVER

Place both thumb tips in the crook of their respective index fingers. The remaining fingers are closed, with the palms facing each other. Move the right hand sharply toward self and the left hand forward.

Memory aid: Suggests the action of *tearing* paper.

Example: Please don't *tear* the newspaper.

TEASE, DAMAGE, PERSECUTE, RUIN, SPOIL, TORMENT

Hold both closed hands to the front with both thumb tips in the crooks of their respective index fingers. Move the knuckles of the right hand forward across the top of the left hand. Repeat according to emphasis required.

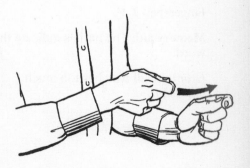

Memory aid: The use of the knuckles suggests repeated harassment.

Examples: Don't *tease* your sister. Gossip can be *damaging*. All this attention is *spoiling* me.

TEETH

Move the tip of the right index finger sideways across the front teeth.

Memory aid: The *teeth* are indicated by pointing to them.

Example: Her *teeth* are healthy.

TELEPHONE, CALL

Position the *Y* hand at the right of the face so that the thumb is near the ear and the little finger near the mouth.

Memory aid: The natural position for using the *telephone*.

Example: What is your *phone* number?

TELEVISION

Fingerspell *T-V*.

Memory aid: The initials indicate the word.

Example: Jill watches too much *television*.

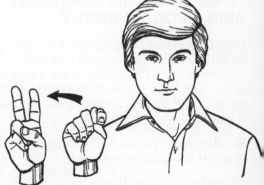

TEMPERATURE, FEVER, THERMOMETER

Rub the right index finger up and down over the central part of the left upright index finger.

Memory aid: Symbolizes the rising and falling of the mercury in a *thermometer*.

Example: June had a *fever* last night.

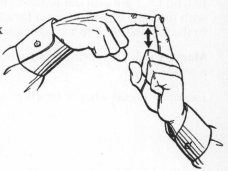

TEMPLE (building)

Place the heel of the right *T* hand on the back of the closed left hand.

Memory aid: The initial indicates the word, and the position suggests that a *temple* has a solid foundation.

Example: We go to the *temple* every Saturday.

TEMPT, ENTICE

Tap close to the left elbow with the right curved index finger.

Memory aid: Suggests a secretive and persistent method of attracting attention.

Example: It's sure *tempting* to have another doughnut.

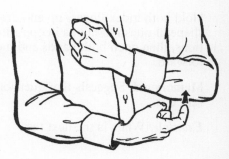

TENNIS

Extend the right arm out to the right side with the hand closed. Move it forward across to the left and back to the right again.

Memory aid: The position and action of a *tennis* player.

Example: I need a better *tennis* racket.

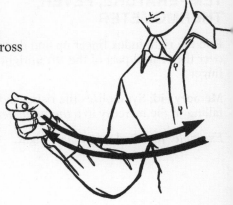

TENT

Form the point of a triangle with the fingers of both *V* hands, then separate them by moving them down and to the sides a short distance. To sign *camp*, repeat the sign a few times while moving the hands to the right.

Memory aid: Symbolizes the shape of a *tent*.

Example: Do you have any *tents*?

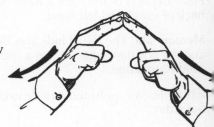

TEST, EXAMINATION, QUIZ

Hold both index fingers up and draw the shape of question marks in opposite directions, then open both hands and move them forward.

Memory aid: Suggests that questions are sent out.

Example: When is the next *test*?

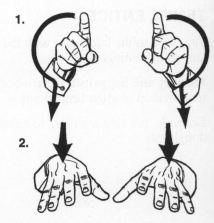

TESTAMENT, WILL (legal statement)

Place the index and thumb side of the right *T* hand on the front of the palm-forward left hand near the top, then move it downward in a small arc until it rests at the base of the left hand. Use the right *W* hand for signing *will*.

Memory aid: The right hand seems to be drawing attention to written statements on the left hand, which can represent the printed page.

Example: Have your parents made their *will* yet?

THAN

Hold the left flat or curved hand to the front with palm facing down. Brush the index-finger edge of the right flat hand down off the fingertips of the left hand.

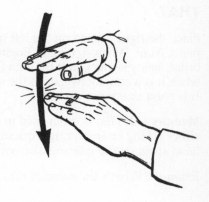

Memory aid: The right hand is both above and below the left hand, thus showing a comparison.

Example: Jim is a better craftsman *than* Pete.

THANKS, THANK YOU, YOU'RE WELCOME

Touch the lips with the fingertips of one or both flat hands, then move the hands forward until the palms are facing up. It is natural to smile and nod the head while making this sign.

Memory aid: A natural expression of affection used when one is grateful.

Example: *Thanks* for your concern.

THANKSGIVING

Touch the lips with the fingertips of one or both flat hands; then move the hands forward until the palms are facing up. Hold both curved hands to the front with palms facing down; then move them forward while simultaneously forming flat hands that point forward with the palms facing up. This sign is a combination of the signs for *thanks* and *give*.

Memory aid: Suggests a natural expression of affection when one is grateful, and a response made by giving.

Example: Thanksgiving is next week.

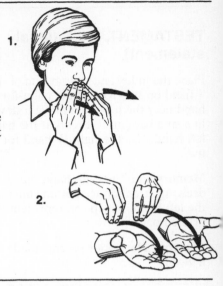

THAT

Place the right *Y* hand on the left upturned palm. *Note:* When signing in English syntax order, many signers omit the sign for *that* when it is a conjunctive, as in the sentence, It is good *that* you trust me.

Memory aid: *That* is often used in relation to either asking or answering a question. The *Y* hand suggests the interrogative *why*?

Example: What's the name of *that* building?

THEATER

Rotate both *A* hands alternately toward the body with the palms facing each other. Form the point of a triangle at head level with both flat hands; then move them apart and straight down simultaneously with the fingers pointing up.

Memory aid: This sign is a combination of the signs for *drama* and *house*.

Example: Don't forget to buy this season's *theater* tickets by Saturday.

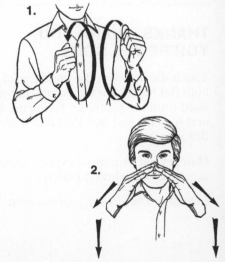

THEN

Point the left *L* hand forward with palm facing right; then touch the left thumb and index finger with the right index finger.

Memory aid: First one location, and *then* another.

Example: First we searched the main streets, *then* the back streets.

THERE

Point with the right index finger when being specific. For a more general reference, move the right flat hand to the right with palm facing forward.

Memory aid: A gesture indicating location.

Example: The oak tree is over *there*.

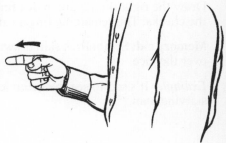

THEY, THEM, THESE, THOSE

Point the right index finger forward or in the direction of the persons or objects referred to, then move it to the right.

Memory aid: The signer directs attention by pointing.

Examples: They are in a jubilant mood today. I see *them* over there.

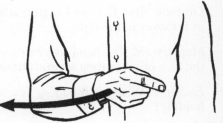

THIEF, BANDIT, BURGLAR, CROOK, ROBBER

Place the index-finger side of both *H* hands under the nose; then draw both hands outward.

Memory aid: Suggests a false mustache that can be used as a disguise.

Example: Our store was held up by *bandits* yesterday.

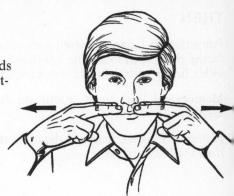

THIN, GAUNT, LEAN, SKINNY

Draw the right thumb and index finger down the cheeks. The remaining fingers are closed.

Memory aid: Symbolizes skin drawn tightly over the face.

Example: It's sad to see the *gaunt* look of a starving man.

THING, SUBSTANCE

Drop the right flat hand slightly a few times as it moves to the right.

Memory aid: The hand movements suggest the idea of presenting several alternatives.

Example: Where is the *thing* you were holding?

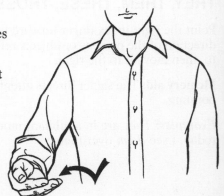

THINK, CONSIDER, REFLECT, SPECULATE

Make a counterclockwise circle with the right index finger just in front of the forehead. This can be done simultaneously with two hands if more intensity of meaning is required.

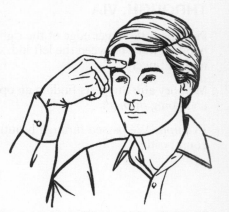

Memory aid: The circular motion indicates action in the mind.

Examples: I am *thinking*. Nancy *reflected* upon her past.

THIRSTY, PARCHED

With the palm facing in, trace a downward line with the right index finger by starting under the chin and ending near the base of the neck. *Note:* Compare *swallow*.

Memory aid: Suggests the direction liquid flows when swallowed.

Example: Exercise makes me *thirsty*.

THIS

Put the right index fingertip into the palm of the flat left hand if something specific is indicated. Drop both *Y* (or flat) hands together with palms facing up if something more abstract is indicated. Sometimes the right *Y* hand by itself is moved downward with palm facing down.

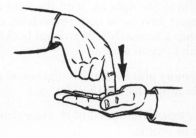

Memory aid: The right index finger points to an object in the left hand. Or both hands seem to be holding something for others to see.

or:

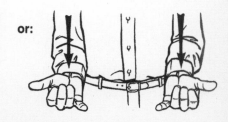

Examples: Specific —*This* is my pencil.
Abstract—What is *this* message you have?

THROUGH, VIA

Pass the little-finger edge of the right flat hand forward between the left index and middle fingers.

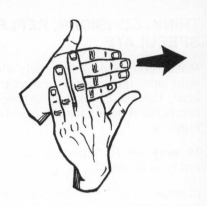

Memory aid: Suggests finding an opening and going *through*.

Example: We passed *through* beautiful countryside.

THROW, TOSS

Place the right *A* hand beside the right side of the head. Move the right hand quickly forward while simultaneously opening it.

Memory aid: A common motion for *throwing*.

Example: Throw the ball here.

THUNDER

Point to the right ear with the right index finger; then move both palm-down closed hands alternately forward and backward with forceful action.

Memory aid: Symbolizes the sound and vibrating effect of *thunder*.

Example: The sound of *thunder* scares a lot of people.

1.

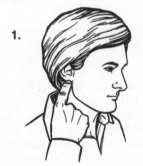

2.

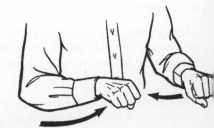

THURSDAY

Make a small clockwise circle with the right *H* hand. *Note:* This is sometimes signed with the manual *T* and *H*, with or without rotation.

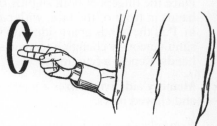

Memory aid: The initial suggests the word, and the circular motion suggests the passing of time.

Example: Come on *Thursday*.

TICKET

Squeeze the little-finger edge of the left palm between the right curved *V* fingers. *Alternative* (not illustrated): Touch the index and thumb tips of both *C* hands with the other fingers closed and palms facing each other. Draw the fingers apart while moving hands to the sides; then bring the thumbs and index fingers together.

Memory aid: The first sign symbolizes the punching of a *ticket* by an official. The second suggests the shape of a *ticket*.

Example: We need four *tickets*, please.

TIE (a knot)

Place both thumb tips in the crook of their respective bent index fingers, with the other fingers closed. Move the hands alternately in small forward circles; then pull the hands apart to the sides.

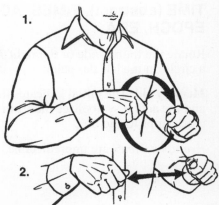

Memory aid: Symbolizes the movements of *tying a knot.*

Example: There are many different ways to *tie a knot.*

TIGER

Place the fingers of both slightly curved open hands in front of the face, with palms facing in. Pull the hands apart sideways while simultaneously changing to claw-shape hands. Repeat a few times.

Memory aid: Symbolizes a *tiger's* stripes and clawed paws.

Example: Our zoo has two *tigers*.

TIME, CLOCK, WATCH

The right curved index fingertip is made to tap the back of the left wrist a few times.

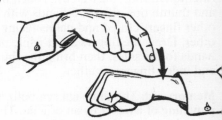

Memory aid: An obvious reference to a *wristwatch*.

Examples: What is the *time*? My *watch* is a present from Sam.

TIME (abstract), TIMES, AGE, EPOCH, ERA

Rotate the thumb side of the right *T* hand in a circle on the left flat palm.

Memory aid: The initial indicates the word, and the action symbolizes the truth that the clock stops for no one.

Example: Times are unpredictable.

TIRED, EXHAUSTED, FATIGUED, WEARY

Place the fingertips of both bent hands on the upper chest, then pivot the hands downward while maintaining contact with the chest. The fingertips point upward in the final position.

Memory aid: Suggests that the body is ready to drop in *exhaustion.*

Example: Joe *wearily* dragged himself up the stairs.

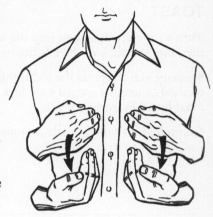

TITHE

Point the right index finger up; then lower the hand to an *A* position and pivot the hand slightly back and forth sideways.

Memory aid: The signs for *1* and *10* indicate the fraction ¹⁄₁₀.

Example: She was surprised to find that *tithing* her income was financially beneficial.

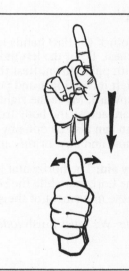

TO

Hold the left index finger up and move the right index finger toward it, but do not touch fingertips.

Memory aid: Suggests the concept of moving closer.

Example: Are you going *to* the concert?

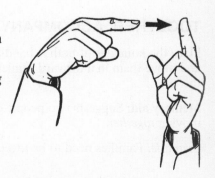

TOAST

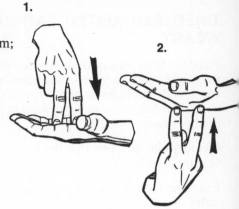

Thrust the right *V* fingers into the left palm; then into the back of the left flat hand.

Memory aid: Suggests the old-fashioned method of using a special long fork to *toast* bread in front of a fire.

Example: I love marmalade on *toast*.

TODAY

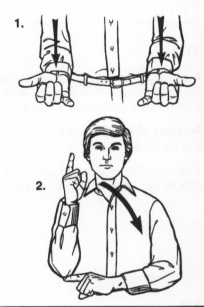

Drop both *Y* (or flat) hands together in front of the chest. Point the left index finger to the right with palm down. Rest the right elbow on the left index finger and point the right index upward. Move the right arm in a partial arc across the body from right to left. This sign can also be done by combining either *now* and *day*, or *this* and *day*.

Memory aid: The horizontal left arm indicates the horizon, while the right arm symbolizes the movement of the sun.

Example: We must finish *today*.

TOGETHER, ACCOMPANY

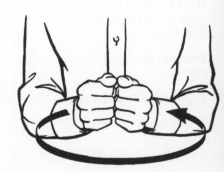

Place the knuckles of both *A* hands together and move them in a forward semicircle to the left.

Memory aid: Suggests two people or things moving *together*.

Example: Families need to be *together*.

TOILET, BATHROOM

Shake the right *T* hand in front of the chest with the palm facing forward. See also *restroom*.

Memory aid: The shaking motion suggests the need to meet a physical requirement.

Example: May I use your *bathroom*?

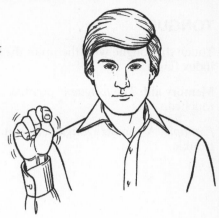

TOMATO

Stroke the lips downward with the right index finger. Hold the left *and* hand with fingers pointing right; then bring the right index finger down past the fingers of the left *and* hand.

Memory aid: Suggests the red color of a *tomato* followed by the action of slicing it with a knife.

Example: There's nothing like homegrown *tomatoes*.

1.

2.

TOMORROW

Touch the right *A* thumb on the right cheek or chin area; then make a forward arc.

Memory aid: The forward movement indicates the future.

Example: What shall we do *tomorrow*?

TONGUE

Touch the tongue with the tip of the right index finger.

Memory aid: The *tongue* is pointed to and touched.

Example: A person's *tongue* can cause much trouble.

TOO, ALSO

Bring both index fingers together with the palms facing down. Repeat slightly to the left. *Note:* Compare *same* and *as*.

Memory aid: The repeated action indicates something extra.

Examples: Is he an expert, *too*? Jim and Barbara are *also* coming.

TOOTHBRUSH, BRUSH TEETH

Shake the right horizontal index finger up and down in front of the teeth.

Memory aid: The action for cleaning teeth.

Example: I'd like a blue *toothbrush*.

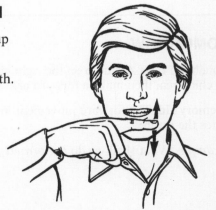

TOTAL, AMOUNT, SUM

Hold the left open curved hand over the right open curved hand with palms facing. Bring the hands together while simultaneously forming *and* hands until the fingertips touch.

Memory aid: The fingers can represent several individual *amounts* that are brought together.

Example: What is your *total*?

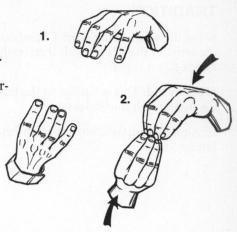

TOUCH, CONTACT

Touch the back of the left downturned curved hand with the right middle finger. The other fingers of the right open hand are extended.

Memory aid: A gesture of *touching.*

Example: Don't *touch* the cookies.

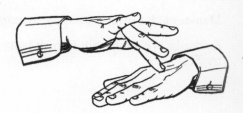

TOWARD

Hold the index finger up and move the right index finger toward it, but do not touch fingertips.

Memory aid: Suggests the concept of moving closer.

Example: The basketball team was headed *toward* certain victory.

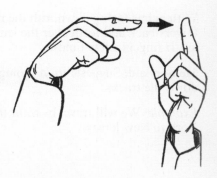

TRADITION

Bring the wrist of the right *T* hand down on the wrist of the left *S* hand; then push both hands down slightly.

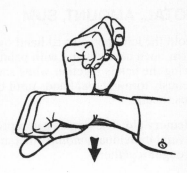

Memory aid: This is similar to the basic sign for *habit,* with the initial added.

Example: Traditions are strong in Pete's family.

TRAFFIC

With the palms facing, move the open hands back and forth a few times.

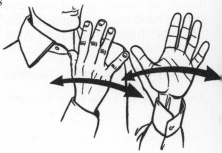

Memory aid: Symbolizes two-way *traffic.*

Example: We got caught in rush-hour *traffic.*

TRAIN, RAILROAD

With palms facing down, rub the right *H* fingers back and forth over the length of the left *H* fingers a few times.

Memory aid: Suggests *trains* going up and down the tracks.

Example: We will travel by *train* from New York to New Jersey.

TRAVEL, JOURNEY, TRIP

With right palm facing down, imitate traveling along a winding road with right curved *V* fingers. *Alternative* (not illustrated): Point down with the right index finger and up with the left. Rotate them around each other in small counterclockwise circles as they are moved to the left.

Memory aid: In the first sign the *V* hand represents the legs of a person who is going somewhere. The alternative sign suggests a continuous moving around.

Example: Will you *travel* with me?

TREASURER

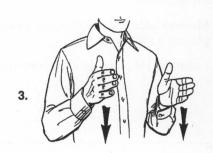

Bring the back of the *and* hand down onto the palm of the left flat hand a few times. Make a scooping movement with the right hand from the fingertips to the heel of the left hand. Finally, bring both flat hands down simultaneously with palms facing. This is a combination of *money, collection,* and *person (personalizing word ending).*

Memory aid: A person who collects money.

Example: A *treasurer* must be elected.

TREE, BRANCH, FOREST, WOODS

Place the right elbow in the left palm with the right fingers pointing up. Pivot the right wrist and wiggle the fingers. Initials can be used for *branch, forest,* and *woods.*

Memory aid: The forearm symbolizes a *tree* trunk, while the moving hand and fingers suggest the *branches* and leaves.

Example: Climbing *trees* can be dangerous.

TRINITY

With palms facing in, slide the right 3 hand down through the left C hand. Bring the right hand from beneath the left C hand and point the right index finger up.

Memory aid: Symbolizes the concept that three become one.

Example: The doctrine of the *trinity* is of Christian origin.

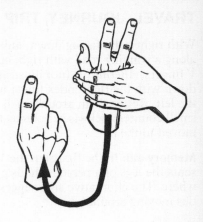

TROMBONE

Place the thumbs of both A hands in the crooks of their respective index fingers. Hold the left hand near the mouth and move the right hand forward and backward in front of the left hand.

Memory aid: The position and movement for playing a *trombone*.

Example: He plays the *trombone* too loud.

TRUE, AUTHENTIC, GENUINE, REAL, REALLY, SINCERE, SURE, TRUTH, VALID

With palm facing left, move the right index finger in a forward arc from the lips.

Memory aid: Symbolizes *true* and straightforward communication.

Examples: We need to know the *true* story. It's a *sure* thing.

TUESDAY

Make a small clockwise circle with the right
T hand.

Memory aid: The initial suggests the word,
and the circular motion suggests the passing
of time.

Example: Come on *Tuesday*.

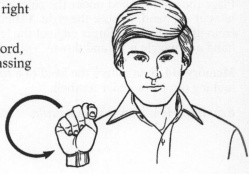

TURKEY

With the palm facing down, shake the right
Q fingers back and forth in front of the chin;
then move the *Q* hand forward and down
with a few small spiraling movements.

Memory aid: Symbolizes the shaking wattle
that hangs from a *turkey's* throat.

Example: Mother bought a large *turkey*
today.

TURN

Hold the left index finger upward with palm
facing in. Move the right index finger around
the left index finger in counterclockwise
circles while simultaneously turning the left
index finger slowly around in the same
direction.

Memory aid: Can symbolize two gears
turning at different speeds.

Example: The model *turned* around gracefully.

TURTLE, TORTOISE

Place the right *A* hand under the palm-down left curved hand. Expose the right *A* thumb from under the little-finger edge of the left hand and wiggle it up and down.

Memory aid: Symbolizes the head of a *turtle* looking out from under its shell.

Example: He is slower than a *turtle*.

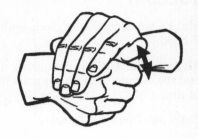

TWICE

Hold the left flat hand at chest level with the palm facing right. Touch the left palm with the second finger of the right *2* hand. Move the right hand upward to a vertical position.

Memory aid: The use of two fingers indicates the meaning.

Example: I tried to contact Phil *twice* today.

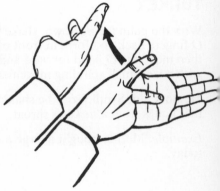

TWINS

Place the thumb side of the right *T* hand first on the left side of the chin, then on the right.

Memory aid: The two *T* positions on the same chin indicate the meaning.

Example: I have a *twin* sister.

UGLY, HOMELY

Cross the index fingers just below the nose with the remaining fingers closed; then bend the index fingers as the hands are pulled apart to the sides. Sometimes only one hand is used. Assume an appropriate facial expression by frowning.

Memory aid: Suggests facial features that are distorted and pulled out of shape.

Example: She thought the dress was *ugly*.

UMBRELLA

Hold the right closed hand over the left closed hand; then raise the right hand a short distance.

Memory aid: Symbolizes opening an *umbrella*.

Example: We don't sell many *umbrellas* in the summer.

UNCLE

With the palm facing forward, place the right *U* hand close to the right temple and shake back and forth from the wrist.

Memory aid: The initial *U* is placed near the *male* sign position.

Example: My *uncle* was an excellent boxer in his youth.

UNDERSTAND, COMPREHEND

With the palm facing in, flick the right index finger up vertically in front of the forehead. *Alternative* (not illustrated): A more formal sign touches the forehead with the *S* hand before flicking up the index finger.

Memory aid: Both signs suggest a figurative light of *understanding* coming on in the mind.

Example: Are you sure you *understand*?

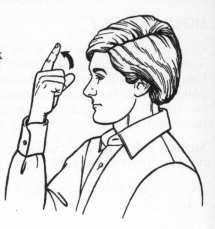

UNFAIR, UNJUST

With palms facing, strike the fingertips of the left *F* hand with the fingertips of the right *F* hand in a downward movement.

Memory aid: The left hand is treated *unfairly*.

Example: That's an *unfair* evaluation.

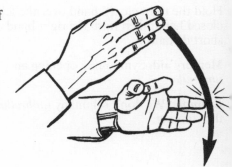

UNITED STATES

With one flowing movement make a three-quarter counterclockwise circle with the right *U* hand, repeating the movement with the right *S* hand as the hand moves to the right.

Memory aid: The initials indicate the words, which require context and simultaneous lipreading for full comprehension.

Example: When did you emigrate to the *United States*?

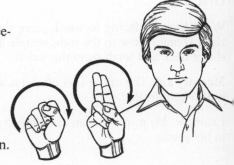

UNIVERSE

Make a forward circle with the right *U* hand around the left *U* hand. End with the little-finger edge of the right *U* hand resting on the thumb side of the left *U* hand. *Note:* Compare *world*.

Memory aid: The initials indicate the word, and the action symbolizes the movement of the *universe*.

Example: The *universe* seems endless.

UNTIL

Hold the left index finger up with palm facing inward. Move the right index finger in a slow forward arc until it touches the tip of the left index finger.

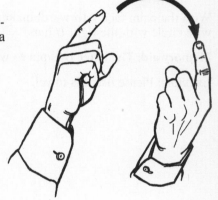

Memory aid: Wait *until* contact is made.

Example: Do your best *until* I get there.

UP

Hold up the right index finger with palm facing forward and move it up slightly. This word is sometimes fingerspelled.

Memory aid: Pointing upward.

Example: Can you reach *up* to that shelf?

UPSET

Place the palm of the right flat hand on the stomach; then move the hand forward and face the palm up.

Memory aid: Symbolizes a stomach turning over in nausea.

Example: She was too *upset* to think clearly.

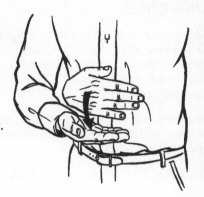

USE, USEFUL, UTILIZE

With the palm facing forward, make a clockwise circle with the right *U* hand.

Memory aid: The letter *U* is put to work.

Example: Please *use* this towel.

USUALLY, USED TO

Point the fingers of the right *U* hand upward. Place the right wrist on the wrist of the left downturned closed hand; then push both hands down slightly.

Memory aid: This is similar to the basic sign for *habit,* with the initial added.

Examples: She *usually* arrives late. I *used to* play baseball.

VACATION, HOLIDAY, LEISURE

Place both thumbs at the armpits and wiggle all the fingers.

Memory aid: A common symbol of *leisure.*

Example: She goes on *vacation* next week.

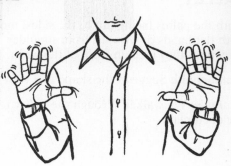

VAIN (characteristic), VANITY

With palms facing in, point the two *V* hands at the face, and bend and unbend the *V* fingers simultaneously a few times.

Memory aid: The *V* hands suggest two pairs of eyes looking at the person.

Example: Have you noticed how *vain* Mary is?

VALENTINE

Outline a heart shape on the chest with the fingers of both *V* hands.

Memory aid: The *V* hands and the heart shape indicate the meaning.

Example: Let's have a *Valentine's* Day party.

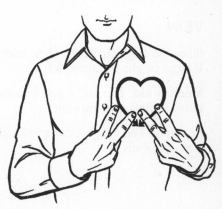

VALLEY

With the palms facing out to the sides, move both flat hands downward from shoulder level until they meet in front of the waist.

Memory aid: Suggests the shape of a *valley*.

Example: We walked through the *valley* to the open plain.

VANILLA

Shake the right *V* hand.

Memory aid: The *V* hand indicates the word, which requires context and simultaneous lipreading for full comprehension.

Example: This cake frosting has a definite *vanilla* flavor.

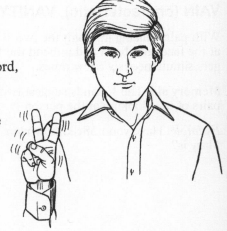

VEIN

Place the fingertip of the right middle-finger *V* hand on the upturned left wrist.

Memory aid: The initial and location combined indicate the meaning.

Example: The weightlifter's *veins* seemed to pop out of his skin.

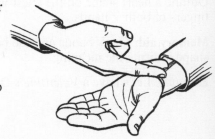

VERY

With the palms facing in, touch the fingertips of both *V* hands; then draw both hands apart to the sides.

Memory aid: The initial plus the same movement as is used for *much* indicate the meaning.

Example: That is a *very* nice dress.

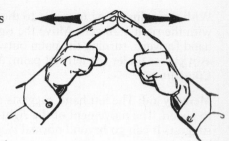

VIDEOTAPE

Rotate the thumb side of the right *V* hand in a clockwise circle on the left flat palm, which is facing right. Make the same movement with the right *T* hand on the left flat palm.

Memory aid: The initialized movement suggests the sign.

Example: Cynthia decided to have her wedding *videotaped.*

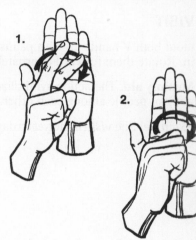

VIOLIN

Hold the left hand up with thumb and fingers curled. Move the right *O* hand back and forth over the bent left elbow.

Memory aid: The position and movement for playing a *violin.*

Example: I learned to play the *violin* at a young age.

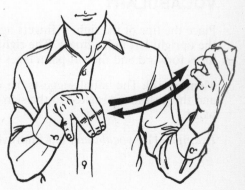

VISION, FORECAST, FORESEE, PROPHECY

With the palm facing in, point to the eyes with the right *V* fingers. Move the right hand forward, turning the palm outward as it passes under the left flat palm. *Note:* Compare *see.*

Memory aid: The left hand suggests a limit to *vision.* The movement of the right hand suggests it can go beyond normal *vision.*

Example: The growth of this university is the result of one man's *vision.*

VISIT

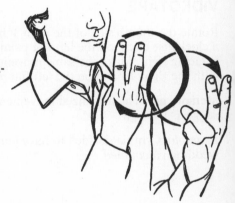

Hold both *V* hands up with palms facing in. Rotate them forward alternately.

Memory aid: The action symbolizes a mingling of people among each other.

Example: She *visited* me yesterday.

VOCABULARY

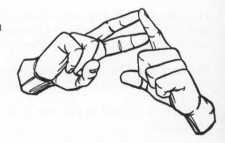

Place the tips of the right *V* fingers against the upright left index finger. The right palm faces forward and the left palm faces right.

Memory aid: The initial suggests the word, and the position is related to the sign for *word.*

Example: Her *vocabulary* has improved.

VOICE, VOCAL

Draw the back of the right *V* fingers up the neck and forward under the chin.

Memory aid: The initial indicates the word, and the action shows the location.

Example: John has a powerful bass *voice*.

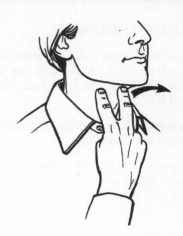

VOLLEYBALL

Hold both flat hands at head level with palms facing forward. Move them forward and upward.

Memory aid: The position and action for playing *volleyball*.

Example: Volleyball gives Vickie the exercise she needs.

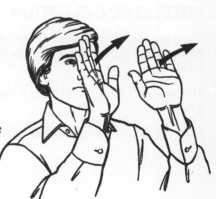

VOLUNTEER, APPLY, CANDIDATE

Take a piece of clothing near the right shoulder between the thumb and index finger of the right hand, and pull it away from the body a few times. If a jacket or suit is worn, the lapel may be used.

Memory aid: Making oneself prominent.

Example: I will *apply* for the job.

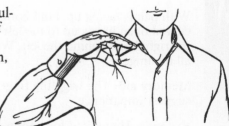

VOMIT, THROW UP

Move both open hands forward and down from the mouth. Sometimes one hand is used and the mouth is opened while the head tilts forward.

Memory aid: Symbolizes the action and direction of *vomiting*.

Example: Overeating can sometimes cause one to *throw up*.

VOTE, ELECT, ELECTION

Place the thumb and index finger of the downturned right *F* hand into the left *O* hand.

Memory aid: Suggests placing a ballot in a box.

Example: Have you registered to *vote*?

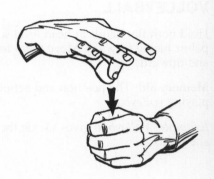

WAIT, PENDING

With palms facing up, hold both curved open hands up to the left with the right hand behind the left. Wiggle all the fingers.

Memory aid: The wiggling fingers suggest impatience.

Example: He *waited* four hours before leaving.

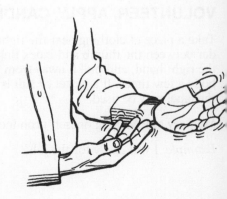

WAITER, SERVANT, WAITRESS

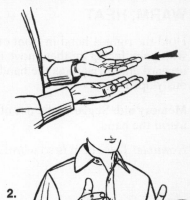

Move both upturned flat hands back and forth alternately. Add the sign for *person* (*personalizing word ending*).

Memory aid: The movement suggests someone who offers something to another.

Example: The *waiter* was very attentive to our needs.

WALK, STEP

Hold both flat hands in front with palms down; then imitate walking by moving each hand forward alternately.

Memory aid: Symbolizes the movement of feet.

Example: Please *walk* with me.

WANT, COVET, DESIRE

With palms facing up, move both open curved hands toward self a few times. *Note:* Compare *don't want*.

Memory aid: Suggests pulling something toward self.

Examples: Jackie *wants* to come and see you. I *covet* your good looks.

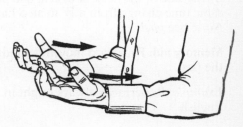

WARM, HEAT

Hold the right *A* hand in front of the mouth with palm facing in; then move it slowly upward and forward as the hand simultaneously opens.

Memory aid: Suggests the use of breath to *warm* the hand.

Example: This room is so *warm*.

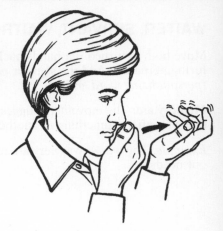

WARN, CAUTION

Pat the back of the left flat hand with the right flat hand a few times.

Memory aid: Suggests slapping the hand as a disciplinary measure.

Example: Calvin was *warned* of the dangers.

WAS

Hold the right *W* hand in front with palm facing left. Move it backward to a position by the side of the neck or cheek, and at the same time change from a *W* to an *S* hand. *Note:* See *past*.

Memory aid: Backward movement indicates the past.

Example: Robert *was* always bright in English.

WASH

Rub the knuckles of both closed hands together with circular movements.

Memory aid: Suggests *washing* clothes by hand.

Example: Your jersey needs *washing*.

WASH DISHES, DISHWASHING

With palms facing, rub the right flat hand in a clockwise circle over the left flat hand.

Memory aid: Symbolizes *washing* a plate with a dishcloth.

Example: It's John's turn to *wash dishes*.

WASHING MACHINE

Hold both curved open hands with palms facing each other vertically. Make twisting circular motions with both hands, which rotate in opposite directions.

Memory aid: Suggests the swirling water and clothes in a *washing machine*.

Example: Let's buy Mother a new *washing machine* for her birthday.

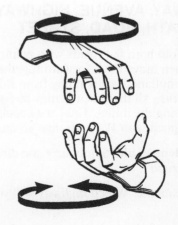

WATER

Touch the mouth with the index finger of the
right *W* hand a few times.

Memory aid: The initial indicates the word,
and the movement points to the location for
drinking.

Example: The *water* level at the dam is high.

WATERMELON

Flick the right middle finger on the back of
the palm-down closed left hand a few times.

Memory aid: Suggests testing a *watermelon*
for ripeness.

Example: I love salt on *watermelon*.

WAY, AVENUE, HIGHWAY, PATH, ROAD, STREET

Hold both flat hands with palms facing;
then move them forward together while
simultaneously winding from side to side.
Note: All these words may be signed by
using the initial. Thus, *way* could be
signed with *W* hands, and so on.

Memory aid: Symbolizes the direction of
a *road*.

Example: Which *highway* will you travel?

WE, US

Touch the right index finger on the right shoulder; then move it in a forward semi-circle until it touches the left shoulder. Often the *W* or *U* hand is used instead of the index finger to indicate either *we* or *us* respectively.

Memory aid: Touching two shoulders suggests more than one person.

Examples: We will see you soon. Allow *us* to come in.

WEAK, FEEBLE, FRAIL

Place the right curved fingers in a standing position in the palm of the left flat hand. Cause the fingers to bend and unbend.

Memory aid: Suggests the buckling of *weak* knees.

Example: He was old and *feeble.*

1.

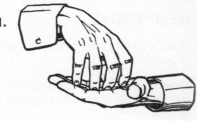

2.

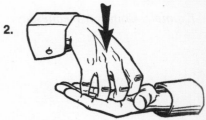

WEATHER

Hold both *W* hands to the front with palms facing; then pivot them up and down from the wrists.

Memory aid: The initials indicate the word, and the action indicates the changeable nature of *weather.*

Example: What's the *weather* forecast for tomorrow?

WEDDING

Point the fingers of both flat hands down from the wrists in the front. Swing the hands toward each other until the left fingers and thumb grasp the right fingers.

Memory aid: Suggests a bride and groom joining hands.

Example: Becky and Tom's *wedding* was very elaborate.

WEDNESDAY

Make a small clockwise circle with the right *W* hand.

Memory aid: The initial suggests the word, and the circular motion suggests the passing of time.

Example: Come on *Wednesday*.

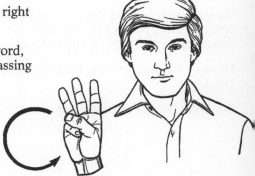

WEEK, NEXT WEEK

Move the right index-finger hand across the left flat palm in a forward movement. For *next week*, let the right hand continue beyond the left hand and point forward.

Memory aid: The five fingers of the left hand plus the thumb and index finger of the right make seven, thus symbolizing a *week*.

Example: This has been a hectic *week*.

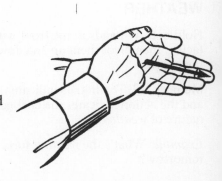

WEIGH

Cross the middle finger of the right *H* hand
over the index finger of the left *H* hand.
Rock the right *H* hand back and forth over
the left *H* hand.

Memory aid: Symbolizes scales.

Example: How much do you *weigh*?

WELCOME

Position the right flat hand forward and to
the right with the palm facing left. Sweep
the hand in toward the body until the palm
is facing in front of the abdomen.

Memory aid: A common gesture of polite-
ness and acceptance.

Example: You are *welcome* here.

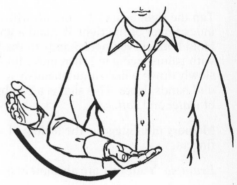

WERE

Hold the right *W* hand slightly to the front
with the palm facing left. Move it backward
to a position at the side of the neck or cheek
while simultaneously changing from a *W* to
an *R* hand. *Note:* See *past*.

Memory aid: Backward movement indicates
the past.

Example: In 1956 they *were* in college.

WEST

Move the *W* hand to the left.

Memory aid: Indicates direction.

Example: The *western* sky was aflame.

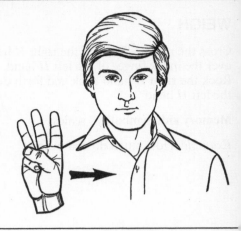

WET, DRENCH, SATURATE, SOAK

Tap the right side of the mouth with the index finger of the right *W* hand a few times. Hold both curved open hands to the front with palms facing up; then move the hands slowly down while simultaneously forming *and* hands. Note: This sign is a combination of *water* and *soft*.

Memory aid: Suggests the feeling of *wet* fingers.

Example: Your feet are absolutely *soaked*.

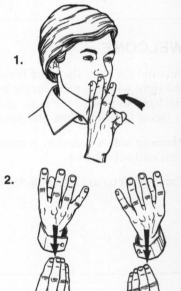

WHAT

Pass the tip of the right index finger down over the left flat hand from index to little finger.

Memory aid: The fingers of the left hand suggest alternative ideas to choose from.

Example: What is today's date?

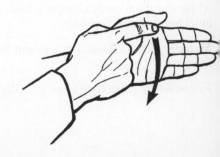

WHEN

Hold the left index finger upright with the palm facing right. Make a clockwise circle around the left index finger with the right index finger.

Memory aid: The right index finger seems to be wondering *when* it can stop circling the left index finger.

Example: When will you be ready to go out?

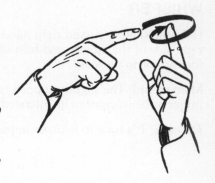

WHERE

Hold the right index finger up with palm facing forward and shake it rapidly back and forth from left to right.

Memory aid: The right index finger seems undecided as to *where* to settle.

Example: Where is the house we are going to visit?

WHICH, EITHER, WHETHER

With the palms facing, move the *A* hands alternately up and down in front of the chest.

Memory aid: Suggests two or more things being compared.

Example: Which team do you think will win?

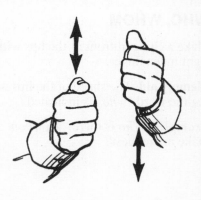

WHISPER

Hold the slightly curved right hand over the right side of the mouth, and lean slightly forward or to the side.

Memory aid: The slightly cupped hand projects the *whisper* to its intended receiver.

Example: It's rude to *whisper* in public.

WHITE

Place the fingers and thumb of the right curved hand on the chest; then move it forward while simultaneously forming the *and* hand.

Memory aid: Can suggest reference to a clean *white* shirt.

Example: Buy some *white* sheets when you go to the store.

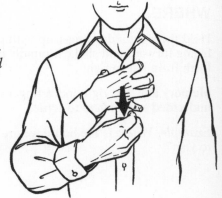

WHO, WHOM

Make a circle in front of the lips with the right index finger.

Memory aid: The shape of the lips when saying the word "*who*" is indicated.

Examples: Who is there? To *whom* should I make my request?

WHY

Touch the forehead with the fingers of the right hand; then move forward while simultaneously forming the Y hand with the palm facing in.

Memory aid: The Y hand coming from the mind suggests a question by its phonetic link to *why*.

Example: Why do you want to leave college?

WIDE, BROAD

Place both flat hands to the front with palms facing and draw them apart to the sides.

Memory aid: The distance created between the hands indicates the meaning.

Example: The workmen were *widening* the road.

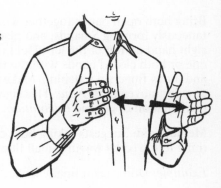

WIFE

Trace the right jawbone from ear to chin with the palm side of the right A thumb. Then clasp the hands in a natural position with the right hand above the left. The latter is the sign for *marriage*.

Memory aid: Indicates a married female.

Examples: John's *wife* is a nurse. All their *wives* are invited.

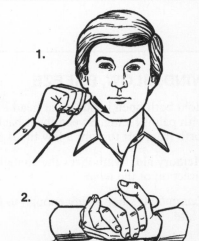

WILL (verb), SHALL, WOULD

Place the right flat hand opposite the right temple or cheek with the palm facing in. Move the hand straight ahead.

Memory aid: The forward movement indicates future intention.

Examples: Tom *will* come on Saturday. We *shall* overcome! I *would* love to be there.

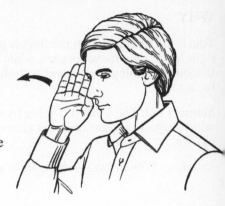

WIN

Bring both open hands together while simultaneously forming *S* hands, and place the right hand on top of the left. Hold up either one or both closed hands with the thumb tip and index fingertip touching. Make small circular movements. *Note:* This sign is a combination of *get* and *celebration*.

Memory aid: Suggests taking hold of something followed by waving small flags.

Example: Don's team finally *won*.

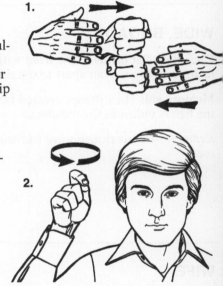

WIND, BLOW, BREEZE

Hold both open hands up at head level with palms facing. Sweep them back and forth from left to right a few times.

Memory aid: Symbolizes the changing direction of the *wind*.

Example: It's not *windy* enough to fly a kite.

WINDOW

Place the little-finger edge of the right flat hand on the thumb edge of the left flat hand with palms facing in. Move the right hand up a short distance.

Memory aid: Suggests raising a sliding *window*.

Example: Please open both *windows*.

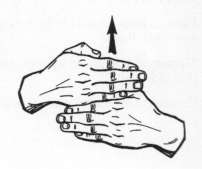

WINE

Make a forward circular movement with the right *W* hand on the right cheek.

Memory aid: Symbolizes the redness of cheeks caused by drinking too much alcohol.

Example: This *wine* is very sweet.

WINGS, ANGEL

Touch the shoulders with the fingertips of both hands (sometimes only one hand is used). Point the fingers of both down-turned hands outward to the sides; then flap the hands up and down a few times.

Memory aid: Suggests the general location and action of *wings*.

Example: An albatross has very large *wings*.

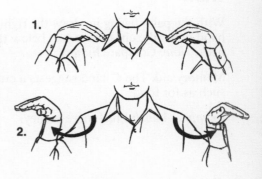

WINTER

Hold up both *S* hands in front of the chest and shake them.

Memory aid: Suggests a person shivering in the cold.

Example: Last *winter* was unusually mild.

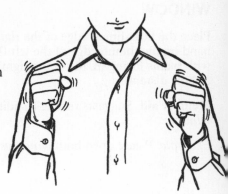

WISDOM, INTELLECTUAL, WISE

Move the right bent finger of the *X* hand up and down slightly just in front of the forehead. Make the movement from the wrist.

Memory aid: Measuring *intellectual* depth.

Example: Dr. Williams has great *wisdom*.

WISH

With the palm facing in, draw the right *C* hand down the chest from just below the neck. *Note:* Compare *hungry*.

Memory aid: The *C* hand suggests a craving, such as for food.

Example: I *wish* I had more money.

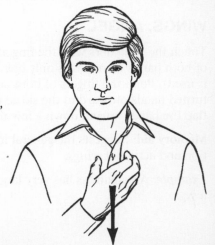

WITH

Bring the two *A* hands together with palms facing.

Memory aid: The two hands are *with* each other.

Example: Come *with* me.

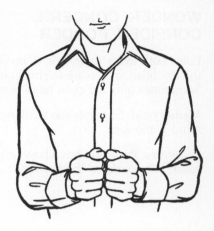

WITHOUT

Make the sign for *with*, then separate the hands and move them outward while simultaneously forming open hands.

Memory aid: The hands end up *without* each other.

Example: We must go *without* luxuries.

WOMAN

Touch the thumb of the right open hand on the chin, then on the chest.

Memory aid: The sign is a combination of *mother* and *fine*. It suggests that it is a fine thing to have a mother who is a real *woman*.

Example: This *woman* was the first to arrive.

WONDER, CONCERN, CONSIDER, PONDER

Point both index fingers or *W* hands toward the forehead and rotate in small circles. Sometimes only the right hand is used.

Memory aid: Suggests the workings of a mind in motion.

Examples: Paul *wondered* how he should react. We *pondered* the problem continually.

WONDERFUL, EXCELLENT, FANTASTIC, GREAT, MARVELOUS, SPLENDID

Move the flat open hands up and forward a few times with the palms facing out.

Memory aid: A gesture symbolizing an attitude of awe that is used in some forms of religious worship.

Example: You are a *fantastic* cook.

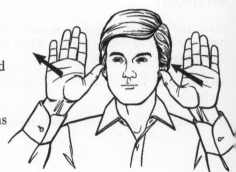

WOOD, LUMBER, SAW

Move the little-finger edge of the right flat hand back and forth across the back of the left hand.

Memory aid: Suggests a *saw* cutting *wood*.

Example: The *lumber* yard may have what we need.

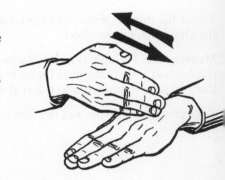

WORD

Hold the left index finger up with palm facing left; then place the thumb and index finger of the right *Q* hand against it.

Memory aid: Symbolizes that a *word* is just a small section of a sentence.

Example: John is fascinated by the origin of *words*.

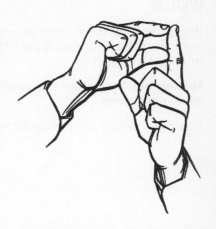

WORK, JOB, LABOR, TASK

With the palms facing down, tap the wrist of the right *S* hand on the wrist of the left *S* hand a few times.

Memory aid: Suggests the action of a hammer.

Example: Sam needs a new *job*.

WORLD

Make a forward circle with the right *W* hand around the left *W* hand. End with the little-finger edge of the right *W* hand resting on the thumb side of the left *W* hand. *Note:* Compare *universe*.

Memory aid: The initials indicate the word, and the action symbolizes the revolving *world*.

Example: His speech caused considerable *world* tension.

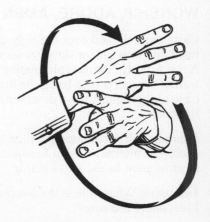

WORM

Wiggle the right index finger as it moves forward along the palm side of the left flat hand from heel to fingertips.

Memory aid: Symbolizes the crawling motion of a *worm*.

Example: I need some *worms* for fishing.

WORRY, ANXIOUS, FRET

Rotate both flat or slightly curved hands in front of the head in opposite directions.

Memory aid: Suggests problems being heaped upon the mind.

Examples: Joe *worries* about his job a lot. Please don't *fret* about it.

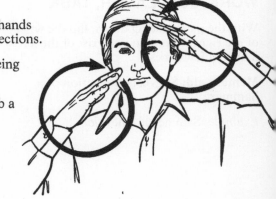

WORSHIP, ADORE, AMEN

Close the left hand over the right closed hand and move them slowly toward self. *Note:* A fairly common alternative (not illustrated) for *amen* is to bring the little finger edge of the right *A* hand down into the left flat palm.

Memory aid: A common position of reverence. The alternative sign for *amen* is similar in movement to the sign for *stop*.

Examples: What time is the *worship* service? I just *adore* red roses.

WORST

Hold both *V* hands in a vertical position with palms facing the body and cross both hands, left hand in front of right hand. Then bring the right *A* hand up quickly, just above the right side of the head.

Memory aid: This is a combination of the signs for *multiply*, and *most*, and suggests that things may be *worse* because they have increased negatively.

Example: Sharon expected the *worst* but was pleasantly surprised.

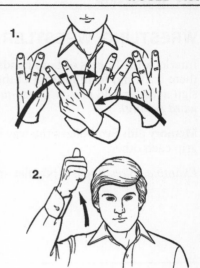

WORTHLESS, USELESS

Bring both *F* hands up from the sides to the center until the thumbs and index fingers touch. Swing the hands away to the sides while simultaneously forming open hands. *Note:* Compare *important*.

Memory aid: This is a combination of the signs for *important* and *finish*. Therefore, the idea is expressed that importance is finished.

Example: This coat is *worthless*.

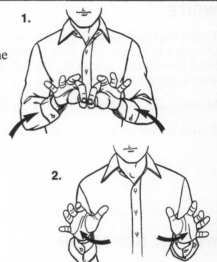

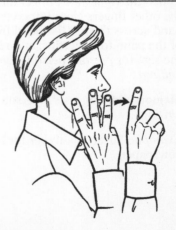

WOULD

With the palm facing left, place the right *W* hand in an upright position close to the side of the right cheek. Move the hand straight forward while simultaneously changing from a *W* to a *D* hand.

Memory aid: The forward movement indicates positive intention.

Example: Would you like to eat now?

WRESTLING, WRESTLER

Interlock the fingers of both hands and move them back and forth in front of the chest. To sign *wrestler,* add *person (personalizing word ending).*

Memory aid: Symbolizes the way *wrestlers* grip each other.

Example: Wrestling is a popular sport.

WRITE

Touch the right index finger and thumb with the other fingers closed; then move the right hand horizontally across the flat left palm with a slight wavy motion.

Memory aid: Symbolizes *writing* on paper.

Example: She *writes* children's stories.

WRITER, REPORTER

Touch the right index finger and thumb with the other fingers closed; then move the right hand across the left flat hand from the base of the palm to fingertips, and repeat. Add the sign for *person (personalizing word ending).*

Memory aid: Suggests a person who is *writing.*

Example: Susan is a *writer* for the local newspaper.

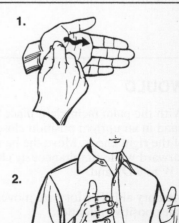

WRONG, ERROR, FAULT, MISTAKE

Place the *Y* hand on the chin with the palm facing in.

Memory aid: The *Y* hand is normally shown with palm facing out, so this position suggests a *mistake*.

Example: Please forgive my *mistake*.

X RAY

Hold the right *X* hand up with palm facing forward; then form an *O* position and twist the hand until the palm faces self. Open the hand as it is moved toward the chest.

Memory aid: The initial indicates the word, and the action suggests *X rays* penetrating the body.

Example: The doctor decided to *X-ray* my ankle.

XYLOPHONE

Hold both modified *A* hands (thumb tips in the crooks of both index fingers) with palms facing. Move the hands up and down alternately.

Memory aid: Suggests the action of striking the bars of a *xylophone* with the hammers.

Example: My aunt plays the *xylophone*.

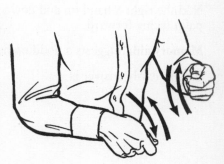

YEAR

Move the right *S* hand in a complete forward circle around the left *S* hand and come to rest with the right *S* hand on top of the left. Repeat the sign for the plural.

Memory aid: The movement of the right hand suggests the earth's revolution around the sun.

Example: What *year* were you born?

YELLOW

Move the right *Y* hand to the right while shaking it from the wrist.

Memory aid: The initial indicates the meaning, which requires context and simultaneous lipreading for full comprehension.

Example: A *yellow* butterfly flitted by.

YES

Nod the right *S* hand up and down with palm facing forward.

Memory aid: Suggests a nodding head.

Example: My answer is *yes*.

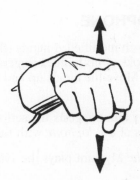

YESTERDAY

With the palm facing forward, place the thumb of the right *A* (or *Y*) hand on the right side of the chin. Move in a backward arc toward the ear.

Memory aid: The backward movement indicates the past.

Example: Yesterday was exciting.

YOU

Point the right index finger to the person being addressed. Or, if referring to several people, make a sweeping motion from left to right.

Memory aid: The person being pointed to clearly understands the reference to self.

Examples: You are right. *You* must play as a united team.

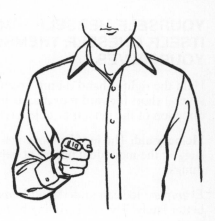

YOUNG, ADOLESCENT, YOUTH

Place the fingertips of both curved hands on the upper chest and quickly pivot them upward from the wrists several times. *Note:* Compare *life.*

Memory aid: Symbolizes a fast pace of life and *youthful* exuberance.

Example: We all experience the joys and trials of *youth.*

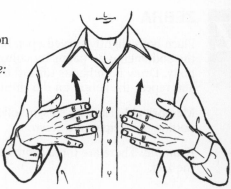

YOUR, YOURS (plural)

Move the flat hand across the front of the body from left to right with the palm facing outward.

Memory aid: The flat hand and the left-to-right movement symbolize possession by several people.

Examples: Is *your* raincoat blue? The professor said to us, Success is *yours* if you will study diligently.

YOURSELF, HERSELF, HIMSELF, ITSELF, ONESELF, THEMSELVES, YOURSELVES

Hold the right *A* hand thumb up and make several short forward movements in the direction of the person or object referred to.

Memory aid: The jerking movement can suggest the individual nature of persons or things.

Examples: Joe can understand *himself* much better lately. The car is rolling by *itself*.

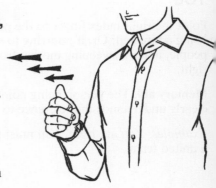

Z   ZEBRA

Place both slightly curved open hands on the abdomen with palms touching the body. Draw both hands toward the sides and repeat the action on the chest.

Memory aid: The fingers symbolically outline the stripes of a *zebra*.

Example: There are three *zebras* at the zoo.

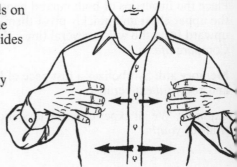

ZIPPER, ZIP UP

Hold both modified *A* hands (thumb tips in the crook of both index fingers) at waist level with palms facing in and the right hand just above the left. Move the right hand straight upward to the upper chest.

Memory aid: Suggests the action of *zipping up* a jacket.

Example: The *zipper* on his jacket is stuck.

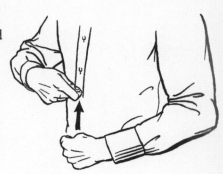

ZOO

Hold the left flat open hand up with palm facing forward. Trace the letter Z across the front of the left hand with the right index finger. This sign is often fingerspelled.

Memory aid: The initial indicates the word, and the open left hand suggests the bars on animal cages.

Example: I've always found *zoos* interesting.

Main Entry and Synonym Index

The Main Entry and Synonym Index is a list of all the main entry words and all the synonyms following the main entries. Main entry words appear in boldface; synonyms are in lightface. This list is not to be considered exhaustive, but the sign language student will find it a rich resource and an invaluable aid to versatility of expression. It will also assist the student in locating a basic sign when he or she can think only of a synonym.

A

A (indefinite article), 27
Abandon
Abhor *See* Hate.
Ability *See* Can.
Able *See* Can.
Abolish *See* Destroy.
Abortion *See* Subtract.
About
Above
Above (comparative degree)
Abraham
Absent *See* Gone.
Accept
Accident
Accompany *See* Together.
Accomplish *See* Success.
Accord *See* Agree.
Accumulate See Collect and Earn.
Accurate *See* Exact.
Accurate *See* Right.
Accuse *See* Blame.
Ache *See* Pain.
Acid *See* Sour.
Acknowledge *See* Confess.
Acquire *See* Get.
Across
Act *See* Drama.
Action *See* Do.
Actor
Actress *See* Actor.

Adam
Adapt *See* Change.
Add
Add *See* Increase.
Address *See* Live.
Address *See* Speech.
Adequate *See* Enough.
Adjacent *See* Near.
Adjust *See* Change.
Admire *See* Like.
Admit *See* Confess.
Adolescent *See* Young.
Adopt
Adore *See* Worship.
Adult
Advance *See* Onward.
Advanced *See* High.
Advertise
Advice
Advise *See* Advice.
Afraid
Africa
African *See* Africa.
After (time)
After a While *See* Later.
Afternoon
Afterward *See* Later.
Again
Against
Age *See* Old.
Age *See* Time (abstract).
Aggravated *See* Discontented.
Ago *See* Past.
Agony *See* Suffer.
Agree

Ahead
Aid *See* Help.
Aim *See* Ambition.
Air Conditioning
Airplane
Algebra *See* Mathematics.
Align
Alike *See* Same.
All
All Along *See* Since.
All Day *See* Day.
All Night
Allow
All Right
Almost
Alphabet *See* Fingerspelling, 20
Already *See* Finish.
Also *See* Too.
Altar
Alter *See* Change.
Although *See* Anyhow.
Although *See* But.
Always
Am
Amaze *See* Surprise.
Ambition
Ambitious *See* Eager.
Amen *See* Worship.
America
American *See* America.
Ameslan (American Sign Language)
Among
Amount *See* Total.

Below
Below (comparative
  degree)
Beneath   *See* Below.
Benefit   *See* Profit.
Benevolent   *See* Kind
  (emotion).
Berry
Be Seated   *See* Sit.
Best
Bestow   *See* Gift.
Bethlehem
Betray   *See* Cheat.
Better
Between
Bewilder   *See* Shock.
Beyond
Bible
Bicycle
Big   *See* Large.
Billiards   *See* Pool.
Bills (currency)   *See*
  Dollars.
Biology   *See* Science.
Bird
Birth
Birthday
Biscuit
Bitter   *See* Sour.
Black
Blackberry
Blame
Blanket
Bleed   *See* Blood.
Bless
Blind
Block   *See* Prevent.
Blood
Bloom   *See* Blossom.
Blossom
Blouse
Blow   *See* Wind.
Blue
Blueberry
Blush
Board   *See* Member.
Boast
Boat
Body
Boil
Bones
Book
Booklet   *See* Magazine.
Boost   *See* Help.
Boots

Boring
Born   *See* Birth.
Borrow
Boss
Boston
Botch   *See* Bungle.
Both
Bother   *See* Disturb.
Bowling
Box
Boxing
Boy
Bracelet
Brag   *See* Boast.
Brain   *See* Mind.
Branch   *See* Tree.
Brave
Bread
Break
Breakdown   *See* Collapse.
Breakfast
Breast
Breath
Breathe   *See* Breath.
Breeze   *See* Wind.
Bridge
Brief   *See* Short (in
  length or time).
Bright   *See* Light.
Bright   *See* Smart.
Brilliant   *See* Smart.
Bring
Broad   *See* Wide.
Broad-minded
Brochure   *See* Magazine.
Broke
Brother
Brown
Brush Teeth   *See*
  Toothbrush.
Bug
Build
Building
Bungle
Bungling   *See* Awkward.
Burden   *See*
  Responsibility.
Burglar   *See* Thief.
Burn   *See* Fire.
Bury
Business
Busy
But
Butter
Butterfly

Buy
By   *See* Near.
By and By   *See* Future.

C

Cabbage
Cake
Calculate   *See* Multiply.
Calculus   *See*
  Mathematics.
California
Call
Call   *See* Telephone.
Called   *See* Name.
Call Out   *See* Shout.
Calm   *See* Quiet.
Camera
Camp
Can
Canada
Canadian   *See* Canada.
Cancel
Candidate   *See* Volunteer.
Candle
Candy
Cannot
Canoeing
Capable   *See* Can.
Capacity   *See* Limit.
Capital   *See* Government.
Capital   *See* Money.
Capsule   *See* Pill.
Captain   *See* Boss.
Caption   *See* Quote.
Capture   *See* Catch.
Car
Care   *See* Supervise.
Careful
Careless
Carry
Cat
Catalog   *See* Magazine.
Catastrophic   *See* Awful.
Catch
Catholic
Caution   *See* Warn.
Cease   *See* Stop.
Celebrate
Celebration   *See*
  Celebrate.
Celestial   *See* Heaven.
Cemetery   *See* Bury.
Cent
Center

Central   *See* Center.
Cents   *See* Cent.
Certificate   *See* License.
Chain
Chair
Chairman   *See* Boss.
Challenge   *See* Game.
Change
Chapel   *See* Church.
Chaplain   *See* Priest.
Chapter
Character (individual)
Character   *See* Personality.
Charge   *See* Cost.
Chase   *See* Follow.
Cheap
Cheat
Check
Check (bank)
Cheer   *See* Celebrate.
Cheese
Chef
Chemistry   *See* Science.
Chewing Gum
Chicago
Chicken
Chief   *See* Prominent.
Child
Children   *See* Child.
Chilly   *See* Cold.
China
China   *See* Glass.
Chinese   *See* China.
Chipmunk   *See* Squirrel.
Chocolate
Choke   *See* Stuck.
Choose
Christ   *See* Lord.
Christen (sprinkling)   *See* Baptize.
Christian
Christmas
Chubby   *See* Fat.
Chuckle   *See* Laugh.
Church
Cigarette
Cinema   *See* Movie.
Circumstance   *See* Environment.
Cite   *See* Quote.
City
Clap
Class   *See* Group.
Clean

Clear   *See* Light.
Clergyman   *See* Priest.
Clever   *See* Smart.
Climb
Clippers   *See* Scissors.
Clock   *See* Time.
Close
Close To   *See* Near.
Clothes
Cloud
Clumsy   *See* Awkward.
Coat
Coax   *See* Persuade.
Cock   *See* Rooster.
Coffee
Coincide   *See* Agree.
Coins
Cold
Cold (sickness)
Collapse
Collar
Collect
College
Collision   *See* Accident.
Colon   *See* Period.
Color
Combine   *See* Match.
Come
Comfort
Comical   *See* Funny.
Comma   *See* Period.
Command
Commandments
Commence   *See* Start.
Commercial   *See* Advertise.
Communicate   *See* Talk.
Communion
Community   *See* City.
Company   *See* Group.
Compare
Compassion   *See* Pity.
Compel   *See* Force.
Compete   *See* Race.
Competent   *See* Can.
Competent   *See* Expert.
Competition   *See* Race.
Complain
Complete
Complete   *See* Finish.
Comprehend   *See* Understand.
Computer
Concentration   *See* Attention.

Concept   *See* Idea.
Concern   *See* Wonder.
Concerning   *See* About.
Conclude   *See* Complete.
Conduct   *See* Do.
Conduct   *See* Guide.
Confer   *See* Gift.
Confess
Confidence
Confidential   *See* Secret.
Conflict
Confuse
Congratulate
Congress   *See* Member.
Connection
Conquer
Conscience
Consent   *See* Agree.
Consider   *See* Evaluate.
Consider   *See* Think.
Consider   *See* Wonder.
Consistent   *See* Regular.
Constantly   *See* Always.
Constitution
Construct   *See* Build.
Consume   *See* Eat.
Contact   *See* Touch.
Content   *See* Satisfaction.
Contest   *See* Race.
Continue
Contradict   *See* Disagree.
Contrary   *See* Opposite.
Contrary To   *See* Disagree.
Contrast   *See* Compare.
Contrast   *See* Opposite.
Contribute   *See* Gift.
Control
Controversy   *See* Argue.
Conversation   *See* Talk.
Conviction   *See* Conscience.
Cook (verb)
Cook (verb)   *See* Boil.
Cook (noun)   *See* Chef.
Cookie
Cool
Cooperate
Cop   *See* Police.
Copy
Cord   *See* String.
Corn
Corner
Correct   *See* Cancel.
Correct   *See* Right.
Correspond   *See* Agree.

Exaggerate
Examination *See* Test.
Examine *See* Search, and Check.
Example *See* Show.
Exceed *See* Above (comparative degree).
Excellent *See* Wonderful.
Except *See* Special.
Exceptional *See* Special.
Exchange
Excite *See* Exciting.
Exciting
Exclamation Point *See* Period.
Excuse
Exempt *See* Excuse.
Exercise
Exercise (mental) *See* Lesson.
Exhausted *See* Tired.
Existence *See* Life.
Expect *See* Hope.
Expelled *See* Fired.
Expense *See* Cost.
Expensive
Experience
Experiment *See* Science.
Expert
Expire *See* Death.
Explain
Express *See* Show.
Expression
Extraordinary *See* Special.
Eye

F

Face
Face to Face *See* Before (location).
Factory *See* Machine.
Fail
Fair *See* Equal.
Faith
Faithful
Fake *See* False.
Fake *See* Hypocrite.
Fall (season)
Fall (verb)
False
Falsehood *See* Lie.
Fame *See* Famous.
Family

Famine *See* Hungry.
Famous
Fantastic *See* Wonderful.
Fantasy *See* Imagination.
Far
Farm
Farmer
Fashion *See* Make.
Fast
Fasting
Fat
Fat *See* Gravy.
Father
Fatigued *See* Tired.
Fault *See* Blame.
Fault *See* Wrong.
Favorite
Fear
Fearful *See* Awful.
Fearless *See* Brave.
Federal *See* Government.
Fed Up *See* Full (physical and emotional).
Fee *See* Cost.
Feeble *See* Weak.
Feeling
Feet
Fellowship *See* Associate.
Female
Fetch *See* Bring.
Fever *See* Temperature.
Fiction *See* Imagination.
Field *See* Land.
Field (occupation) *See* Major.
Fifteen, 22
Fighting *See* Boxing.
Figure *See* Multiply.
Filled *See* Full.
Film *See* Movie.
Filthy *See* Dirty.
Final *See* Last.
Finances *See* Money.
Find
Fine
Fine *See* Cost.
Fingerspelling
Fingerspelling, 20
Finish
Finish *See* Complete.
Fire
Fired
Fireworks

First
Fish (noun)
Fishing
Fit *See* Match.
Five, 21
Five Dollars, 25
Fix *See* Make.
Flag
Flame *See* Fire.
Flat Tire *See* Deflate.
Flee *See* Escape.
Flesh *See* Meat.
Flirt
Flood
Floor
Florida
Flower
Fly (insect)
Fly *See* Airplane.
Focus *See* Attention.
Foe *See* Enemy.
Follow
Food *See* Eat.
Fool (verb)
Foolish
Football
For
Forbid
Force
Forecast *See* Vision.
Foreign
Foreseen *See* Vision.
Forest *See* Tree.
Forever
Forfeit *See* Surrender.
Forget
Forgive *See* Excuse.
Fork
Forlorn *See* Sad.
Formerly *See* Past.
Forsake *See* Abandon.
Forsake *See* Forget.
Forward *See* Onward.
Foul *See* Dirty.
Foul Up *See* Bungle.
Foundation
Founded *See* Establish.
Fountain
Four, 21
Fourteen, 22
Fox
Fracture *See* Break.
Fragrance *See* Smell.
Frail *See* Weak.
France

Fraud   *See* Cheat.
Free   *See* Rescue.
Freeze   *See* Ice.
French   *See* France.
French Fries
Frequent   *See* Often.
Freshman
Fret   *See* Worry.
Friday
Friend
Friendship   *See* Friend.
Frightened   *See* Afraid.
Frigid   *See* Cold.
Frog
From
Fruit
Frustrate
Fry   *See* Cook (verb).
Full
Full (physical and emotional)
Fume   *See* Anger.
Fumes   *See* Smell.
Fun
Funds   *See* Money.
Funeral
Funny
Furniture
Future

G

Gain   *See* Profit.
Gain Weight   *See* Increase.
Gale   *See* Cloud.
Gallaudet
Game
Garden
Gardening
Garment   *See* Clothes.
Gasoline
Gate
Gaunt   *See* Thin.
Gaze   *See* Look.
Gender Signs, 15
General   *See* Boss.
Generation
Gentle   *See* Kind (emotion).
Gentleman
Genuine   *See* True.
Geography   *See* Earth.
Geometry   *See* Mathematics.

German   *See* Germany.
Germany
Get
Get   *See* Become.
Get In
Get Off   *See* Get Out.
Get Out
Get To   *See* Arrive.
Get Up   *See* Rise.
Get Up   *See* Stand Up.
Ghost   *See* Spirit.
Gift
Giggle   *See* Laugh.
Giraffe
Girl
Give
Give Up   *See* Surrender.
Glad   *See* Happy.
Glass (drinking)
Glass (substance)
Glasses   *See* Gallaudet.
Globe   *See* Earth.
Glorious   *See* Glory.
Glory
Gloves
Go
Goal   *See* Ambition.
Goat
God
God's Book   *See* Bible.
Gold
Golf
Gone
Good
Gospel
Gossip
Govern   *See* Control.
Government
Governor
Gown   *See* Clothes.
Grab   *See* Catch.
Grace
Gracious   *See* Kind (emotion).
Graduate
Grandfather
Grandmother
Grant   *See* Allow.
Grapes
Grasp   *See* Catch.
Grass
Gratify   *See* Please.
Grave   *See* Bury.
Gravy
Gray

Grease   *See* Gravy.
Great   *See* Large.
Great   *See* Wonderful.
Greedy   *See* Selfish.
Green
Grief
Grin   *See* Smile.
Gripe   *See* Complain.
Grouchy   *See* Cross.
Ground   *See* Soil.
Group
Grow   *See* Spring.
Grumble   *See* Complain.
Grumpy   *See* Cross.
Guard   *See* Defend.
Guess
Guide
Guilty
Guitar
Gun   *See* Hunt.

H

Habit
Had   *See* Have.
Haircut
Half
Hallelujah
Hallowed   *See* Holy.
Halt   *See* Stop.
Hamburger
Hands
Handsome   *See* Beautiful.
Hanger   *See* Hang Up.
Hang Up
Happen
Happy
Hard
Hard   *See* Difficult.
Hard-of-Hearing
Harp
Has   *See* Have.
Hat
Hate
Haughty   *See* Proud.
Have
Have To   *See* Must.
Hawaii
He
Head
Healthy
Hear   *See* Ear.
Hear   *See* Listen.
Hearing (person)
Hearing Aid

O

Obedience   *See* Obey.
Obese   *See* Fat.
Obey
Object   *See* Complain.
Objective   *See* Ambition.
Obligation   *See* Responsi-
   bility.
Observe   *See* Look.
Observe   *See* Notice.
Obstinate   *See* Stubborn.
Obstruct   *See* Prevent.
Obtain   *See* Get.
Obvious   *See* Light.
Occasionally   *See* Some-
   times.
Occur   *See* Happen.
Ocean
Odd
Odor   *See* Smell.
Off
Offer
Officer   *See* Boss.
Often
Ohio
Oil   *See* Gravy.
OK   *See* All Right.
Old
Olympics
On
Once
Once In a While   *See*
   Sometimes.
Once Upon a Time   *See*
   Past.
One, 21
One Another   *See*
   Associate.
One Cent (penny), 25
One Dollar, 25
One-Half, 24
One Hundred, 24
One-Fourth, 24
Oneself   *See* Yourself.
Onion
Onward
Open
Open-minded   *See* Broad-
   minded.
Operate   *See* Control.
Operation
Opinion   *See* Idea.
Opponent   *See* Enemy.
Opportunity

Oppose   *See* Against.
Opposite
Or
Oral   *See* Lipreading.
Orange (color and fruit)
Orbit
Order   *See* Command,
   and Plan.
Organization   *See* Group.
Originate   *See* Invent.
Other   *See* Another.
Ought To   *See* Must.
Our
Ourselves
Out
Outstanding   *See* Special.
Ovation   *See* Clap.
Oven   *See* Bake.
Over   *See* Above.
Over   *See* Above (com-
   parative degree).
Over   *See* Across.
Overcoat   *See* Coat.
Overcome   *See* Conquer.
Overnight   *See* All Night.
Owe
Owl
Own   *See* Have.
Own   *See* My.

P

Pain
Paint
Pair   *See* Both.
Pajamas
Pamphlet   *See* Magazine.
Pancake   *See* Cook
   (verb).
Pants
Paper
Parade   *See* Funeral.
Parade
Paragraph
Parallel
Parched   *See* Dry.
Parched   *See* Thirsty.
Pardon   *See* Excuse.
Parents
Park (a vehicle)
Parliamentary   *See*
   Constitution.
Part   *See* Some.
Party
Pass

Passover
Past
Pastor   *See* Minister.
Path   *See* Street.
Patience   *See* Patient.
Patient
Patient (noun)
Pay
Pay Attention   *See*
   Attention.
Peace
Peaceful   *See* Quiet.
Peach
Peanuts   *See* Nuts.
Pear
Peculiar   *See* Odd.
Pending   *See* Wait.
Penitentiary   *See* Prison.
Penny   *See* Cent.
People
Pepper
Perceive   *See* See.
Perfect
Perform   *See* Do.
Perform   *See* Drama.
Perhaps   *See* May.
Peril   *See* Danger.
Period
Period   *See* Menstruation.
Perish   *See* Death.
Permanent   *See*
   Continue.
Permit   *See* Allow.
Perplexed   *See* Puzzled.
Persecute   *See* Tease.
Persevere   *See* Continue.
Person
**Person (personalizing
   word ending)**
*Person (personalizing word
   ending) sign, The*, 15
Personal   *See* My.
Personal   *See* Secret.
Personality
Perspire   *See* Sweat.
Persuade
Philanderer   *See* Flirt.
Philosophy
Photograph   *See* Picture.
Photographer
Physical   *See* Body.
Physician   *See* Doctor.
Physics   *See* Electricity.
Piano
Pick   *See* Choose.

Picture
Pie
Pig
Pill
Pilot
Pineapple
Ping-Pong
Pink
Pity
Pizza
Place
Plan
Plant
Plate
Play
Play   *See* Drama.
Playing Cards
Plead   *See* Beg.
Please
Pleasure   *See* Please.
Plenty   *See* Enough.
Plump   *See* Fat.
Plural   *See* Many.
Pneumonia
Pocketbook   *See* Purse.
Poem   *See* Poetry.
Poetry
Poison
Police
Polite
Politics   *See* Government.
Ponder   *See* Wonder.
Pool
Poor
Poor (person or thing)
    See Pity.
Pop   *See* Soda.
Pop Up   *See* Appear.
Popcorn
Porcelain   *See* Glass.
Portion   *See* Some.
Positive
Possess   *See* Have.
Possible   *See* Can.
Possibly   *See* May.
Poster
Postpone   *See* Delay.
Potato
Poverty   *See* Poor.
Powerful   *See* Strong.
Practice
Practice   *See* Habit.
Praise   *See* Clap.
Pray
Prayer   *See* Pray.

Preach
Precious   *See* Important.
Precise   *See* Exact.
Prefer
Pregnant
Prepare   *See* Plan.
Presbyterian
Prescription   *See*
    Medicine.
Presence   *See* Before
    (location).
Present   *See* Gift.
Present   *See* Now.
Present   *See* Offer.
*Present, Past, and Future
    Time,* 16
President
Pressure
Pretty   *See* Beautiful.
Prevent
Previously   *See* Past.
Price   *See* Cost.
Priest
Principal
Principle   *See*
    Constitution.
Printer
Printing
Prison
Private   *See* Secret.
Probably   *See* May.
Problem
Procedure   *See* Process.
Proceed   *See* Onward.
Process
Procession   *See* Funeral.
Proclaim   *See* Announce.
Procrastinate   *See* Delay.
Prod   *See* Persuade.
Profession
Professional   *See*
    Profession.
Profit
Program
Progress   *See* Process.
Prohibit   *See* Forbid.
Project
Prominent
Promise
Promotion   *See* High.
Proof
Prophecy   *See* Vision.
Prophet
Propose   *See* Offer.
Prosper   *See* Success.

Protect   *See* Defend.
Protest   *See* Complain.
Protestant   *See* Kneel.
Proud
Prove   *See* Proof.
Pseudo   *See* False.
Psychiatrist
Psychiatry
Psychologist
Psychology
Publicize   *See* Advertise.
Publishing   *See*
    Printing.
Punctuation, 15
Punish
Purchase   *See* Buy.
Pure   *See* Clean.
Purple
Purpose   *See* Mean
    (verb).
Purse
Pursue   *See* Follow.
Push
Put
Put Off   *See* Delay.
Puzzled

Q

Quarrel
Queen   *See* Lord.
Quest   *See* Search.
Question
Quick   *See* Fast.
Quiet
Quit   *See* Resign.
Quiz   *See* Test.
Quote

R

Rabbi
Rabbit
Race
Radio
Rage   *See* Anger.
Railroad   *See* Train.
Rain
Rainbow
Raking   *See* Gardening.
Rapid   *See* Fast.
Rat
Rather   *See* Prefer.
Reach   *See* Arrive.
Read

Ready   *See* Plan.
Real   *See* True.
Really   *See* True.
Reason
Rebellion   *See* Strike.
Recall   *See* Remember.
Receive
Recently
Reckless   *See* Careless.
Recline   *See* Lie Down.
Recognize   *See* Know.
Recollect   *See* Remember.
Recreation   *See* Play.
Red
Redeem   *See* Rescue.
Reduce   *See* Decrease.
Reflect   *See* Think.
Refresh   *See* Cool.
Refrigerator
Refuse
Regardless   *See* Anyhow.
Register   *See* Signature.
Regret   *See* Sorry.
Regular
Regularly   *See* Regular.
Regulate   *See* Control.
Regulations
Rehabilitation
Reign   *See* Control.
Reject
Relationship   *See*
   Connection.
Relax   *See* Rest.
Release   *See* Disconnect.
Religion
Religious   *See* Religion.
Rely   *See* Depend.
Remain   *See* Stay.
Remark   *See* Say.
Remember
Remind
Remote   *See* Far.
Remove   *See* Subtract.
Repeat   *See* Again.
Repent
Replace   *See* Exchange.
Reply   *See* Answer.
Reporter   *See* Writer.
Represent   *See* Show.
Reprimand   *See* Scold.
Republican
Request   *See* Ask.
Require   *See* Demand.
Rescue
Research   *See* Search.

Reservation   *See*
   Appointment.
Reside   *See* Live.
Residence   *See* House.
Resign
Respect
Respond   *See* Answer.
Responsibility
Rest
Restaurant
Restless
Restrict   *See* Limit.
Restroom
Resurrection
Retire   *See* Leave.
Reveal   *See* Show.
Revenge
Reverse Interpret   *See*
   Interpret.
Revival
Revive
Revolt   *See* Strike.
Revolting   *See*
   Discontented.
Reward   *See* Gift.
Rhythm
Rich
Righteous   *See* Holy.
Ride (on an animal)
Ride (in a vehicle)
Ridiculous   *See* Foolish.
Rifle   *See* Hunt.
Right (adjective)
Right (direction)
Rigid   *See* Ice.
Rip   *See* Tear.
Ripe   *See* Soft.
Rise
Rise   *See* Appear.
Rise   *See* Stand Up.
Rival   *See* Enemy.
Rivalry   *See* Race.
River
Road   *See* Street.
Roar   *See* Shout.
Robber   *See* Thief.
Robust   *See* Healthy.
Rock
Rocket
Roller Skating
Romp   *See* Play.
Room
Rooster
Rope
Rotten   *See* Lousy.

Round   *See* Ball.
Row   *See* Quarrel.
Rowing
Royal   *See* Lord.
Rub
Rubber
Ruin   *See* Tease.
Rule   *See* Control.
Rules
Run
Run Off   *See* Escape.
Rush   *See* Hurry.
Russia
Russian   *See* Russia.

S

Sacrifice
Sad
Safe   *See* Saviour.
Salary   *See* Collect.
Salary   *See* Earn.
Sale   *See* Sell.
Salt
Salvation   *See* Saviour.
Same
Sanctified   *See* Holy.
Sandwich
Satan   *See* Devil.
Satisfaction
Saturate   *See* Wet.
Saturday
Save
Save   *See* Savior.
Savior
Saw   *See* Wood.
Say
Scared   *See* Afraid.
Scatter
Scent   *See* Smell.
Schedule
School
Science
Scissors
Scold
Scores   *See* Many.
Scramble   *See* Confuse.
Scream   *See* Shout.
Sea   *See* Ocean.
Seal
Search
Season
Seat   *See* Sit.
Second (time)
Secret

Textbook   *See* Book.
Than
Thanks
Thanksgiving
Thank You   *See* Thanks.
That
The (definite article), 27
Theater
Their   *See* His.
Them   *See* They.
Theme   *See* Quote.
Themselves   *See* Yourself.
Then
Theory   *See* Imagination.
There
Thermometer   *See* Temperature.
These   *See* They.
They
Thief
Thin
Thing
Think
Thirsty
Thirteen, 22
Thirty, 23
This
Those   *See* They.
Thoughtless   *See* Careless.
Thousand, 24
Thread   *See* String.
Thread   *See* Spaghetti.
Three, 21
Thrill   *See* Exciting.
Thrilling   *See* Exciting.
Through
Throw
Throw Up   *See* Vomit.
Thunder
Thursday
Ticket
Tie (a knot)
Tiger
Time
Time (abstract)
Times   *See* Time (abstract).
Tiny   *See* Small.
Tired
Tithe
Title   *See* Quote.
To
Toast
Today
Together

Toilet
Tomato
Tomorrow
Tongue
Tongue   *See* Language.
Too
Toothbrush
Topic   *See* Quote.
Topsy-turvy   *See* Bungle.
Torment   *See* Tease.
Tortoise   *See* Turtle.
Toss   *See* Throw.
Total
Touch
Toward
Town   *See* City.
Trade   *See* Exchange.
Tradition
Traffic
Tragic   *See* Awful.
Train
Training   *See* Practice.
Transport   *See* Carry.
Tranquil   *See* Quiet.
Translate   *See* Interpret.
Trapped   *See* Stuck.
Travel
Treasurer
Tree
Trial   *See* Judge.
Tricycle   *See* Bicycle.
Trigonometry   *See* Mathematics.
Trinity
Trip   *See* Travel.
Triumph   *See* Celebrate.
Trombone
Trousers   *See* Pants.
True
Trust   *See* Confidence.
Truth   *See* True.
Try   *See* Attempt.
Tuesday
Turkey
Turn
Turtle
Twice
Twelve, 22
Twenty, 23
Twenty-one, 23
Twenty-two, 23
Twenty-three, 23
Twine   *See* String.
Twins
Two, 21

U

Ugly
Umbrella
Unable   *See* Cannot.
Uncle
Under   *See* Below.
Under   *See* Below (comparative degree).
Understand
Unfair
Unique   *See* Special.
Unite   *See* Join.
United States
Universe
Unjust   *See* Unfair.
Unlike   *See* Different.
Unsure   *See* Skeptical.
Until
Unwind   *See* Rest.
Up
Uphold   *See* Support.
Upset
Upside Down   *See* Bungle.
Urge   *See* Persuade.
Us   *See* We.
Use
Used To   *See* Past.
Used To   *See* Usually.
Useful   *See* Use, and Important.
Useless   *See* Worthless.
Usually
Utilize   *See* Use.

V

Vacant   *See* Empty.
Vacation
Vaccination   *See* Injection.
Vain (characteristic)
Valentine
Valid   *See* True.
Valley
Valuable   *See* Important.
Vanilla
Vanity   *See* Vain.
Varied   *See* Different.
Variety   *See* Kind (type).
Vein
Very
Via   *See* Through.
Victory   *See* Celebrate.

Videotape
Village   *See* City.
Violin
Vision
Vision   *See* See.
Visit
Vital   *See* Must.
Vocabulary
Vocal   *See* Voice.
Voice
Volleyball
Volume   *See* Book.
Volunteer
Vomit
Vote

W

Wag   *See* Tail.
Wages   *See* Collect.
Wages   *See* Earn.
Wait
Waiter
Waitress   *See* Waiter.
Wake Up   *See* Awake.
Walk
Wander   *See* Stray.
Want
War   *See* Battle.
Warm
Warn
Was
Was   *See* Past.
Wash
Wash Dishes
Washing Machine
Waste   *See* Spend.
Watch   *See* Look.
Watch   *See* Time.
Water
Watermelon
Way
We
Weak
Wealthy   *See* Rich.
Wear   *See* Clothes.
Weary   *See* Tired.
Weather
Wedding
Wednesday
Week
Weep   *See* Cry.
Weigh
Weighty   *See* Heavy.
Weird   *See* Odd.

Welcome
Well   *See* Healthy.
Well   *See* Good.
Were
Were   *See* Past.
West
Wet
What
When
Where
Whether   *See* Which.
Which
While   *See* During.
While Ago, A   *See*
   Recently.
Whiskey   *See* Liquor.
Whisper
White
Who
Whole   *See* All.
Wholesome   *See* Healthy.
Whom   *See* Who.
Why
Wicked   *See* Evil.
Wide
Wife
Will (verb)
Will (legal statement),
   See Testament.
Willing   *See* Please.
Win
Wind
Window
Wine
Wings
Winter
Winter   *See* Cold.
Wire   *See* Spaghetti.
Wisdom
Wise   *See* Wisdom.
Wish
With
Withdraw   *See* Leave.
Without
Woman
Wonder
Wonderful
Won't   *See* Refuse.
Wood
Woods   *See* Tree.
Word
Work
World
Worm
Worry

Worse   *See* Multiply.
Worsen   *See* Deteriorate.
Worship
Worst
Worthless
Worthy   *See* Important.
Would
Would   *See* Will (verb).
Wound   *See* Pain.
Wrath   *See* Anger.
Wreck   *See* Accident.
Wrestler   *See* Wrestling.
Wrestling
Write
Writer
Wrong

X

X Ray
Xylophone

Y

Yard   *See* Garden.
Year
Yellow
Yes
Yesterday
Yet   *See* Still.
Yield   *See* Surrender.
You
Young
Your   *See* His.
You're Welcome   *See*
   Thanks.
Yours (singular)   *See* His.
Your, Yours (plural)
Your Fault   *See* Blame.
Yours   *See* Your.
Yourself
Yourselves   *See* Yourself.
Youth   *See* Young.

Z

Zeal   *See* Eager.
Zebra
Zero, 21
Zip Up   *See* Zipper.
Zipper
Zoo

Available wherever books are sold

SIGNING IS FUN by Mickey Flodin

From the premiere publishers of sign language books: a primer for children in grades 1 to 3 that introduces them to the wonders of signing.

THE POCKET DICTIONARY OF SIGNING (Revised Edition)
by Rod R. Butterworth and Mickey Flodin

The first easy-to-use pocket reference guide to sign language.

THE PERIGEE VISUAL DICTIONARY OF SIGNING, 3rd Edition
by Rod R. Butterworth and Mickey Flodin

This revised and expanded edition is the most comprehensive alphabetized reference work available of American Sign Language.

SIGNING FOR KIDS by Mickey Flodin

For eight- to fourteen-year-olds, an invaluable guide for learning American Sign Language. Illustrated with more than 1,000 signs aimed specifically at kids' interests.

SIGNING ILLUSTRATED: THE COMPLETE LEARNING GUIDE
by Mickey Flodin

A complete learning guide that teaches American Sign Language by "category," the most popular and preferred method of teaching and learning.

SIGNING EVERYDAY PHRASES by Mickey Flodin

The easy way to learn basic sign language in English word order for everyday life.

SIGNING MADE EASY
by Rod R. Butterworth, M.A., M.Ed., and Mickey Flodin

A complete program for learning sign language. Includes drills and exercises for increased comprehension and signing skills.

PERIGEE
An imprint of Penguin Group (USA) Inc.
penguin.com

T32.0208